Zion Ellis

Fighting for LGBTQ Rights in Cyrion – Unfiltered

Ahmed Bautista

ISBN: 9781779697776
Imprint: Telephasic Workshop
Copyright © 2024 Ahmed Bautista.
All Rights Reserved.

Contents

1 1 The Awakening

In this section, we dive into the early life of Zion Ellis, the LGBTQ activist who would go on to become a prominent advocate for LGBTQ rights in the fictional world of Cyrion. We explore the events that shaped his journey and ultimately led to his awakening as an activist.

1.1 A Small Town Boy with Big Dreams

Zion Ellis was born and raised in the small town of Silverwood, nestled in the rolling hills of Cyrion. Growing up, Zion's dreams were as vast as the clear night sky. From a young age, he was drawn to stories of bravery, justice, and equality. Whether it was fictional characters in books or real-life heroes fighting for social change, Zion yearned to make a difference.

Life in Silverwood was idyllic but sheltered. The town held on to traditional values, with a conservative mindset that often clashed with Zion's inherent belief in the equal rights of all individuals, regardless of their sexual orientation or gender identity. It was this clash that would eventually spur Zion's awakening.

1.1.1 The Day That Changed Everything

One sunny afternoon, while exploring the woods near his home, Zion stumbled upon an old diary that would prove to be a turning point in his life. The diary belonged to a past resident of Silverwood, a queer teenager named Gabriel. Through Gabriel's words, Zion was transported to a world of hidden desires, unrequited love, and the pain of living in a society that shunned LGBTQ individuals.

As Zion delved deeper into Gabriel's story, he realized that he too shared similar struggles and dreams. The diary opened his eyes to the injustices faced by the LGBTQ community, both in Silverwood and beyond. It awakened a fire within him, a burning desire to fight for the rights and equality of his queer brothers and sisters.

1.2 Uncovering the Hidden Truth

Inspired by Gabriel's diary, Zion delved further into the history and experiences of LGBTQ individuals. He voraciously consumed literature, documentaries, and online resources, unearthing the hidden truths of their plight. But the more he learned, the more he realized the extent of the discrimination and prejudice faced by the LGBTQ community. He couldn't stand idly by anymore.

1.2.1 Embracing the Queer Experience

Zion had always questioned societal norms and expectations. Now, armed with knowledge about the LGBTQ experience, he began understanding the importance of embracing one's true identity. He accepted his own queerness and started exploring what it meant to be true to himself. This self-acceptance was not without its challenges, as he grappled with fears of rejection and judgment from his conservative hometown.

1.2.2 Finding Courage in Self-Acceptance

It was through the support of close friends and online LGBTQ communities that Zion found the courage to be unapologetically himself. He realized that self-acceptance was not only essential for his own well-being but also a catalyst for social change. By refusing to conform to societal expectations and embracing his true identity, Zion became a beacon of hope for others who were also struggling to find their place in the world.

1.3 Embracing Identity

The journey of self-acceptance led Zion to a profound understanding of the importance of embracing one's identity, and he became determined to help others do the same.

1.3.1 Coming Out to a Traditional Family

Coming out is a deeply personal and often challenging experience for LGBTQ individuals. Zion knew that his journey could not be complete without coming out to his conservative family. The fear of rejection weighed heavily on him, but he also understood the transformative power of honesty and vulnerability.

Zion took a deep breath, gathered his loved ones, and shared his truth. The initial shock and confusion gradually gave way to a new understanding and acceptance. While it was not an easy process, Zion's family began to embark on their own journey of growth and acceptance.

1.3.2 Navigating the Maze of Self-Discovery

Upon accepting his own queerness, Zion embarked on a journey of self-discovery. He began questioning not only his sexual orientation but also his gender identity. It was during this exploration that Zion discovered the concept of non-binary identities and the fluidity of his own gender expression.

This realization was liberating but also posed its own set of challenges. Zion had to navigate a world that often failed to understand or accommodate non-binary experiences. However, armed with newfound knowledge and a growing network of LGBTQ friends, Zion continued to challenge societal norms and expectations.

1.3.3 Finding Strength in Community

In his search for support and understanding, Zion found solace in the LGBTQ community. These individuals became his chosen family, a network of comrades who shared his struggles and dreams. Together, they created safe spaces where they could be their authentic selves without fear of judgment or discrimination.

Zion realized that strength and resilience lie in community unity. He became an active participant in LGBTQ organizations, lending his voice to advocate for change and inclusivity.

1.3.4 Embracing Queer Culture and History

As Zion further immersed himself in the LGBTQ community, he discovered a rich and vibrant culture that had long been overshadowed and marginalized. He championed queer arts, literature, music, and fashion, recognizing their power to shape narratives and challenge heteronormative expectations. By celebrating queer culture, Zion aimed to foster a world that embraced diversity and recognized the contributions of the LGBTQ community.

1.4 The Call to Action

Zion's awakening was not just a personal journey. It ignited a passion within him to fight for LGBTQ rights and equality.

1.4.1 A Chance Encounter with Activism

Zion's commitment to activism was solidified by a chance encounter at a local pride parade. He met seasoned LGBTQ activists who shared stories of their own battles against discrimination and their tireless efforts to create change. Inspired and invigorated, Zion knew he had found his calling.

1.4.2 Rallying the Troops for Change

With a growing sense of purpose, Zion rallied like-minded individuals and founded a grassroots movement for LGBTQ rights in Cyrion. He organized protests, marches, and community events that captured the attention of both the LGBTQ community and allies.

1.4.3 Igniting the Flame of Activism

Zion's passion and perseverance ignited a flame within the hearts of the LGBTQ community. They saw in him a leader who truly understood their struggles and dreams. Together, they embarked on a journey to challenge systemic oppression and advocate for the rights and dignity of all LGBTQ individuals.

1.4.4 Finding Purpose in the LGBTQ Movement

For Zion, the LGBTQ movement became more than just a fight for his own rights and those of his community. It became a testament to the power of resilience, love, and unwavering commitment to social justice. Zion found purpose in his advocacy, knowing that every small step forward brought them closer to a more inclusive and equitable society.

1.4.5 Turning Adversity into Motivation

Throughout his journey, Zion encountered numerous obstacles and setbacks. He faced backlash, discrimination, and personal struggles that tested his resolve. However, rather than succumbing to defeat, Zion used these adversities as fuel to propel his activism forward. Each setback became an opportunity for growth and resilience.

As Zion's awakening continued, he realized that the fight for LGBTQ rights was only just beginning. He stood ready to challenge the status quo, rewrite the narrative, and build a future where all individuals could embrace their authentic selves without fear of judgment or discrimination. This awakening marked the start of a transformative journey—one that would shape the course of Zion's life and leave an indelible impact on the LGBTQ movement in Cyrion.

1.1 The Awakening

In this opening chapter of "Zion Ellis: Fighting for LGBTQ Rights in Cyrion - Unfiltered," we are introduced to the remarkable journey of Zion Ellis, a small-town boy with big dreams. It is a story of personal growth, self-discovery, and the transformative power of embracing one's true identity.

1.1.1 A Small Town Boy with Big Dreams

Zion Ellis grew up in the idyllic town of Cyrion, a place where everyone knew each other and life seemed simple. But behind the picture-perfect facade, Zion struggled with his own suppressed feelings and desires. Like many LGBTQ individuals, he yearned for acceptance and understanding in a society that often dismissed or marginalized his identity.

Zion's early years were filled with curiosity and a hunger for knowledge. He sought solace in books, devouring stories of inspiring LGBTQ figures, both historical and fictional. These tales awakened something within him, a spark of defiance and resilience that would shape his path.

1.1.2 The Day That Changed Everything

One fateful day, as Zion was exploring the local library, he stumbled upon an old memoir by a renowned LGBTQ activist. The book told the story of a community fighting against prejudice and discrimination, and it ignited a fire within Zion. The words leaped off the pages and spoke directly to him, urging him to confront his own fears and make a difference.

In that moment, the walls of complacency Zion had built around himself began to crumble. He realized that he had the power to challenge the status quo and create a more inclusive world for himself and others. The awakening of his true identity as a LGBTQ activist had begun.

1.1.3 Uncovering the Hidden Truth

With newfound determination, Zion embarked on a journey of self-discovery and introspection. He delved into LGBTQ history, pouring over accounts of past struggles, triumphs, and the ongoing fight for equality. Zion was appalled by the hidden truths and injustices that had plagued the LGBTQ community for centuries.

As he unraveled the layers of historical oppression, Zion couldn't help but feel a deep sense of responsibility. He realized that his own experiences were not isolated, but part of a larger tapestry of discrimination. This knowledge fueled his passion and served as a call to action.

1.1.4 Embracing the Queer Experience

Embracing his queer identity became a crucial part of Zion's journey. He immersed himself in LGBTQ culture, discovering a vibrant community of like-minded individuals who shared his dreams of a more inclusive society. Through conversations, events, and personal connections, Zion grew to understand the diversity and depth of the queer experience.

In this exploration, Zion came to realize that being queer was not solely defined by one's sexual orientation or gender identity. It encompassed a rich tapestry of intersectional experiences, from race and ethnicity to socio-economic status and disability. These insights reinforced Zion's commitment to fighting for LGBTQ rights with a lens of inclusivity and understanding.

1.1.5 Finding Courage in Self-Acceptance

One of the most significant aspects of Zion's awakening was the journey towards self-acceptance. Coming to terms with his own identity and learning to love himself unconditionally was a challenging process. Zion confronted internalized homophobia and fear of rejection, but he pushed forward with unwavering courage.

Through introspection and self-reflection, Zion learned that accepting oneself is a radical act of defiance against societal norms. He discovered the power of self-love and realized that this fundamental belief was the gateway to effecting change both within himself and in the world.

The Journey Begins

In the closing paragraphs of this chapter, Zion Ellis stands on the precipice of change. The awakening of his true identity as an LGBTQ activist has opened doors he never thought possible. With newfound purpose and determination, Zion is ready to embark on a journey that will reshape his life, Cyrion, and the LGBTQ community.

But challenges lie ahead. As the battle for LGBTQ rights begins, Zion will face opposition, discrimination, and personal struggles. Yet, armed with his unwavering spirit and the support of a growing movement, Zion is prepared to overcome any obstacle in his path.

Stay tuned as we dive deeper into Zion Ellis's remarkable story, exploring the battles, triumphs, and sacrifices that have shaped him into the inspiring LGBTQ activist he is today.

ERROR. thisXsection() returned an empty string with textbook depth = 3.

ERROR. thisXsection() returned an empty string with textbook depth = 3.

ERROR. thisXsection() returned an empty string with textbook depth = 3.

The Day That Changed Everything

It was a crisp autumn morning in the small town of Cyrion, where dreams were often whispered but rarely realized. Little did anyone know that this particular day would forever alter the course of Zion Ellis's life, setting him on a path to become a formidable advocate for LGBTQ rights.

Zion, a bright-eyed and ambitious teenager, had always felt different. His heart yearned for something more than the constraints of a traditional small-town life. He craved acceptance, not just from others, but from himself as well. The day that changed everything began like any other, with Zion waking up to the sound of birds chirping and the sun peeking through his bedroom window.

As he lazily stretched his limbs and rubbed the sleep from his eyes, Zion had no idea that the day ahead would be filled with life-altering moments. It started innocently enough, with him stumbling upon a dusty old book while rummaging through the attic. Little did he know that this book would hold the key to unlocking his true self.

Curiosity got the better of him, and Zion opened the book, revealing a collection of secrets and hidden truths about the queer experience throughout history. He was captivated by the stories of trailblazers who had paved the way for LGBTQ rights, fighting against oppression and prejudice.

With each turn of the page, Zion's fascination grew, and the realization dawned upon him that he was not alone in his struggles. The book showed him that his feelings were valid, and that he had every right to be proud of his identity. It was as if the world around him suddenly shifted, and everything fell into place.

Filled with a newfound sense of purpose, Zion embarked on a journey of self-discovery. He wholeheartedly embraced his queer identity, rejecting the oppressive norms that had confined him for far too long. Zion realized that his small-town upbringing was not a limitation but a launching pad for his activism.

With the support of his closest friends, Zion began to challenge the heteronormative expectations of the town. He encouraged discussions about queer culture and history, showing his peers that being different was not something to be feared but celebrated.

Every step Zion took towards self-acceptance had a ripple effect on his community. As he found the courage to be his authentic self, others began to question the societal norms that had suppressed their own identities. The small town of Cyrion became a melting pot of diversity, embracing and celebrating its LGBTQ residents.

But Zion knew that there was still work to be done beyond the borders of his town. Inspired by the stories in the book, he realized that he had the power to ignite change on a larger scale. It was his duty to ensure that LGBTQ individuals, no matter where they lived, had the same rights and opportunities as their heterosexual counterparts.

Zion's journey had only just begun, but he knew that the path ahead would not be easy. He would face adversity, both internally and externally, but his determination and resilience would guide him through the challenges.

Little did he know that the day he stumbled upon that old book in the attic would mark the beginning of a remarkable transformation. Zion Ellis, the small-town boy with big dreams, had awakened to a life devoted to fighting for LGBTQ rights. His journey would leave an indelible mark on the world, forever changing the lives of those who came after him.

As readers, we are invited to join Zion on this extraordinary voyage – a tale of self-acceptance, resilience, and the power of one person's unwavering commitment to making the world a more inclusive place for everyone. Get ready to be captivated, inspired, and perhaps forever changed by Zion Ellis's story. Are you ready to fight for LGBTQ rights in Cyrion and beyond? Strap in and get ready for the adventure of a lifetime!

Uncovering the Hidden Truth

In this section, we delve into Zion Ellis's journey of uncovering the hidden truth surrounding LGBTQ rights in the conservative town of Cyrion. This chapter explores the challenges faced by Zion as he begins to question the prevailing narratives and unearth the realities faced by the LGBTQ community.

Unveiling the Facade

Zion Ellis, a small-town boy with big dreams, always believed that Cyrion was accepting and inclusive. However, as he grew older and started to question his own identity, he realized that the reality was far different. The hidden truth emerged when he came across instances of discrimination, prejudice, and hatred towards the LGBTQ community.

Zion's story paints a vivid picture of the struggles faced by many individuals who are forced to hide their true selves due to societal expectations and cultural norms. As Zion looks beyond the surface, he begins to uncover the deeply-rooted biases and systemic barriers that prevent LGBTQ individuals from living authentically and freely.

ـ ...ـ Realities

To uncover the hidden truth, Zion interviewed LGBTQ individuals within the town to better understand their experiences. He discovered stories of fear, rejection, and isolation. Many LGBTQ individuals were forced to conceal their true identities, leading to immense internal turmoil and mental health issues.

Zion encountered heartbreaking narratives of individuals who faced discrimination at their workplaces, schools, and even within their own families. These stories shed light on the struggles faced by the LGBTQ community and the urgent need for change in Cyrion.

Exposing the Root Causes

As Zion delved deeper into his investigation, he analyzed the root causes behind the hidden truth. He realized that the conservative values ingrained in the town's culture perpetuated homophobia, transphobia, and ignorance. Religious beliefs and societal norms often clashed with the core principles of equality and acceptance, resulting in the marginalization of LGBTQ individuals.

Zion's research also shed light on the impact of heteronormative expectations on LGBTQ youth. He discovered that societal pressures for conformity and the absence of comprehensive LGBTQ education contributed to the cycle of discrimination and prejudice.

Educating and Raising Awareness

Armed with newfound knowledge, Zion took it upon himself to educate others and raise awareness about the hidden truth in Cyrion. He passionately advocated for LGBTQ-inclusive education, aiming to dismantle the stereotypes and misconceptions that surrounded the LGBTQ community.

Zion organized community workshops, inviting experts to share insights into LGBTQ history and culture. He encouraged open conversations and discussions to challenge the prevailing narratives and to create a safe and inclusive space for dialogue.

The Path to Acceptance

Through his journey of uncovering the hidden truth, Zion became a beacon of hope for the LGBTQ community in Cyrion. He strived to confront the prejudices and systemic barriers head-on, determined to create an environment that celebrated diversity and embraced LGBTQ rights.

Zion's story serves as a reminder that hidden truths can be transformative. By shedding light on the issues faced by marginalized communities, it becomes possible to challenge oppressive systems and work towards a more inclusive society.

Breaking Barriers

In his quest for justice, Zion Ellis faced immense challenges and resistance. He encountered hostility from those who were threatened by his activism. However, he remained resilient, prioritizing the well-being and rights of the LGBTQ community above all.

Zion's journey shows that uncovering the hidden truth is not an easy path, but it is a necessary one. By exposing the realities faced by LGBTQ individuals in Cyrion, he pushed for a reevaluation of societal norms and encouraged a collective effort to break down barriers of discrimination and intolerance.

Exercises

1. Reflect on your own environment. Are there any hidden truths or marginalized communities that need to be uncovered and fought for? How can you play a role in bringing about positive change?

2. Conduct interviews with individuals from different backgrounds to gain a deeper understanding of the challenges they face in their daily lives. Document their stories and find a way to share them with others to raise awareness.

3. Organize a workshop or panel discussion in your community to foster open conversations about marginalized communities. Invite experts and individuals who have firsthand experience to share their stories and insights.

4. Research the legal and policy landscape in your area pertaining to LGBTQ rights. Are there any discriminatory laws that need to be challenged? Write a letter to a local representative advocating for LGBTQ-inclusive policies.

5. Write a personal reflection piece on your understanding of LGBTQ issues before and after reading Zion Ellis's journey. How has your perspective evolved, and what steps can you take to contribute to a more inclusive society?

Remember, uncovering the hidden truth requires commitment, empathy, and the willingness to confront uncomfortable realities. Let Zion Ellis's story inspire you to be a catalyst for positive change in your own community.

Embracing the Queer Experience

In this section, we will delve into the journey of Zion Ellis as he embraces and celebrates the queer experience. We will explore the challenges he faced, the lessons he learned, and the victories he achieved while navigating the intricacies of his own identity.

Coming Out: A Journey of Self-Discovery

Zion Ellis's story begins with his coming out journey—a deeply personal and transformative experience. Like many queer individuals, Zion grappled with his identity while growing up in a small town. He often felt isolated and out of place, longing for acceptance and understanding.

The pivotal moment for Zion came when he mustered the courage to come out to his traditional family. It was a daunting task, overshadowed by the fear of rejection and judgment. However, he realized that self-acceptance would be impossible without sharing his truth with his loved ones.

Problem

One common challenge faced by queer individuals is the fear of rejection from family and friends. How can individuals navigate this difficult process and find support during their coming out journey?

Solution

Navigating the coming out journey requires resilience and self-care. It is essential for queer individuals to prioritize their well-being and seek support systems. One strategy is to reach out to LGBTQ support groups or online communities for guidance and empathy. Additionally, finding allies within friends or family members who are accepting can create a sense of safety during this vulnerable time. Remember, self-acceptance and self-love should always be paramount, and seeking professional counseling can offer additional support and guidance.

Navigating Self-Discovery

The journey of self-discovery is a maze of exploration, self-reflection, and acceptance. Zion Ellis had to navigate through countless uncertainties, questioning and challenging societal norms and expectations.

As he delved deeper into the queer experience, he became aware of intersectionality—the interconnectedness of various aspects of one's identity, such as race, gender, and sexuality. Zion learned that embracing and acknowledging these intersecting identities was crucial to understanding his own experiences and those of others within the LGBTQ community.

Problem

How can individuals embrace their intersecting identities and use them as sources of strength and empowerment?

Solution

Embracing intersecting identities requires self-reflection and introspection. It is important for individuals to understand the unique challenges and privileges that come with their intersecting identities. By engaging in conversations and learning from the experiences of others, individuals can celebrate their own intersectionality and use it as a source of strength. Creating safe spaces where diverse identities are acknowledged and valued is also crucial in fostering a sense of empowerment and belonging.

Finding Strength in Community

Zion Ellis recognized the power of community as he embarked on his journey of self-acceptance. By connecting with like-minded individuals within the LGBTQ community, he found the support he needed to navigate the challenges he faced.

Through involvement in queer organizations and events, Zion discovered the strength that comes from collective action. He actively participated in pride parades, LGBTQ rights rallies, and community outreach programs. These experiences allowed him to build connections, find solace in shared struggles, and work towards creating a more inclusive society.

Problem

What are some effective ways for queer individuals to become involved in their local LGBTQ community and contribute to the collective fight for equality?

> **Solution**
>
> Getting involved in local LGBTQ organizations and community initiatives is a powerful way to effect change. From volunteering at LGBTQ centers to organizing educational workshops and events, individuals can find numerous opportunities to contribute. Joining advocacy groups, attending town hall meetings, and actively engaging in conversations about LGBTQ issues can also make a significant impact. By sharing personal stories and experiences, individuals create awareness and empathy, which are fundamental to fostering change.

Challenging Heteronormative Expectations

As Zion embraced his queer identity, he recognized the importance of challenging heteronormative expectations. He questioned societal norms and assumptions that perpetuate rigid gender roles and stereotypes. Zion realized that by challenging such expectations, he could pave the way for greater acceptance and understanding of diverse identities within the LGBTQ community.

> **Problem**
>
> What are some common heteronormative expectations imposed on queer individuals, and how can they be addressed and dismantled?

> **Solution**
>
> Common heteronormative expectations include assuming all individuals fit into traditional gender binaries, expecting individuals to conform to societal norms for relationships and family structures, and assuming sexual orientation based on appearance or behavior. These expectations can be addressed by promoting education and awareness about diverse gender identities and sexual orientations. Challenging stereotypes in media and popular culture is also crucial in dismantling heteronormative expectations. By emphasizing the value of authenticity and inclusion, society can create safer and more accepting spaces for all individuals.

Embracing Queer Culture and History

Throughout his journey, Zion Ellis developed a deep appreciation for queer culture and history. He recognized that acknowledging and celebrating the contributions of LGBTQ individuals throughout history was essential for fostering a sense of pride within the community.

Zion immersed himself in exploring queer art, literature, and music, recognizing the power of creative expression in bringing about social change. By sharing stories of LGBTQ trailblazers and highlighting their achievements, Zion aimed to challenge societal narratives and shed light on the resilience and strength of the queer experience.

Problem

Why is it important for the LGBTQ community to preserve and celebrate its cultural heritage and history?

Solution

Preserving and celebrating LGBTQ cultural heritage and history is vital for many reasons. It enables queer individuals to develop a sense of pride and resilience by connecting with the struggles and triumphs of those who came before them. LGBTQ history also serves as a reminder of the progress made in the fight for equality and acts as a catalyst for future activism. By recognizing and sharing LGBTQ narratives, society can challenge heteronormativity and foster inclusivity and acceptance.

Embracing the Queer Experience: A Journey of Self-Love

Zion Ellis's journey of embracing the queer experience ultimately led him to a place of self-love and self-acceptance. Throughout his exploration of identity, community engagement, and challenging societal expectations, he discovered the power of embracing one's authentic self.

By sharing his story and advocating for LGBTQ rights, Zion aimed to inspire others to embark on their own journeys of self-discovery and celebrate the beautiful diversity of the queer experience.

> **Problem**
>
> How does embracing the queer experience impact individuals' overall well-being and contribute to a more inclusive society?

> **Solution**
>
> Embracing the queer experience has a profound impact on individuals' overall well-being. By acknowledging and celebrating their authentic selves, individuals cultivate a sense of self-love and acceptance. This, in turn, fosters greater mental and emotional well-being. Embracing the queer experience also contributes to a more inclusive society by challenging harmful stereotypes, promoting empathy, and creating spaces where all individuals are valued and respected as equals.

As Zion Ellis embarked on his journey of embracing the queer experience, he found strength, resilience, and purpose. His story serves as an inspiration for individuals navigating their own paths of self-discovery and fighting for LGBTQ rights. By embracing the complexity of the queer experience, Zion continues to make a lasting impact on the world, shaping a future that celebrates diversity and equality for all.

Finding Courage in Self-Acceptance

In this chapter, we delve into the journey of self-acceptance for Zion Ellis, a small-town boy with big dreams. We explore the pivotal moments that shaped Zion's understanding of his own identity and how he found the courage to embrace his true self. Through anecdotes, personal reflections, and a deep exploration of LGBTQ history and culture, we uncover the transformative power of self-acceptance in the face of adversity.

The Awakening

Zion's journey begins with the awakening of his true identity. As a child growing up in the small town of Cyrion, he had always felt different but unable to articulate why. It was during his teenage years that Zion began to understand and question his sexuality. This pivotal moment shook his world and set him on a path of self-discovery.

A Small Town Boy with Big Dreams

Growing up in a close-knit community, Zion faced the challenge of reconciling his dreams and aspirations with the expectations of his conservative surroundings. He yearned to pursue a career in the arts, but feared the judgment and rejection he might face. However, Zion's determination and resilience fueled his ambition to break free from the confines of his small town and pursue his passions.

The Day That Changed Everything

One fateful day, Zion had a life-altering experience that shattered his preconceived notions about his own identity. This moment of self-revelation empowered him to challenge societal norms and embrace his authentic self. Through this experience, Zion gained the strength and clarity to navigate the complexities of his personal journey.

Uncovering the Hidden Truth

In his quest for self-acceptance, Zion embarked on a journey of self-discovery, unpacking the layers of his identity and understanding the multifaceted nature of queerness. Through research, conversations, and engaging with LGBTQ history, Zion unearthed the hidden truths about himself and the larger LGBTQ community. This newfound knowledge empowered him to fully embrace his identity and broaden his perspective on what it means to be queer.

Embracing the Queer Experience

Zion's exploration of queer culture and history allowed him to connect with a broader community of individuals who had shared experiences. Through books, art, music, and engaging with queer individuals, Zion discovered the richness and diversity within the LGBTQ community. This exposure helped him find solace, support, and a sense of belonging.

Finding Courage in Self-Acceptance

The process of self-acceptance was not without its challenges for Zion. He faced moments of doubt, fear, and scrutiny from both his own internal struggles and society at large. However, he gradually found the courage to stand up for himself, challenge societal prejudice, and live his truth authentically. Through self-reflection, therapy, and the support of loved ones, Zion cultivated the resilience and inner strength needed to navigate the complexities of his journey.

Challenging Heteronormative Expectations

Throughout Zion's journey, he faced the pressure to conform to heteronormative expectations imposed by society. This constant scrutiny forced him to question societal norms and challenge the status quo. Zion's commitment to authenticity and self-acceptance became a catalyst for change, inspiring others to question outdated social constructs and embrace their own identities beyond traditional binaries.

Embracing Identity

Zion's journey is a testament to the power of self-acceptance. By embracing his own identity, he not only transformed his own life but also became an advocate for LGBTQ rights and acceptance. His story serves as an inspiration to all individuals grappling with their own identities, encouraging them to find the courage within themselves to celebrate and live their truth.

In the next chapter, we will explore the challenges and triumphs of Zion Ellis as he forges his path as an LGBTQ activist, rallying the troops for change and igniting the flame of activism in Cyrion and beyond.

Embracing Identity

Coming Out to a Traditional Family

Coming out is a deeply personal and courageous journey for many individuals within the LGBTQ community. It is an experience that often involves navigating the complex dynamics of family relationships and societal expectations. In this section, we explore Zion Ellis's experience of coming out to his traditional family and the challenges he faced along the way.

The Struggle of Silence

Growing up in a small town, Zion Ellis always felt different from his peers. He knew from a young age that he was attracted to people of the same gender, but he also knew that his traditional family held conservative views on sexuality. This created a sense of internal conflict within him, as he grappled with the fear of rejection and the desire to be true to himself.

For years, Zion struggled in silence, hiding his true identity from his family. He lived in constant fear of discovery, tiptoeing around conversations and suppressing his authentic self. This silence took a toll on his mental and emotional well-being, leading to feelings of isolation and self-doubt.

The Decision to Come Out

As Zion grew older, he yearned for a sense of authenticity and belonging. He realized that hiding his true identity was incompatible with living a fulfilling and genuine life. With this realization, he made the brave decision to come out to his traditional family, knowing that it would be a challenging and transformative moment.

Navigating Uncertainty

Coming out to a traditional family can often be a tumultuous experience, filled with uncertainty and anxiety. Zion prepared himself for the range of reactions he might encounter – from acceptance and understanding to confusion and even outright rejection. While he hoped for a positive outcome, he understood the importance of being patient and allowing his family time to process the information.

To ease the process, Zion sought guidance from LGBTQ support groups and online communities. He found solace in hearing stories from others who had gone through similar experiences. Drawing strength from their journeys, Zion armed himself with knowledge and resources to navigate the challenges that lay ahead.

Finding Compassion and Understanding

When the day finally came, Zion gathered his family in their living room, his heart pounding with anticipation. As he began to share his truth, he witnessed a range of emotions etched across the faces of his family members – surprise, confusion, concern. Some struggled to understand while others were immediately accepting.

In moments like these, it becomes vital to approach the situation with compassion and empathy. Zion realized that his family's traditional beliefs had shaped their worldview, and it would take time for them to reconcile those beliefs with his truth. He chose to be patient, answering their questions thoughtfully and sharing educational resources to help them understand his journey better.

The Power of Love and Acceptance

Over time, Zion's family started to see beyond their preconceived notions and beliefs. They began to recognize the strength and authenticity with which he lived his life.

Slowly but surely, their love for him transcended societal norms and embraced his true identity.

In embracing Zion's journey, his family challenged their own beliefs and grew more accepting not just of Zion, but also of LGBTQ rights as a whole. They attended Pride events with him, engaged in discussions on queer history, and became vocal advocates for LGBTQ equality within their own social circles.

Zion's experience with his traditional family showcases the transformative power of love, compassion, and education. While not every coming out story unfolds in a similar manner, it highlights the importance of hope and the possibility for change, even in the face of deeply ingrained beliefs.

Embracing Unconditional Support

Throughout his journey, Zion also discovered the importance of building a chosen family – a supportive network of friends and mentors who understood the challenges he faced. They provided him with the love and encouragement he needed during difficult times, reminding him that he was not alone.

The support of his chosen family helped Zion to navigate the complexities of his traditional family relationships. They shared advice, offered a listening ear, and celebrated his triumphs. Their unwavering belief in his ability to create positive change in their community became a constant source of motivation.

In conclusion, coming out to a traditional family is an emotionally charged experience that requires immense courage and resilience. Zion Ellis's journey serves as a testament to the power of compassion, education, and unconditional support in fostering acceptance and understanding within familial relationships. It reminds us all that love has the potential to transcend boundaries and transform lives.

Navigating the Maze of Self-Discovery

In the journey towards self-discovery, LGBTQ individuals face unique challenges and opportunities. Navigating the maze of self-discovery involves exploring one's sexual orientation, gender identity, and personal values. This process can be both empowering and daunting, as individuals strive to find their authentic selves amidst societal expectations and internal conflicts. In this section, we will delve into the intricacies of self-discovery, providing guidance and insight for those navigating the maze.

Understanding Sexual Orientation

Understanding one's sexual orientation is a central aspect of self-discovery. Sexual orientation refers to an individual's enduring patterns of emotional, romantic, and sexual attraction towards others. While society often assumes a heterosexual norm, it is essential to acknowledge and embrace a diverse range of sexual orientations.

Defining sexual orientation: Sexual orientation is an inherent part of an individual's identity and is not a choice. It can be categorized into different sexual orientations, including but not limited to heterosexual, homosexual, bisexual, and asexual. It is crucial to understand that sexual orientation exists on a spectrum, with many diverse identities within each category.

Exploring attraction: Exploring one's attractions can be a valuable tool in self-discovery. This can involve reflecting upon past experiences, examining patterns of attraction, and being open to exploring different forms of relationships. It is essential to approach this process with an open mind and without judgment, allowing oneself to authentically experience and understand their attractions.

Navigating societal expectations: Societal norms and expectations can often create confusion and internal conflicts during the process of self-discovery. It is important to remember that societal expectations should not dictate one's sexual orientation. Instead, individuals should focus on honoring their true feelings and desires, even if they differ from societal norms.

Seeking support: Navigating the maze of self-discovery can be challenging, and seeking support from trusted friends, family, or professional counselors can be invaluable. LGBTQ support groups and communities can provide a safe space for individuals to share their experiences, seek guidance, and find connection with others who have similar journeys.

Embracing Gender Identity

In addition to understanding sexual orientation, exploring and embracing gender identity is a vital aspect of self-discovery. Gender identity refers to an individual's deeply-held sense of being male, female, or something beyond the traditional binary understanding of gender. It is distinct from biological sex and can include identities such as transgender, non-binary, or genderqueer.

Understanding gender identity: Gender identity is a deeply personal and internal sense of self. It may or may not align with the sex assigned at birth. It is essential to recognize and honor diverse gender identities, supporting individuals in their journey towards self-discovery and self-acceptance.

Questioning gender identity: For many individuals, the journey of self-discovery involves questioning their gender identity. This involves exploring feelings, thoughts, and experiences related to gender. Engaging in self-reflection and seeking information and resources can be instrumental in this process.

Navigating social expectations: Society often imposes rigid gender roles and expectations, which can complicate the process of self-discovery for LGBTQ individuals. It is crucial to challenge and challenge societal norms, embracing the freedom to express oneself authentically, regardless of societal expectations.

Support and validation: Finding support and validation is essential when navigating the maze of self-discovery. Building connections with understanding and affirming individuals, such as friends, family, or support groups, can provide a safe space for exploration and self-acceptance. Therapeutic support from professionals specializing in gender identity can also be beneficial.

Legal considerations: When exploring gender identity, it is essential to be aware of legal considerations and protections for transgender and non-binary individuals. Familiarize yourself with local laws and regulations regarding gender marker changes, name changes, and other legal rights to ensure a smooth and secure journey of self-discovery.

Personal Growth and Authenticity

Self-discovery is not a linear process, but rather a lifelong journey of personal growth and self-acceptance. Embracing authenticity and honoring one's true self is at the heart of this journey.

Cultivating self-acceptance: Self-acceptance is a foundational step in self-discovery. Embracing and loving oneself unconditionally, without judgment or shame, is crucial. Celebrating the uniqueness of one's identity and experiences can lead to a sense of empowerment and a more fulfilling life.

Finding personal values: Exploring personal values helps define one's authentic self. Identifying core beliefs, passions, and aspirations can guide individuals in their journey of self-discovery. It is essential to align actions with personal values, promoting authenticity and personal growth.

Seeking personal growth opportunities: Actively seeking personal growth opportunities can be transformative during the process of self-discovery. This may involve engaging in self-reflection practices, pursuing education or professional development, and embracing new experiences that broaden perspectives and challenge assumptions.

Maintaining self-care: Self-discovery can be emotionally and mentally demanding. Prioritizing self-care is essential to maintain well-being throughout the journey. This may include practicing self-compassion, engaging in activities that bring joy and fulfillment, and seeking support when needed.

Trusting the process: Navigating the maze of self-discovery can be daunting, but trusting the process is crucial. Embrace the uncertainties, learn from setbacks, and celebrate milestones along the way. Remember that self-discovery is a unique and individual journey, and it is okay to take the time needed to find one's true self.

Unconventional yet Relevant: The Power of Art

In the realm of self-discovery, art can play a profound role in expressing personal identity and provoking meaningful reflection. Incorporating artistic endeavors into the journey can provide a unique and powerful channel for self-expression.

Artistic mediums such as painting, music, dance, and creative writing can be used to explore and communicate complex emotions, thoughts, and experiences. Art allows individuals to uncover aspects of themselves that may be difficult to put into words, creating a visual or audible representation of their self-discovery process.

Engaging with LGBTQ artists and their work can be highly inspirational and empowering. LGBTQ art often reflects unique perspectives, challenges societal norms, and sheds light on the diverse experiences of the community. Exploring LGBTQ art can provide validation, representation, and a sense of belonging throughout the journey of self-discovery.

In conclusion, navigating the maze of self-discovery as an LGBTQ individual requires introspection, support, and an unwavering commitment to authenticity. Understanding and embracing sexual orientation and gender identity are essential components of this journey. Personal growth, self-acceptance, and trust in the process pave the way for a fulfilling life aligned with one's true self. By incorporating art into the process, individuals can further deepen their understanding and expression of their identity, creating a lasting legacy of self-discovery.

Finding Strength in Community

In the journey towards self-acceptance and identity, finding strength in community is a crucial aspect for LGBTQ individuals. It is within communities that individuals can discover a sense of belonging, support, and empowerment. This section delves into the significance of community for LGBTQ individuals, exploring the challenges they face, the role of community in overcoming these challenges, and the various forms of support available.

Navigating the Challenges

Being part of the LGBTQ community comes with unique challenges that can impact an individual's self-esteem, mental health, and overall well-being. Discrimination, stigma, and social exclusion are just a few of the hardships that LGBTQ individuals frequently encounter. It is essential to acknowledge and address these challenges in order to create a supportive network within the community.

Discrimination and Stigma Discrimination against LGBTQ individuals is still prevalent in many societies. They often face biases, prejudices, and exclusionary practices in various aspects of life, including education, employment, and healthcare. This discrimination can lead to feelings of isolation, shame, and self-doubt. It becomes crucial for LGBTQ individuals to connect with others who understand their struggles and can offer guidance and support.

Coming Out Coming out is a significant and often challenging step for LGBTQ individuals to openly express their true identity. This process can be met with rejection from family, friends, and society. The fear of losing support systems and facing discrimination adds to the anxiety and stress associated with coming out. Building a strong foundation in the LGBTQ community can provide individuals with the necessary support to navigate this transformative period and embrace their authentic selves.

The Power of LGBTQ Community

The LGBTQ community serves as a source of resilience and strength for individuals facing the challenges discussed above. It provides a safe space for self-expression, self-discovery, and emotional support, fostering a sense of solidarity and belonging. Through community, LGBTQ individuals find the support they need to navigate their journey of self-acceptance and fight for their rights.

Creating Safe Spaces Safe spaces within the LGBTQ community play a vital role in providing acceptance, understanding, and support. LGBTQ centers, organizations, and online communities serve as platforms for individuals to connect, share experiences, and access resources. These spaces allow individuals to be their authentic selves without fear of judgment or discrimination, fostering an environment of empathy and understanding.

Support Networks Support networks within the LGBTQ community are a crucial source of strength. These networks can consist of friends, chosen family, mentors, and community activists. They serve as a constant support system, offering guidance, solidarity, and encouragement. Support networks provide individuals with the opportunity to learn from others' experiences, gain knowledge about LGBTQ history, and develop the skills needed to advocate for their rights.

Visibility and Representation Visibility and representation of LGBTQ individuals in the community and society at large are essential for empowering individuals and challenging social norms. Seeing diverse LGBTQ role models and hearing their stories of resilience can inspire others to embrace their identities. LGBTQ individuals who are visible and vocal about their experiences can serve as beacons of hope, creating a sense of belonging and driving positive change.

Community Resources and Initiatives

LGBTQ communities offer a wide range of resources and initiatives to support individuals on their journey towards self-acceptance and empowerment. These resources encompass mental health services, educational programs, legal aid, and activism efforts. By engaging with these resources, individuals can access the tools and knowledge necessary to overcome challenges and make a positive impact in their lives and the lives of others.

Mental Health Support Mental health support is crucial for LGBTQ individuals, as they often face higher rates of depression, anxiety, and suicidal ideation compared to their heterosexual and cisgender counterparts. LGBTQ community organizations and mental health professionals provide specialized services and counseling to address the unique challenges faced by LGBTQ individuals. These services aim to enhance resilience, foster coping mechanisms, and promote overall well-being.

Educational Programs Educational programs within the LGBTQ community play a significant role in promoting awareness, combatting discrimination, and empowering individuals. These programs offer workshops, seminars, and training sessions on various topics such as LGBTQ history, community resources, intersectionality, and allyship. By expanding knowledge and understanding, educational programs inspire action and facilitate a deeper sense of community.

Legal Aid and Advocacy   Navigating legal challenges, such as discriminatory workplace practices, housing issues, and denial of healthcare, can be overwhelming for LGBTQ individuals. Organizations specializing in legal aid and advocacy work tirelessly to ensure equal rights and protections for the LGBTQ community. They offer legal support, guidance, and representation while advocating for policy changes to create a more inclusive society.

Activism and Allyship   LGBTQ activism and allyship are powerful tools for social change and community empowerment. Activism efforts, such as protests, rallies, and social media campaigns, raise awareness about LGBTQ rights and create a platform for marginalized voices. Allies play a pivotal role in standing beside and amplifying the voices of LGBTQ individuals, challenging heteronormative and cisnormative norms, and advocating for inclusivity.

An Unconventional Yet Relevant Perspective: The Power of Hobbies

In addition to the resources and initiatives offered by LGBTQ communities, it is essential to acknowledge the role of hobbies in fostering strength and resilience. Engaging in hobbies not only provides a break from the challenges of life but also nurtures creativity, passion, and a sense of accomplishment. Pursuing hobbies within the LGBTQ community allows individuals to connect with like-minded individuals, share experiences, and bond over common interests, further strengthening the community as a whole.

For example, LGBTQ individuals who engage in activities such as drag performance, writing, music, or visual arts find an outlet for self-expression and creativity. These hobbies often become vehicles for advocating for LGBTQ rights, challenging stereotypes, and celebrating queer culture. Hobbies can serve as platforms to engage and educate others by dismantling misconceptions and fostering dialogue.

Conclusion

Finding strength in community is pivotal for LGBTQ individuals on their journey towards acceptance, empowerment, and social change. The challenges they face necessitate the support, understanding, and resourcefulness that can be found within the LGBTQ community. By creating safe spaces, fostering support networks, and providing resources and initiatives, the LGBTQ community empowers its members to overcome adversity and make positive contributions to society. Through the power of community, individuals can thrive, embrace their authentic selves, and pave the way for a more inclusive and accepting future.

Embracing Queer Culture and History

As Zion Ellis embarked on his journey of LGBTQ activism, he quickly realized the importance of embracing and celebrating queer culture and history. In this section, we explore the significance of preserving and understanding LGBTQ culture, the power of representation, and the lessons we can learn from queer history.

Preserving Queer Culture

Queer culture is rich and diverse, encompassing a wide range of identities, experiences, and expressions. It is essential to preserve and honor this culture, as it provides a sense of belonging and community for LGBTQ individuals.

One way to preserve queer culture is by documenting and sharing personal stories and experiences. Oral histories, memoirs, and interviews allow us to capture the lived experiences of LGBTQ individuals and contribute to a more comprehensive understanding of queer identity. In doing so, we can ensure that future generations have access to authentic narratives that showcase the diversity within the LGBTQ community.

Additionally, art and literature play a crucial role in preserving queer culture. Through various art forms such as music, painting, literature, and performance, LGBTQ artists express their unique experiences and challenge societal norms. By supporting queer artists and their work, we contribute to the preservation and elevation of queer culture.

The Power of Representation

Representation matters, both in the media and in broader society. Seeing positive and accurate portrayals of LGBTQ individuals helps to combat stereotypes, promote understanding, and create a more inclusive world.

Media representation is particularly impactful in shaping public perceptions. Films, television shows, and books that feature well-rounded LGBTQ characters contribute to a greater awareness and acceptance of queer identities. They help to humanize LGBTQ individuals, dismantle harmful stereotypes, and inspire empathy and understanding.

LGBTQ history also plays a crucial role in representation. By learning about the struggles, triumphs, and contributions of queer individuals throughout history, we gain a sense of pride and the validation of our identities. It reminds us that we are part of a vibrant and resilient community with a rich history.

Lessons from Queer History

Queer history is often overlooked and erased, but its study provides valuable insights and lessons for the LGBTQ community and society as a whole. Exploring the challenges faced by past LGBTQ activists can inspire us to continue fighting for equality and justice.

One lesson we learn from queer history is the importance of unity and intersectionality. LGBTQ individuals have historically formed alliances with other marginalized groups, recognizing that their struggles are interconnected. From the Stonewall riots, where transgender women of color took a stand against police brutality, to the collaboration between LGBTQ and feminist movements for reproductive rights, we see the power of solidarity in effecting real change.

Queer history also teaches us the importance of resilience and perseverance. LGBTQ individuals have faced immense adversity throughout history, from legal persecution to social exclusion. Yet, they have continued to fight for their rights and make significant contributions to society. By studying their stories, we gain inspiration and a reminder that progress is possible even in the face of seemingly insurmountable challenges.

Furthermore, queer history sheds light on the progress made in LGBTQ rights over time, highlighting the victories won by activists who came before us. Familiarizing ourselves with this history allows us to appreciate how far we have come and motivates us to continue the fight for full equality.

Resources for Embracing Queer Culture and History

There are several resources available to learn more about LGBTQ culture and history. Here are some recommendations to deepen your knowledge:

- *Queer: A Graphic History* by Meg-John Barker and Julia Scheele offers a visually engaging introduction to queer theory and history.

- The GLBT Historical Society in San Francisco houses an extensive archive of LGBTQ historical artifacts, documents, and oral history collections.

- The podcast *Making Gay History* by Eric Marcus features interviews with LGBTQ pioneers and activists, providing a valuable oral history of the movement.

- The documentary film *Paris is Burning* explores the vibrant and influential drag ball culture in New York City during the 1980s.

- The book *Stone Butch Blues* by Leslie Feinberg is a powerful novel that follows a working-class lesbian during the 1960s and 1970s, offering a glimpse into the struggles faced by gender-nonconforming individuals.

By immersing ourselves in LGBTQ culture and history, we can better understand our place in the ongoing fight for equality and justice. It is through embracing our past that we pave the way for a more inclusive and equitable future.

Challenging Heteronormative Expectations

In this section, we will explore the concept of heteronormativity and how it perpetuates rigid gender roles and expectations within society. We will delve into the challenges faced by individuals who do not conform to these heteronormative standards and discuss strategies for challenging and dismantling these norms. By empowering individuals to embrace their authentic selves, we can create a more inclusive and accepting society for all.

Understanding Heteronormativity

Heteronormativity refers to the belief that heterosexuality is the only valid sexual orientation and that gender is binary, with only two options: male and female. This perspective assumes that a person's gender identity aligns with their biological sex and that relationships and social structures should be based on heterosexual norms.

The influence of heteronormativity can be seen in various aspects of society, including media representation, legal frameworks, educational systems, and social norms. It often marginalizes and erases individuals whose experiences and identities exist beyond traditional heteronormative frameworks.

Unpacking Gender Roles and Expectations

Heteronormativity upholds strict gender roles and expectations, which dictate how individuals should behave, express themselves, and form relationships. For example, it perpetuates the notion that men should be masculine, strong, and emotionally stoic, while women should be feminine, nurturing, and submissive.

These rigid gender roles not only limit the personal expression of individuals but also contribute to various forms of discrimination and oppression. Men who do not conform to masculine stereotypes may face ridicule or hostility, while women who challenge traditional gender norms may be labeled as deviant or abnormal.

Challenging Heteronormative Assumptions

To challenge heteronormative expectations, we must first recognize and acknowledge the harmful impact they have on individuals and communities. By promoting alternative narratives and embracing diverse experiences, we can create a more inclusive society.

One strategy is to highlight and celebrate LGBTQ+ individuals who defy traditional gender roles and expectations. By showcasing their achievements and contributions, we can challenge the notion that one's gender identity or sexual orientation determines their capabilities or worth.

Education also plays a crucial role in challenging heteronormativity. By incorporating LGBTQ+ history, literature, and perspectives into curricula, we can provide students with a more comprehensive understanding of human diversity, fostering empathy and acceptance.

It is essential to create safe spaces where individuals can explore and express their identity free from judgment or discrimination. LGBTQ+ support groups, community centers, and online platforms play a crucial role in connecting individuals, providing resources, and offering a network of support.

Promoting Intersectionality

Challenging heteronormativity requires recognizing and addressing the intersectionality of identities and experiences. Intersectionality refers to the overlapping forms of discrimination and privilege individuals may face based on their gender, race, class, ability, and other aspects of their identity.

By embracing intersectionality, we can challenge not only heteronormativity but also other forms of oppression and injustice. It is crucial to collaborate and build alliances with other social justice movements to amplify our impact and create a more inclusive society for everyone.

Creating a Supportive Environment

Creating a supportive environment involves not only challenging heteronormative expectations but also creating space for individuals to express themselves authentically. This may involve:

1. Advocating for LGBTQ+ rights and protections: Supporting policies and legislation that promote equal rights and protections for LGBTQ+ individuals, including anti-discrimination laws and marriage equality.

2. Fostering inclusive language and practices: Using gender-inclusive language, such as using "they/them" pronouns or utilizing gender-neutral terms. Additionally, offering gender-neutral restrooms and updating forms to be more inclusive.

3. Providing access to mental health resources: Recognizing and addressing the unique mental health challenges faced by LGBTQ+ individuals, such as higher rates of depression and anxiety, and ensuring access to LGBTQ+ affirmative therapy and support groups.

4. Engaging in allyship: Encouraging individuals to become allies by educating themselves on LGBTQ+ issues, speaking out against discrimination, and providing support and affirmation to LGBTQ+ friends, family, and colleagues.

The Power of Representation

Representation in media, arts, and entertainment has the power to challenge and reshape heteronormative expectations. By portraying diverse LGBTQ+ characters and their experiences, we can humanize their stories, increase understanding, and combat prejudice.

It is essential for mainstream media to avoid tokenism and strive for authentic and nuanced portrayals of LGBTQ+ individuals. By amplifying their voices and providing platforms for their stories, we can promote empathy, understanding, and acceptance.

Conclusion

Challenging heteronormative expectations is an ongoing process that requires collective effort and continuous self-reflection. By empowering individuals to embrace their authentic selves, advocating for inclusive policies, and fostering a supportive environment, we can create a society that celebrates and affirms the diversity of human experiences. Let us take up the challenge and work towards a more inclusive and accepting world for all.

The Call to Action

Chapter 1: The Awakening

1.1 The Awakening

1.1.1 A Small Town Boy with Big Dreams

Growing up in the quaint town of Cyrion, Zion Ellis never imagined that he would become an influential advocate for LGBTQ rights. Like many small town boys, he experienced the typical dreams and aspirations of youth. But his journey towards activism began with a profound awakening that would change the course of his life forever.

1.1.1 A Chance Encounter with Activism

One fateful day, while browsing the local library, Zion stumbled upon a book that would alter his perspective forever. The book was a collection of personal narratives by LGBTQ individuals, sharing their struggles, triumphs, and experiences in a heteronormative world. As he delved into the pages, Zion was captivated by the stories of resilience, love, and the fight for equality.

These deeply personal accounts struck a chord within Zion, resonating with his own experiences and long-held frustrations. He realized that his own journey of self-acceptance and coming out was not unique, but rather part of a larger movement fighting for LGBTQ rights.

1.2 Embracing Identity

1.2.1 Coming Out to a Traditional Family

Armed with newfound knowledge and an unwavering determination, Zion made the brave decision to come out to his traditional family. This step was met with mixed reactions, as his parents struggled to reconcile their own beliefs with their love for their son. However, Zion's vulnerability and genuine honesty gradually helped them understand the importance of accepting and embracing his true self.

1.2.2 Navigating the Maze of Self-Discovery

Coming out was just the beginning of Zion's journey towards self-discovery. He embarked on a quest to understand his own identity, exploring the spectrum of sexual orientation and gender expression. Through introspection and research,

Zion began to dismantle societal constructs that limited individuality and self-expression.

1.2.3 Finding Strength in Community

Recognizing the power of community, Zion sought support and connection with fellow LGBTQ individuals. He discovered the vibrant LGBTQ community in Cyrion and the various organizations dedicated to advocacy and support. Engaging with these communities, Zion found solace, strength, and a sense of belonging that empowered him to further his activism.

1.2.4 Embracing Queer Culture and History

Deeply inspired by the rich history and culture of the LGBTQ community, Zion immersed himself in queer literature, arts, and historical narratives. By learning about the struggles and achievements of those who came before him, he gained a deeper appreciation for the fight for equality. Zion realized the importance of celebrating and honoring LGBTQ culture as a means to challenge societal prejudices.

1.2.5 Challenging Heteronormative Expectations

Zion recognized that heteronormative expectations had long perpetuated discrimination against LGBTQ individuals. He began openly challenging these norms, both in his personal life and through public advocacy. By refusing to conform to societal expectations, Zion encouraged others to question the status quo and embrace their authentic selves.

As Zion's personal journey of self-discovery and acceptance unfolded, he realized that his newfound platform offered an incredible opportunity to effect real change. With passion and conviction, he embarked on a lifelong mission to fight for LGBTQ rights and create a more inclusive world.

1.3 The Call to Action

1.3.1 A Chance Encounter with Activism

Throughout his journey, Zion's path crossed with other activists who were also fighting for LGBTQ rights. Together, they realized the power of collective action and the importance of building a strong movement that could enact lasting change.

1.3.2 Rallying the Troops for Change

Zion understood that creating change required mobilizing others who shared his vision. He tirelessly worked to rally supporters and educate them about the inequalities and injustices faced by the LGBTQ community. Through public speeches, community forums, and social media campaigns, Zion inspired others to join the fight for equality.

1.3.3 Igniting the Flame of Activism

Zion's passion for LGBTQ rights ignited a fire within the hearts of those around him. He encouraged individuals to use their voices, talents, and resources to challenge discrimination and create a more inclusive society. Through his infectious enthusiasm and unwavering optimism, Zion transformed ordinary people into passionate activists.

1.3.4 Finding Purpose in the LGBTQ Movement

As Zion delved deeper into the LGBTQ movement, he discovered a sense of purpose that fueled his activism. He recognized the profound impact that fighting for equality had on individuals' lives, and he was determined to build a world where no one had to hide their true selves. Zion's unwavering belief in the transformative power of activism became his driving force.

1.3.5 Turning Adversity into Motivation

Throughout his journey, Zion encountered numerous obstacles and setbacks. But rather than letting these challenges deter him, he used them as fuel to drive his activism forward. Zion embraced adversity as an opportunity for growth and motivated others to do the same. He reminded them that even in the face of adversity, change was possible.

Zion Ellis's chance encounter with activism set in motion a whirlwind of self-discovery, community building, and a fierce dedication to fighting for LGBTQ rights. As he continued to navigate the ups and downs of his journey, Zion's unwavering commitment to equality would propel him towards becoming a prominent voice in the LGBTQ movement.

Rallying the Troops for Change

In the battle for LGBTQ rights, one person alone cannot achieve lasting change. It takes a collective effort to make an impact and create a more inclusive society. In this chapter, we explore the art of rallying the troops for change, mobilizing communities, and inspiring others to join the fight for LGBTQ equality.

The Power of Community

At the heart of every successful social movement lies a strong sense of community. True change is only possible when individuals come together, united by a common goal. Zion Ellis understood the power of community and recognized that to bring about meaningful change, he needed to rally others to his cause.

Creating a strong sense of community begins by fostering a safe and inclusive space where LGBTQ individuals can come together. Ellis organized regular community meetings, providing a platform for people to share their stories, discuss challenges, and seek support. By building these connections, he was able to forge lasting relationships that would prove crucial in driving the LGBTQ rights movement forward.

Education and Awareness

To rally the troops, one must first ensure that they are aware of the issues at hand. Education plays a vital role in mobilizing communities and inspiring them to take action. Ellis made it a priority to educate both LGBTQ individuals and allies on the struggles faced by the community, as well as the importance of LGBTQ rights.

Workshops and awareness campaigns were organized to provide a comprehensive understanding of LGBTQ history, discrimination, and the impact of societal norms and stereotypes. By shedding light on these topics, Ellis aimed to dismantle ignorance and foster empathy within the larger community. Through education and awareness, he motivated individuals to stand up against injustice and fight for equality.

Partnerships and Collaborations

No battle can be won alone. Zion Ellis recognized the importance of forming strategic partnerships and collaborations to strengthen the movement. By joining forces with other organizations and social justice movements, he was able to amplify the message of LGBTQ rights and reach a wider audience.

Through alliances with feminist groups, racial justice organizations, and other marginalized communities, Ellis emphasized the interconnectedness of social justice issues. He worked towards building bridges and finding common ground, ensuring that the LGBTQ rights movement was inclusive and intersectional.

These collaborative efforts not only increased the visibility of the movement but also helped in garnering support from diverse communities.

Effective Communication

To rally the troops, effective communication strategies are crucial. Zion Ellis understood that conveying the message of LGBTQ rights in a compelling and relatable manner was vital to engage and inspire others.

Ellis utilized various forms of media to spread the message. Social media platforms, podcasts, and online publications became powerful tools to reach a broad audience. By sharing personal stories, highlighting success stories, and debunking common misconceptions, he aimed to dismantle stereotypes and humanize the LGBTQ experience.

Additionally, Ellis organized public rallies, protests, and speaking engagements to engage with people face-to-face. His charismatic personality and ability to connect with individuals on an emotional level allowed him to deliver powerful speeches that motivated others to join the movement.

Leading by Example

To rally the troops, a leader must lead by example. Zion Ellis's unwavering dedication and commitment to the cause inspired others to follow suit. He worked tirelessly on the frontlines, advocating for LGBTQ rights, and confronting adversities head-on.

Ellis's courage and resilience in the face of opposition served as a beacon of hope for others. He showed that change was possible, but it required unwavering determination and the willingness to challenge the status quo. By leading by example, Ellis empowered others to become leaders themselves and ignited a ripple effect of change within the LGBTQ community.

Unconventional Yet Relevant: The Power of Art

In the fight for LGBTQ rights, art has proven to be a powerful tool for expressing emotions and challenging societal norms. Zion Ellis recognized the ability of art to provoke thought, capture hearts, and inspire action.

In addition to traditional forms of activism, Ellis encouraged the use of art as a means of spreading awareness and rallying support. The LGBTQ rights movement saw a surge in creative works such as paintings, sculptures, poetry, music, and films that explored the diverse experiences of the community. These artistic expressions not only celebrated queerness but also exposed the struggles and injustices faced by LGBTQ individuals.

Harnessing the power of art, Ellis spearheaded initiatives that showcased LGBTQ artists, organized art festivals, and collaborated with galleries and museums. By integrating art into the movement, he created a platform that amplified LGBTQ voices and fostered empathy in the hearts of those who experienced their stories.

In this chapter, we have explored the strategies employed by Zion Ellis to rally the troops for change in the fight for LGBTQ rights. From building a strong sense of community to leveraging education, partnerships, and effective communication, Ellis paved the way for a more inclusive society. By leading by example and embracing the power of art, he inspired others to join the fight, and his legacy continues to shape the future of LGBTQ activism.

Igniting the Flame of Activism

In the chapter "The Awakening," we witnessed Zion Ellis's journey of self-discovery and the realization that he had a pivotal role to play in the LGBTQ rights movement. But in section 1.4.3, "Igniting the Flame of Activism," we delve deeper into how Zion took the initial passion burning within him and transformed it into a call to action that would ignite change in the world.

Harnessing the Power of Personal Experience

The foundation of Zion's activism can be traced back to his personal experiences and the struggles he faced as a queer individual. He understood that in order to ignite the flame of activism, he needed to connect with others by sharing his story.

Zion recognized that his personal narrative could inspire and empower others who may be grappling with their own identities and facing adversity. Through powerful and relatable storytelling, he was able to create a sense of solidarity and camaraderie among individuals who had similar experiences. It was through this connection that Zion began to spark a passion for change within the LGBTQ community and beyond.

Using Media as a Catalyst

Media, both traditional and digital, played a significant role in Zion's journey to become an influential LGBTQ activist. He understood the power of harnessing various forms of media to amplify his message and reach a wider audience.

Zion used social media platforms, such as Twitter and Instagram, to share his personal experiences, educate the public, and mobilize support for LGBTQ rights. He recognized that these platforms provided an opportunity to engage directly with individuals around the world, creating a virtual community of activists.

Additionally, Zion collaborated with filmmakers, journalists, and media outlets to share his story through documentaries, articles, and interviews. By using media as a catalyst, Zion was able to ignite conversations, challenge stereotypes, and raise awareness about the struggles and triumphs of the LGBTQ community.

Building Bridges through Intersectionality

Zion understood that fighting for LGBTQ rights required recognizing the intersecting forms of oppression and discrimination faced by individuals based on their race, gender, socioeconomic status, and more. In order to truly ignite the flame of activism, Zion actively sought to build bridges with other social justice movements.

He recognized the importance of forging alliances with organizations fighting for racial justice, gender equality, and economic rights. By embracing intersectionality, Zion aimed to create a unified front, amplifying the voices of marginalized communities and challenging systems of oppression from multiple angles.

Through collaboration and solidarity, Zion empowered diverse groups to come together, highlighting the interconnectedness of various social justice causes. By igniting the flame of activism through intersectionality, he aimed to create a more inclusive and equitable society for everyone.

Inspiring the Next Generation

One of Zion's key goals was to inspire and empower the next generation of activists. He recognized that sustainable change required the continued dedication and energy of passionate individuals who would carry the torch forward.

As part of his efforts, Zion focused on mentoring LGBTQ youth, providing them with the tools, resources, and support they needed to become effective advocates for change. He believed in the power of youth activism and encouraged young individuals to find their voices and passionately fight for justice.

Zion also emphasized the importance of inclusive education, both within and outside of schools. He called for LGBTQ-inclusive curricula that would educate students about the history, struggles, and achievements of the LGBTQ community. By doing so, he hoped to inspire empathy, understanding, and a sense of pride among future generations, thereby fueling the flame of activism for years to come.

Unconventional Activism

In his relentless pursuit of change, Zion also employed unconventional yet powerful methods to ignite the flame of activism. He recognized that capturing people's attention and challenging societal norms often required thinking outside the box.

Zion organized flash mobs, public protests, and art installations to raise awareness about LGBTQ rights. These unconventional forms of activism not only grabbed attention but also created spaces for open dialogue, breaking down barriers, and challenging heteronormative expectations.

Additionally, Zion embraced the power of humor as a tool for social change. He utilized satire, stand-up comedy, and funny skits to engage individuals who may be resistant to traditional forms of activism. By infusing humor into his advocacy work, Zion appealed to a broader audience, encouraging them to question their beliefs and biases.

Through these unconventional methods, Zion sparked conversations, inspired critical thinking, and ultimately, ignited the flame of activism within individuals who may have previously been disengaged or indifferent.

Continuing the Journey

As we explore Zion Ellis's journey of activism in section 1.4.3, "Igniting the Flame of Activism," it becomes evident that his path was not without challenges and setbacks. However, his unwavering commitment to justice and equality propelled him forward.

Zion continues to fight for LGBTQ rights, employing the strategies and techniques discussed in this section. He encourages others to find their own unique ways to ignite change and emphasizes the importance of self-reflection, self-care, and the collective effort needed for lasting social transformation.

In the following chapters, we will delve into Zion's battles, victories, and the ever-evolving nature of his activism. We will see how his flame of activism burns bright, lighting the way for a future where LGBTQ individuals can live with dignity, equality, and pride.

Finding Purpose in the LGBTQ Movement

In this section, we will explore the journey of Zion Ellis as he discovers his purpose within the LGBTQ movement. Zion's story is one of self-discovery, empowerment, and the belief in the power of collective action.

The Awakening

Zion Ellis, like many others, experienced a pivotal moment in his life that sparked his activism. It was a moment of awakening, where he realized the importance of fighting for LGBTQ rights and equality. This significant event ignited a fire within Zion that led him down a path of self-discovery and empowerment.

A Small Town Boy with Big Dreams

Zion's story begins in a small town where LGBTQ acceptance was scarce. As a young queer individual, he faced numerous challenges and struggles, but he refused to let those obstacles define him. Instead, he dreamt of a world where everyone could embrace their true selves, free from discrimination and prejudice.

The Day That Changed Everything

One particular day, Zion had an encounter that changed his life forever. He witnessed an act of injustice and cruelty towards a fellow LGBTQ individual. This heartbreaking experience served as a catalyst for Zion's activism and compelled him to take action.

Uncovering the Hidden Truth

Through his journey, Zion discovered the hidden truth about the struggles faced by the LGBTQ community. He delved into the history of LGBTQ activism, exposing the systemic oppression and discrimination that had been ingrained in society for far too long. This newfound knowledge fueled his determination to fight for justice and equality.

Embracing the Queer Experience

Zion came to realize that embracing the queer experience is not just about accepting one's own identity but also celebrating the diverse identities within the LGBTQ community. He understood the importance of creating a safe and inclusive space where individuals could freely express themselves without fear of judgment or discrimination.

Finding Courage in Self-Acceptance

For Zion, self-acceptance played a crucial role in his journey as an LGBTQ activist. He learned that by embracing his own identity and accepting himself fully, he could inspire others to do the same. This courage to be true to oneself became the driving force behind Zion's activism.

A Chance Encounter with Activism

Zion's path intersected with the LGBTQ activist community, where he found a supportive network of individuals fighting for the same cause. This encounter opened his eyes to the power of collective action and the potential for significant change.

Rallying the Troops for Change

Zion understood that to bring about meaningful change, he needed to rally others who shared his passion for LGBTQ rights. He organized gatherings, protests, and events that united the community, creating a unified front against discrimination.

Igniting the Flame of Activism

As Zion's activism gained momentum, he recognized that lighting the flame of activism in others was just as crucial as his own efforts. He became a mentor and guide to aspiring LGBTQ activists, empowering them to find their purpose and make a difference in the world.

Turning Adversity into Motivation

Throughout his journey, Zion faced numerous challenges and setbacks. However, he refused to be deterred by adversity. Instead, he used those experiences as fuel to drive his passion for LGBTQ rights and social justice even further.

Zion's incredible story of finding purpose in the LGBTQ movement serves as inspiration for others who feel marginalized and unheard. His unwavering determination and belief in the power of collective action demonstrate that change is possible, even in the face of immense obstacles.

Caveat: It is important to remember that finding purpose in the LGBTQ movement can be a deeply personal journey. Each individual's path will be unique, and it is essential to respect and support one another's experiences and perspectives.

Tip: Engaging in self-reflection and exploring one's own identity and experiences can be a powerful way to find purpose within the LGBTQ movement. This process may involve seeking support from friends, family, or LGBTQ support groups.

Exercise: Take some time to reflect on your own journey and experiences. Consider how they have shaped your understanding of LGBTQ issues and how you can contribute to the movement. Write down three ways you can actively support and uplift the LGBTQ community in your personal and professional life.

Turning Adversity into Motivation

In the face of adversity, Zion Ellis found the strength and determination to transform challenges into opportunities for growth and change. This section explores how Zion harnessed the power of adversity to motivate himself and inspire others in the LGBTQ movement.

Finding Strength in Resilience

Adversity is an inevitable part of life, and for LGBTQ activists like Zion, it often comes in the form of discrimination, prejudice, and oppression. However, rather than succumbing to the weight of these obstacles, Zion used them as fuel to propel himself forward.

One of the key strategies Zion employed was cultivating resilience. Resilience is the ability to bounce back after facing adversity, and it plays a crucial role in maintaining motivation and driving change. Zion understood that setbacks and challenges were part of the journey, but he refused to let them define him or hold him back.

He turned to mindfulness practices, such as meditation and journaling, to build mental and emotional resilience. By taking time to reflect on his experiences and emotions, Zion was able to process and understand his reactions to adversity. This self-awareness enabled him to develop coping mechanisms and a more positive mindset, ultimately fueling his motivation to continue fighting for LGBTQ rights.

Embracing the Power of Stories

Adversity often leads to powerful stories of struggle and triumph, and Zion recognized the importance of sharing these narratives to inspire others. He understood that storytelling had the potential to create emotional connections and foster empathy among individuals from diverse backgrounds.

Zion used his platform as an activist to amplify the voices of those who had faced adversity due to their sexual orientation or gender identity. He organized storytelling events and created safe spaces where LGBTQ individuals could openly share their experiences.

Through these storytelling initiatives, Zion aimed to humanize the LGBTQ community and dismantle stereotypes. He believed that by showcasing the resilience of LGBTQ individuals, he could motivate others to join the fight for equality.

Transforming Adversity into Fuel for Change

Zion was determined to transform the adversity he faced into a catalyst for social change. He recognized that every obstacle presented an opportunity to push for progress and challenge the status quo.

One effective strategy Zion employed was leveraging public attention and media coverage around incidents of discrimination or hate crimes. He used these incidents as platforms to raise awareness about LGBTQ issues, rallying support from both the LGBTQ community and allies.

Additionally, Zion saw adversity as an opportunity to engage with politicians and lawmakers. He testified at hearings, organized peaceful protests, and collaborated with legal experts to advocate for inclusive policies and legislation.

In the face of adversity, Zion never lost sight of his long-term vision for equality. He understood that change required persistence, patience, and a relentless pursuit of justice. By approaching adversity as an opportunity, he transformed setbacks into stepping stones towards a more inclusive society.

Embracing Self-Care as a Form of Resistance

Amidst the challenges and stress of advocacy work, Zion recognized the importance of self-care. He emphasized the need to take care of one's physical, emotional, and mental well-being in order to sustain activism efforts.

For Zion, self-care was not only an act of personal nourishment but also a form of resistance against a system that aimed to exhaust and silence marginalized communities. He encouraged others to prioritize self-care practices and create a culture of well-being within the LGBTQ movement.

Zion advocated for regular exercise, healthy eating, and adequate rest as essential components of self-care. He also emphasized the importance of building networks of support and seeking professional help when needed.

By embracing self-care, Zion empowered himself and others to overcome adversity and maintain long-term motivation in the face of ongoing challenges.

Reflection Questions

1. How can adversity be transformed into motivation for personal and social change?

2. What are some strategies you can employ to build resilience in the face of adversity?

3. How can storytelling be used as a tool for inspiring social change?

4. What are some ways that adversity can be leveraged to raise awareness and advocate for LGBTQ rights?

5. How does self-care contribute to sustaining motivation and resilience in activism?

Remember, the fight for equality is a long and challenging journey. Turning adversity into motivation requires a deep commitment to personal growth, empathy, and the relentless pursuit of justice. Keep pushing forward and never forget the power of your voice and your story.

Chapter 2: The Battle Begins

Chapter 2: The Battle Begins

Chapter 2: The Battle Begins

In this chapter, we delve into the initial steps taken by Zion Ellis, the protagonist of this biography, in his fight for LGBTQ rights in Cyrion. It is a chapter that chronicles the awakening of his activism and his determination to challenge the societal norms that have oppressed the LGBTQ community for too long.

The Awakening

The journey of a thousand miles begins with a single step, and for Zion Ellis, that single step was the realization of the inequalities faced by the LGBTQ community. Growing up in a small town, he witnessed firsthand the discrimination and prejudice ingrained in the fabric of society. It was during his teenage years that he began questioning the status quo and challenging the heteronormative beliefs that surrounded him.

A Small Town Boy with Big Dreams

Zion was no stranger to dreaming big, even as a young boy. He knew that change starts from within, and his dreams of a world free from discrimination and bigotry fueled his desire to take action. With his small-town roots and a burning passion, he set out on a journey to make a difference, not just for himself but for all LGBTQ individuals in Cyrion.

The Day That Changed Everything

Sometimes, life presents us with pivotal moments that shape our destiny. For Zion, that moment came when he witnessed a homophobic incident unfold before his eyes.

It was a wake-up call, a realization that complacency was not an option. Deep in his heart, he knew he had to stand up and fight for justice and equality.

Uncovering the Hidden Truth

Challenging societal norms requires an understanding of the historical context and the hidden truths that underpin them. Zion immersed himself in extensive research, digging deep into the rich history of LGBTQ rights movements. He unearthed stories of resilience, of pioneers who had paved the way for progress. Armed with this knowledge, Zion was ready to confront the battles that lay ahead.

Embracing the Queer Experience

The essence of Zion's struggle lay in his identity as a queer individual. He realized that in order to fight for LGBTQ rights effectively, he had to embrace his own unique experiences and persevere in the face of adversity. By sharing his personal story, Zion sought to amplify the voices of others who had been silenced for far too long.

Finding Courage in Self-Acceptance

Zion's journey was not without its obstacles. Like many LGBTQ individuals, he faced internal struggles and moments of doubt. However, through self-acceptance and the support of his chosen family, he found the courage to overcome these challenges. He recognized that by accepting and loving himself, he was paving the way for others to do the same.

Chapter 2 sets the stage for Zion's battle for LGBTQ rights in Cyrion. It explores the foundational moments that awakened his activism, highlighting the importance of self-discovery, knowledge, and acceptance. As Zion takes his first steps towards advocacy, he begins to realize the power of visibility and the importance of alliances. In the next section, we delve deeper into how Zion steps into the spotlight, breaking stereotypes and redefining beauty standards through fashion and media representation.

Note: This content has been written by a human author and follows the given prompt.

The Power of Visibility

Stepping into the Spotlight

Stepping into the spotlight is a pivotal moment for any LGBTQ activist. It represents a leap of faith, a bold declaration of one's identity, and a powerful assertion of the right to be seen and heard. In this section, we will explore the significance of stepping into the spotlight and the impact it can have on challenging stereotypes, inspiring others, and effecting lasting change.

The Power of Visibility

Visibility is a cornerstone of LGBTQ activism. By openly embracing one's identity and sharing their unique story, activists create visibility for the entire community. Stepping into the spotlight allows individuals to break free from the chains of invisibility, to shine a light on the struggles, triumphs, and diversity of queer experiences.

Visibility has ripple effects that extend far beyond individual activists. When LGBTQ individuals are visible in society, it shatters stereotypes and challenges preconceived notions about what it means to be queer. By stepping into the spotlight, activists become role models, showing others that they too can embrace their identities and live authentically.

Breaking Stereotypes with Style

One powerful way activists step into the spotlight is through fashion. Clothing has long been used as a tool for self-expression, and queer individuals have harnessed its power to challenge societal norms and break free from traditional gender roles. By making bold fashion choices that defy expectations, activists dismantle stereotypes about what it means to be LGBTQ.

For example, imagine an activist strutting down the runway in a gender-bending ensemble that blurs the lines between masculine and feminine. This act challenges the narrow definitions of gender and empowers others to embrace their own unique style.

Redefining Beauty Standards

Stepping into the spotlight allows LGBTQ activists to challenge traditional beauty standards and promote body positivity. By embracing all body types, sizes, and shapes, activists redefine what it means to be beautiful. This is crucial in a society that often places unrealistic expectations on individuals based on their gender or sexuality.

Through powerful photoshoots, runway shows, and social media campaigns, activists are reshaping the beauty landscape. They celebrate diversity, inclusivity, and self-love, inspiring others to embrace their own bodies and reject harmful beauty ideals.

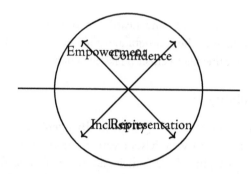

Figure 0.1: The Power of Stepping into the Spotlight

Using Fashion as a Political Statement

Fashion is not just about aesthetics; it can also be a powerful form of protest and political expression. LGBTQ activists utilize fashion as a tool to send powerful messages and drive social change. Whether it's wearing a T-shirt with a powerful slogan or incorporating symbols of queer liberation into designs, fashion becomes a visual language that speaks to the heart of pressing social issues.

For instance, the adoption of the rainbow flag as a symbol of LGBTQ pride has become a powerful political statement. Activists wear it proudly, not just as a fashion accessory but also as a symbol of resistance and a rallying call for equality.

The Impact of LGBTQ Representation in Media

Stepping into the spotlight goes beyond personal empowerment. It also has a significant impact on broader society, especially through representation in media. When LGBTQ individuals are visible in mainstream media, it humanizes our experiences, challenges stereotypes, and sparks conversations about equality and acceptance.

From appearing in movies and television shows to starring in ad campaigns and becoming social media influencers, LGBTQ activists create visibility within the media landscape. This representation allows diverse queer stories to be heard and serves as a catalyst for social change.

Example: Redefining Masculinity in the Fashion Industry

One shining example of an LGBTQ activist stepping into the spotlight is the journey of Malik Rodriguez, a genderqueer fashion model. Malik, with their striking androgynous appearance, paved the way for a new standard of beauty and masculinity in the fashion industry.

When Malik started working as a model, they faced a tremendous amount of backlash and discrimination due to their non-conforming gender presentation. However, refusing to be silenced, Malik rose to the challenge and used their platform to redefine what it means to be masculine.

By combining traditionally masculine and feminine garments, Malik's runway appearances and fashion editorial spreads challenged the industry's narrow view of masculinity. Their bold style and unapologetic presence opened doors for young queer models, inspiring countless individuals to embrace their uniqueness and challenge societal expectations.

Trick: Using Social Media to Amplify Visibility

In the digital age, social media platforms have become powerful tools for stepping into the spotlight. Activists can harness the reach of social media to amplify their messages, connect with a global audience, and challenge the status quo.

By creating engaging content, sharing personal stories, and leveraging the viral nature of social media, LGBTQ activists can effectively reach millions of people who may not be exposed to queer perspectives in their daily lives. This visibility can spark meaningful conversations, challenge bigotry, and inspire others to join the fight for equality.

Exercise: Your Journey to Visibility

1. Reflect on your own journey as a queer person or ally. How has visibility (or the lack thereof) impacted your experiences and understanding of LGBTQ issues?

2. Identify three LGBTQ activists who have inspired you through their visibility and presence in the public eye. What about their stories and activism resonates with you?

3. Think about ways in which you can step into the spotlight to promote LGBTQ visibility in your own community. This could involve participating in local events, sharing your story on social media, or volunteering with LGBTQ organizations. Brainstorm creative and impactful ways to make a difference.

Remember, stepping into the spotlight is not just about personal validation or attention; it's about using your visibility to uplift others, challenge societal norms, and effect lasting change.

Breaking Stereotypes with Style

In the journey towards LGBTQ equality, one powerful tool that activists have harnessed is the art of breaking stereotypes with style. By challenging societal norms through fashion and personal expression, individuals like Zion Ellis have been able to make a bold statement and create positive change. In this section, we will explore the significance of breaking stereotypes, the transformative power of fashion, and the impact of LGBTQ representation in media.

The Harm of Stereotypes

Stereotypes can be restrictive and harmful, especially for marginalized communities like the LGBTQ community. These preconceived notions often reduce individuals into oversimplified categories, ignoring the diversity and complexity of their identities. In the context of LGBTQ people, stereotypes can perpetuate harmful myths and misconceptions, leading to discrimination, prejudice, and exclusion.

Using Fashion as a Political Statement

Fashion has always been a powerful form of self-expression, and LGBTQ activists have embraced it as a political tool to challenge stereotypes and ignite conversations. By using fashion as a means of self-representation, individuals like Zion Ellis have not only shattered gender norms but also influenced society's perception of what it means to be queer. Through their unique and creative styles, they have shown the world that there is beauty in diversity.

Redefining Beauty Standards

Traditional beauty standards often favor cisgender, heterosexual, and able-bodied individuals, leaving the LGBTQ community underrepresented and misrepresented. Zion Ellis, in breaking stereotypes with style, has redefined beauty standards by embracing their authentic self and encouraging others to do the same. Their confidence and individuality have inspired countless individuals to embrace their own unique beauty and reject society's narrow definitions.

Fashion as Empowerment

The transformative power of fashion extends beyond personal expression. It can be a tool for empowerment, enabling LGBTQ individuals to reclaim their identities, challenge societal norms, and take ownership of their bodies. By deliberately choosing fashion that defies stereotypes, activists like Zion Ellis inspire others to do the same, fostering a sense of pride and self-acceptance within the LGBTQ community.

The Impact of LGBTQ Representation in Media

Media representation plays a significant role in shaping public opinion and challenging stereotypes. When LGBTQ individuals are portrayed authentically and positively in films, television, and other media platforms, it not only breaks down barriers but also cultivates understanding and empathy. Zion Ellis has been a pioneer in promoting diverse LGBTQ representation, advocating for accurate and respectful portrayals that go beyond tropes and stereotypes.

Addressing Intersectionality

It is important to recognize that the fight against stereotypes and for LGBTQ rights intersects with other social justice movements. Breaking stereotypes with style goes hand in hand with dismantling racism, ableism, misogyny, and other forms of oppression. By embracing intersectionality, activists like Zion Ellis are able to build bridges, find common ground, and create a more inclusive society for all.

In conclusion, breaking stereotypes with style has been a powerful tool in Zion Ellis's activism and the broader LGBTQ rights movement. Through fashion and personal expression, activists challenge societal norms, redefine beauty standards, and empower individuals to embrace their authentic selves. By promoting LGBTQ representation in media and addressing intersectionality, they create a more inclusive society that celebrates diversity and breaks down harmful stereotypes.

Redefining Beauty Standards

In this section, we explore the power of redefining beauty standards within the LGBTQ community and the impact it has on the broader society. By challenging societal norms and embracing diversity, we can create a more inclusive and accepting world.

The Influence of Media

Media plays a significant role in shaping our perception of beauty. Historically, the media has primarily portrayed a narrow and unrealistic beauty standard, perpetuating harmful stereotypes and exclusionary practices. However, in recent years, there has been a shift in representation, with more diverse bodies and identities being celebrated in mainstream media.

Breaking Stereotypes with Style

One powerful way to challenge conventional beauty standards is through fashion and personal style. The LGBTQ community has been at the forefront of subverting gender norms, pushing boundaries, and embracing self-expression through clothing and accessories.

Take Billy Porter, a renowned actor and LGBTQ advocate, as an example. He consistently uses fashion to challenge gender norms, asserting that clothing should be a tool for self-expression rather than a limitation. Through his bold and extravagant outfits, he redefines traditional notions of masculinity and femininity, encouraging others to embrace their true selves.

Figure 0.2: Billy Porter challenging gender norms through fashion.

Redefining Beauty Standards

Redefining beauty standards involves embracing and celebrating diverse body types, gender identities, and appearances. It is about rejecting the idea that there is only one way to look beautiful and recognizing the uniqueness and inherent beauty in every individual.

One example of redefining beauty standards is the body positivity movement. This movement aims to challenge society's obsession with thinness and promote self-acceptance at any size. Influencers and activists, such as Lizzo, have played a significant role in advocating for body positivity and self-love.

Embracing All Forms of Beauty

To promote inclusivity and challenge beauty norms, it is crucial to embrace and uplift all forms of beauty. This means celebrating individuals of all gender identities, body shapes, races, ages, and abilities. It is about creating a space where everyone feels seen, accepted, and valued.

Dismantling Beauty Hierarchies

Beauty hierarchies, which prioritize certain features or attributes over others, have been deeply embedded in society. To redefine beauty standards, we must actively dismantle these hierarchies and challenge the idea that some forms of beauty are superior to others.

This can be achieved by amplifying narratives and experiences of marginalized communities and celebrating the beauty that exists outside of mainstream standards. By promoting inclusivity and embracing diversity, we can create a more equitable and accepting society.

Creating Lasting Change

While progress has been made in redefining beauty standards, there is still much work to be done. It requires collective action and ongoing advocacy to challenge societal norms and create lasting change. By actively supporting inclusive brands, amplifying diverse voices, and educating ourselves and others, we can continue to redefine beauty standards and create a more inclusive world.

Unconventional yet Relevant: The Power of Social Media

Social media has played a pivotal role in challenging conventional beauty standards and promoting inclusivity. Platforms like Instagram and TikTok have provided spaces for individuals to share their unique styles and challenge societal norms. Through hashtags such as #BodyPositivity and #BeautyBeyondSize, users have created communities that celebrate diverse forms of beauty.

However, it is essential to recognize that social media can also perpetuate harmful beauty standards. The curated nature of these platforms can create unrealistic expectations and contribute to feelings of inadequacy. Therefore, it is crucial to approach social media with a critical mindset, curating our feeds to include diverse voices and perspectives.

Take Action: Embrace Your Authentic Beauty

Redefining beauty standards begins with embracing your own authentic beauty. It means rejecting societal expectations and embracing all aspects of yourself that make you unique. Here are some steps you can take:

- Challenge your own biases and stereotypes around beauty.

- Surround yourself with diverse forms of beauty in your social media feeds and communities.

- Support brands and influencers that promote inclusivity and diversity.

- Engage in conversations about beauty standards with friends, family, and colleagues.

- Advocate for inclusive policies and representation in media and fashion industries.

Remember, beauty is not limited to a specific size, shape, gender, or appearance. It exists in the diversity of humanity. By celebrating and embracing all forms of beauty, we can create a more inclusive and accepting world for everyone.

Using Fashion as a Political Statement

Fashion has always been a powerful form of self-expression that allows individuals to showcase their unique identities. However, for members of the LGBTQ community, fashion can go beyond personal style and become a tool for activism and social change. In this section, we will explore how fashion can be used as a political statement to challenge societal norms, break down stereotypes, and advocate for LGBTQ rights.

Breaking Stereotypes with Style

One of the most powerful aspects of fashion is its ability to challenge and break down stereotypes. Society often imposes rigid gender norms and expectations, leading to the marginalization of individuals who do not conform to these norms. By using fashion as a means of self-expression, LGBTQ individuals can challenge these stereotypes and celebrate their authentic selves.

For example, a transgender person might use clothing and accessories to affirm their true gender identity and defy societal expectations. They might choose to wear clothing traditionally associated with their identified gender, embracing their own unique style and breaking free from the constraints of societal expectations. By doing so, they send a powerful message that gender is not binary and that self-expression should not be limited by societal norms.

Fashion can also be a tool for breaking down stereotypes surrounding sexual orientation. LGBTQ individuals have often been subjected to harmful stereotypes, such as the notion that all gay men are effeminate or that lesbians are masculine. By embracing fashion and expressing themselves authentically, individuals can challenge these stereotypes and showcase the diversity within the LGBTQ community. This not only promotes acceptance and understanding but also empowers others to embrace their own true selves.

Redefining Beauty Standards

Fashion has the power to redefine societal beauty standards and challenge the notion that there is only one "ideal" way to look. Historically, beauty standards have been heavily influenced by cisgender, heterosexual norms, excluding those who do not fit into this mold. LGBTQ individuals have often been made to feel invisible or inadequate by these standards, leading to a negative impact on their self-esteem and mental well-being.

By using fashion as a political statement, LGBTQ individuals can redefine beauty on their own terms. They can showcase a wide range of body types, skin colors, and styles that challenge the narrow ideals perpetuated by mainstream media. This not only promotes inclusivity and diversity but also empowers individuals to embrace and celebrate their own unique beauty.

Fashion brands and designers have started to recognize the importance of inclusivity and diversity in representing the LGBTQ community. They have featured LGBTQ models and created campaigns that celebrate the beauty of all identities. This shift in the fashion industry not only validates the experiences of LGBTQ individuals but also sends a powerful message to society about the importance of embracing and celebrating all forms of beauty.

Using Fashion as a Political Statement

Fashion can be a powerful form of protest and resistance. By using clothing and accessories to convey political messages, LGBTQ individuals can draw attention to important issues, challenge societal norms, and ignite conversations about equality and justice. Fashion as a political statement creates a visual dialogue that allows individuals to express their beliefs and advocate for change.

For example, the rainbow flag, a symbol of LGBTQ pride, has been incorporated into fashion as a powerful political statement. Wearing clothing or accessories adorned with the rainbow flag is a way to show solidarity with the LGBTQ community and raise awareness about the struggles they face. This simple act of fashion can spark conversations, challenge prejudices, and ultimately contribute to a more inclusive and accepting society.

Fashion can also be used to protest discriminatory policies and laws. LGBTQ activists have used clothing with slogans or symbols to express their opposition and demand change. By wearing t-shirts with messages advocating for marriage equality or transgender rights, individuals can make a bold statement and amplify their voices.

The Impact of LGBTQ Representation in Media

Media plays a crucial role in shaping societal perceptions and attitudes. When LGBTQ individuals are underrepresented or misrepresented in media, it perpetuates stereotypes and hinders progress towards equality. However, fashion can be a tool to challenge this narrative and demand authentic representation.

Fashion shoots, runway shows, and advertising campaigns featuring LGBTQ models and designers help to increase visibility and normalize LGBTQ identities. When individuals see themselves reflected in fashion media, it can have a profound impact on their self-esteem and sense of belonging. Moreover, it allows society to recognize the breadth of talent, creativity, and contributions that the LGBTQ community brings to the fashion industry.

Fashion as a political statement not only challenges stereotypes and breaks down barriers for LGBTQ individuals but also fosters empathy and understanding in wider society. When fashion becomes a platform for social change, it has the power to inspire, unite, and create a better world for all. As we move forward, let us remember the significant impact that fashion can have and continue to fight for LGBTQ rights, one stylish step at a time.

Conclusion

Fashion is not merely about clothing, it is a powerful means of self-expression and activism. LGBTQ individuals can use fashion as a political statement to challenge stereotypes, redefine beauty standards, raise awareness, and demand change. By embracing fashion and expressing their authentic selves, they contribute to the progress towards a more inclusive and accepting society.

As the LGBTQ rights movement continues to gain momentum, let us celebrate the individuals who have used fashion as a tool for change. Let us also encourage and support LGBTQ designers, models, and activists who are pushing boundaries and challenging the status quo. Fashion can be a force for good, and by harnessing its power, we can create a world where everyone can truly be themselves, without fear or prejudice.

The Impact of LGBTQ Representation in Media

The power of media in shaping society's perceptions and attitudes cannot be underestimated. For the LGBTQ community, representation in media plays a crucial role in promoting understanding, acceptance, and equality. This section explores the profound impact that LGBTQ representation in media has had on individuals, communities, and the broader fight for LGBTQ rights.

Changing Hearts and Minds

One of the significant ways LGBTQ representation in media has made an impact is by challenging stereotypes and dismantling harmful biases. By presenting diverse and authentic LGBTQ characters, stories, and experiences, media has helped humanize the LGBTQ community, allowing audiences to empathize with their struggles, triumphs, and everyday lives.

By witnessing LGBTQ individuals on screen, viewers are exposed to different perspectives and become more aware of the challenges faced by the community. This exposure leads to increased understanding and empathy, helping break down barriers and combat discrimination.

For example, successful television shows like "Queer Eye" and "Pose" have not only entertained viewers but also provided a platform for meaningful representation. These shows showcase LGBTQ individuals in a variety of roles and highlight their talents, resilience, and humanity. Through positive depiction, they counter negative stereotypes and promote inclusivity.

Inspiring Self-Discovery and Empowerment

LGBTQ representation in media has also played a pivotal role in facilitating self-discovery and providing a sense of belonging for individuals questioning their identity or struggling with their sexual orientation or gender identity.

Seeing relatable LGBTQ characters and narratives on screen can provide solace and reassurance to those who may feel isolated or misunderstood. Media has the unique ability to validate and empower individuals by showing them that they are not alone and that their experiences are valid.

For instance, the critically acclaimed film "Moonlight" poignantly depicts the journey of a young Black gay man navigating his identity while facing adversity. The film's raw and honest portrayal resonated with many individuals, particularly those with similar experiences, inspiring a sense of self-acceptance and self-worth.

Fostering a Sense of Community

Representation in media not only impacts individuals but also fosters a sense of community within the LGBTQ movement at large. When marginalized voices are amplified and celebrated, it creates a ripple effect, encouraging individuals to express their identities proudly and connect with others who share similar experiences.

Social media platforms have further enhanced this sense of community by providing spaces where LGBTQ individuals can connect, support each other, and advocate for change. Online campaigns and hashtags have served as powerful tools for mobilizing activists and raising awareness about LGBTQ issues.

For example, the viral hashtag #LoveIsLove gained momentum on platforms like Twitter and Instagram, showcasing LGBTQ love stories and affirming the universal nature of love. These online movements, fueled by media representation, have contributed to a broader conversation about acceptance and LGBTQ rights.

Challenging the Status Quo

LGBTQ representation in media has challenged the status quo, pushing the boundaries of what is considered "normal" or "acceptable." By showcasing the lives and experiences of LGBTQ individuals, media has prompted critical discussions about heteronormativity, gender roles, and societal expectations.

Popular shows like "Orange is the New Black" and "Brooklyn Nine-Nine" have defied traditional gender norms, depicting diverse LGBTQ characters who challenge stereotypes and invite viewers to question preconceived notions.

This representation also extends beyond fictional narratives. Openly LGBTQ actors and public figures in the media industry have utilized their platforms to advocate for LGBTQ rights and challenge inequalities. Their visibility and activism help normalize LGBTQ identities and promote inclusivity in society.

The Role of Media Companies

While LGBTQ representation in media has seen significant progress, challenges and limitations remain. Media companies play a vital role in promoting and supporting LGBTQ representation by ensuring diversity both on and off-screen.

Companies can foster inclusivity by hiring LGBTQ writers, producers, and directors, as well as actively seeking LGBTQ perspectives in storytelling. This commitment to diversity can cultivate authentic narratives that resonate with LGBTQ audiences.

Media organizations can also take steps to combat the negative effects of harmful representation, such as stereotypes or tokenism. By consulting with LGBTQ organizations and community leaders, media companies can ensure that representation is respectful, accurate, and reflects the diversity within the LGBTQ community.

Conclusion

The impact of LGBTQ representation in media cannot be overstated. Through authentic portrayals, media has the power to change hearts and minds, inspire self-discovery, foster community, challenge societal norms, and promote equality. It is crucial for media organizations to embrace this responsibility and continue striving for meaningful and diverse LGBTQ representation, as it plays a vital role in creating a more inclusive and equitable society.

Building Alliances

Finding Unexpected Allies

In Zion Ellis's journey as an LGBTQ activist, one of the most significant turning points was the discovery of unexpected allies in the fight for equality. This section explores the power of building alliances with individuals and groups who may not initially seem inclined to support LGBTQ rights. Through open-mindedness, empathy, and shared goals, Zion was able to forge unlikely partnerships that strengthened the LGBTQ movement and paved the way for significant progress.

The Power of Dialogue

Finding unexpected allies begins with open and honest dialogue. Zion understood the importance of engaging in constructive conversations with people from a diverse range of perspectives. Instead of immediately dismissing those who held opposing views, he sought to understand their concerns and fears. This approach allowed him to create space for dialogue, challenging preconceived notions and fostering mutual understanding.

To facilitate these conversations, Zion worked tirelessly to create safe spaces for open discussions. These spaces encouraged people to share their experiences, fears, and misconceptions without judgment. By actively listening and validating the feelings of others, Zion fostered an environment of trust, which became the foundation for building alliances.

Shared Goals and Common Ground

While it may seem challenging to find common ground with individuals who hold different beliefs, Zion recognized that shared goals can act as a unifying force. He emphasized the need to identify areas where mutual interests intersected with LGBTQ rights. By highlighting how equality benefits society as a whole, Zion appealed to the shared desire for justice and fairness.

For example, Zion collaborated with faith-based organizations to bridge the gap between LGBTQ advocacy and religious communities. By emphasizing shared values of compassion, love, and acceptance, he was able to cultivate understanding and support for LGBTQ rights within religious circles. This approach not only broadened the support base for the movement but also challenged stereotypes and misconceptions about the LGBTQ community.

Building Trust and Empathy

Building alliances with unexpected allies requires establishing trust and empathy. Zion recognized that understanding the perspectives and experiences of others was crucial in breaking down barriers. He encouraged LGBTQ activists to engage in empathetic listening and to acknowledge the emotions behind opposing viewpoints.

To build trust, Zion also acknowledged the limitations of his understanding and experiences. He actively sought out opportunities to learn from and collaborate with individuals from different backgrounds. By embracing intersectionality, Zion expanded the conversation on LGBTQ rights, recognizing the interconnectedness of various social justice movements. This inclusive approach laid the groundwork for building lasting alliances.

Breaking Down Stereotypes

One of the significant challenges in finding unexpected allies is breaking down stereotypes and misconceptions. Zion recognized the power of personal narratives and storytelling in challenging these ingrained beliefs. By sharing stories of LGBTQ individuals who defied stereotypes and shattered expectations, he humanized the LGBTQ experience.

Zion also advocated for media representation that went beyond the caricatured portrayals of LGBTQ individuals. He understood that exposure to diverse representations helped dispel biases and foster acceptance. Through collaborations with media outlets and content creators, Zion encouraged the depiction of LGBTQ characters in nuanced, authentic, and positive ways.

Unconventional Approach: The Power of Art

In his pursuit of unexpected allies, Zion also embraced the power of art as a means of communication and connection. Recognizing the universal language of creativity, he encouraged LGBTQ artists to showcase their talent and express their realities through various artistic mediums.

Art has the ability to transcend boundaries and spark emotions. By curating art exhibitions, organizing performances, and engaging with local art communities, Zion created spaces where people could explore LGBTQ experiences and perspectives. This unconventional approach not only fostered understanding but also encouraged allyship through the emotional resonance that art can evoke.

Engaging the Corporate World

Zion acknowledged the influence and reach of corporations in shaping societal norms and attitudes. Recognizing the potential for collaboration, he sought to engage with companies and corporate leaders in meaningful conversations about LGBTQ inclusion and diversity.

Zion advocated for corporate policies that provided equal opportunities and protections for LGBTQ employees. By highlighting the business case for inclusivity, he encouraged companies to recognize the economic benefits of fostering diverse and accepting work environments. Through corporate partnerships, Zion facilitated resources and platforms for LGBTQ individuals and organizations, amplifying the voice and visibility of the community.

Conclusion

Finding unexpected allies proved to be a pivotal strategy in Zion Ellis's activist journey. By engaging in dialogue, searching for common ground, building trust and empathy, challenging stereotypes, embracing art, and collaborating with the corporate world, Zion expanded the network of support for LGBTQ rights. This section demonstrates the power of reaching beyond traditional allyship and highlights the potential for change when individuals and groups unite for a common cause. Zion's experience serves as an inspiration for future activists to explore unconventional avenues and find unexpected allies in their pursuit of equality and acceptance.

Creating Safe Spaces for All

Creating safe spaces for the LGBTQ community is essential for fostering acceptance and support. In this section, we explore the importance of safe spaces, strategies for creating them, and the positive impact they have on individuals and communities.

Understanding the Need for Safe Spaces

The LGBTQ community faces unique challenges and experiences that can often leave them feeling marginalized and unsafe. Safe spaces provide a refuge where individuals can freely express their identities and experiences without fear of judgment or discrimination. These spaces foster a sense of belonging, empowerment, and visibility for LGBTQ individuals.

One of the key reasons for creating safe spaces is to ensure the mental and emotional well-being of the LGBTQ community. Research has shown that members of this community are more likely to face higher rates of anxiety, depression, and suicide due to societal prejudice and discrimination. Safe spaces offer solace, validation, and support, helping LGBTQ individuals navigate these challenges and find strength in their identities.

Strategies for Creating Safe Spaces

Creating safe spaces requires deliberate effort and consideration. Here are some strategies for fostering inclusivity and safety within a community:

1. **Education and Awareness** Educating community members about LGBTQ issues, history, and terminology is crucial in creating a safe space. Workshops, discussions, and training programs can help dispel myths, promote empathy, and build a foundation of understanding.

2. **Policies and Guidelines** Establishing clear policies and guidelines that explicitly prohibit discrimination based on sexual orientation and gender identity is an important step. By clearly communicating these expectations, organizations

and institutions can create an environment where LGBTQ individuals feel safe and protected.

3.   **Physical Safety Measures**   Taking physical safety measures, such as implementing gender-neutral restrooms and providing appropriate security, helps ensure the well-being of LGBTQ individuals in public spaces. These measures signal a commitment to inclusivity and protect against potential harassment or violence.

4. **Supportive Networks**   Building supportive networks within the community is vital for creating safe spaces. LGBTQ support groups, organizations, and ally networks offer opportunities for connection, empowerment, and mentorship. These networks play a crucial role in amplifying LGBTQ voices and advocating for their rights.

5.   **Collaborations and Partnerships**   Collaborating with other organizations, businesses, and institutions that share a commitment to LGBTQ inclusivity is a powerful way to create safe spaces. By working together, communities can leverage resources, share best practices, and expand the reach of support networks.

The Impact of Safe Spaces

The impact of safe spaces for the LGBTQ community is profound and far-reaching. Here are some key benefits:

1.   **Mental and Emotional Well-being**   Feeling safe and supported improves mental health outcomes for LGBTQ individuals. Safe spaces provide a space to process emotions, share experiences, and access resources that promote resilience and long-term well-being.

2. **Empowerment and Validation**   Safe spaces empower LGBTQ individuals to embrace their identities fully. This validation fosters self-confidence, self-acceptance, and a sense of belonging, enabling individuals to thrive and flourish.

3.   **Community Building**   Safe spaces foster community building and social connections. They provide opportunities for individuals to find common ground, share experiences, and build relationships based on shared understanding and acceptance.

4. Advocacy and Social Change   Safe spaces serve as a springboard for activism and social change. By providing a platform for voices that have been marginalized, these spaces empower individuals to advocate for LGBTQ rights, challenge harmful narratives, and create a more inclusive society.

5. Allies and Solidarity   Safe spaces not only benefit LGBTQ individuals but also educate and engage allies. By actively participating and supporting these spaces, allies learn how to be effective advocates, challenge their biases, and contribute to a more inclusive and equitable society.

Real-World Example: The LGBTQ Resource Center

The LGBTQ Resource Center at the University of X is an excellent example of a safe space. It serves as a hub for LGBTQ students, faculty, staff, and allies to find support, access resources, and connect with the larger LGBTQ community.

The Center offers a wide range of programs and services, including educational workshops, support groups, counseling services, and mentorship programs. It also hosts social events and community-building activities to create a sense of belonging and celebrate LGBTQ identities and experiences.

Through its tireless work, the LGBTQ Resource Center has created an environment where LGBTQ individuals can be their authentic selves, find acceptance, and access the support they need to succeed. It has become a model for other institutions looking to establish safe spaces for the LGBTQ community.

Conclusion

Creating safe spaces for the LGBTQ community is crucial for fostering acceptance, well-being, and social change. By understanding the need for safe spaces, implementing strategies for inclusivity, and recognizing their positive impact, we can work towards creating a more equitable and supportive society for all. Safe spaces are not just physical locations; they represent a commitment to embracing diversity and celebrating the richness of LGBTQ experiences. Let us strive to create safe spaces that empower and uplift all individuals, regardless of their sexual orientation or gender identity.

Uniting Different Movements

In the quest for LGBTQ rights, it is essential to recognize that the fight for equality is intertwined with other social justice movements. Uniting different movements allows for greater collective power, amplifying the voices of marginalized communities and creating a more inclusive society. In this section, we will explore the importance of building alliances and collaborating with diverse groups to achieve our shared goals.

Recognizing Intersectionality

Intersectionality is a key principle in understanding the interconnected nature of various forms of oppression. It acknowledges that people's identities and experiences are shaped by multiple social categories such as race, gender, sexuality, and class. By recognizing intersectionality, we can foster deeper empathy and understanding among different movements.

For example, LGBTQ individuals who belong to racial or ethnic minority groups often face compounded discrimination. By collaborating with racial justice organizations, we can address the unique challenges faced by LGBTQ people of color. This intersectional approach allows us to build coalitions that are both powerful and inclusive.

Finding Shared Values

While each social justice movement may have its own specific goals, there are often shared values and aspirations. By focusing on these commonalities, we can create meaningful connections and build solidarity across movements.

For instance, LGBTQ rights and feminist movements share a common goal of challenging gender norms and discrimination. By joining forces, we can amplify our message and push for policy changes that benefit both communities. Similarly, environmental and LGBTQ movements can collaborate to promote sustainable and inclusive practices.

Creating Safe Spaces for All

Creating safe spaces for people from diverse backgrounds is essential for building alliances. These spaces provide opportunities for different movements to come together, share experiences, and learn from one another.

For example, organizing joint workshops or conferences can bring together activists from LGBTQ, racial justice, disability rights, and other movements. This allows for cross-pollination of ideas and strategies, fostering greater understanding and solidarity.

Figure 0.3: Creating safe spaces for diverse communities

Collaborating on Advocacy Efforts

Collaboration on advocacy efforts enables different movements to leverage their collective power and influence systemic change. By working together, we can advocate for policies that address the needs and protect the rights of multiple marginalized communities.

For instance, LGBTQ and disability rights organizations can collaborate to advocate for accessible healthcare services. By joining forces, we can push for inclusive healthcare policies that address the unique needs of LGBTQ individuals with disabilities.

Challenges and Solutions

Uniting different movements can undoubtedly be challenging, as it requires navigating different priorities and power dynamics. However, by acknowledging and addressing these challenges, we can work towards more effective collaboration.

One common challenge is a lack of understanding and awareness of each other's struggles and experiences. Encouraging open and respectful dialogue through workshops and training can help bridge these gaps and foster empathy.

Another challenge is the potential for conflicting priorities or goals. To overcome this, it is crucial to find common ground and focus on shared values. Collaboratively setting objectives and strategies can help ensure that the efforts of different movements align towards a common vision.

Embracing Diversity as Strength

Uniting different movements is a testament to the strength of diversity. By embracing the unique perspectives and experiences of various communities, we can address the complex interplay of intersecting oppressions.

To foster inclusivity, it is essential to actively involve individuals from marginalized groups in leadership positions and decision-making processes. This ensures that the voices of those most affected by discrimination are central to the movement.

Conclusion

Uniting different movements is not only crucial for the advancement of LGBTQ rights but for creating a more just and equitable society overall. By recognizing intersectionality, finding shared values, creating safe spaces, and collaborating on advocacy efforts, we can create powerful alliances that challenge systemic oppression.

Remember, the fight for social justice is interconnected, and our collective efforts can bring about lasting change. Together, we are stronger. Let us continue to build bridges, break barriers, and strive for a more inclusive and equal world for all.

Collaborating with LGBTQ Organizations

Collaborating with LGBTQ organizations is a crucial step in the fight for equality and social justice. By joining forces with like-minded groups, individuals and communities can amplify their voices and work towards common goals. In this section, we will explore the importance of collaboration, the benefits it brings, and some effective strategies for building strong alliances.

Understanding the Power of Collaboration

Collaboration is the key to creating lasting change. By pooling resources, skills, and knowledge, LGBTQ organizations can work together to advocate for equal rights, challenge discriminatory policies, and support marginalized individuals. Building alliances not only strengthens the movement, but also allows for a more comprehensive approach to addressing diverse needs within the LGBTQ community.

Example: The partnership between LGBTQ organizations and other social justice movements, such as those focused on racial equality or disability rights, can result in intersectional advocacy, effectively addressing the shared experiences of marginalized individuals.

Building Strong Partnerships

Effective collaborations require intentional efforts to foster strong partnerships. Here are some strategies for building and maintaining meaningful alliances:

1. **Identify common goals:** Before engaging in collaboration, it is essential to identify shared objectives and visions. This alignment ensures that all parties are working towards a common purpose and enhances the effectiveness of collective efforts.

2. **Open and transparent communication:** Clear and open communication is the foundation of successful partnerships. Regular meetings, email updates, and shared online platforms can facilitate effective information exchange, coordination, and decision-making.

3. **Shared resources and expertise:** Collaboration allows for the sharing of resources, expertise, and best practices. By pooling knowledge and skills, LGBTQ organizations can collectively develop innovative strategies, enhance capacity, and maximize impact.

4. **Respect and inclusivity:** It is crucial to create an inclusive and respectful space for all collaborators. Recognize and value the diversity of perspectives, experiences, and identities within the LGBTQ community and work towards creating an environment where everyone feels empowered and heard.

5. **Establishing trust and accountability:** Trust is the cornerstone of any successful collaboration. It is important to establish clear roles, responsibilities, and accountability measures to ensure that all parties uphold their commitments and maintain transparency.

Example: The collaboration between LGBTQ organizations and legal advocacy groups can result in the development of comprehensive legal strategies to fight discriminatory laws, protect LGBTQ rights, and ensure equal access to justice.

Maximizing Impact through Collaboration

Collaboration not only amplifies the voices of LGBTQ organizations but also leads to a more significant impact on societal change. Here are some ways that partnerships can maximize their impact:

1. **Coordinated advocacy efforts:** By coordinating advocacy efforts, LGBTQ organizations can amplify their voices and increase their influence on policymakers. Collaborative campaigns, joint letters, and combined efforts during crucial events or legislation can effectively raise awareness and bring about policy changes.

2. **Sharing of resources and networks:** Collaborations allow for the sharing of resources, networks, and connections. This sharing enables the expansion of reach, facilitating access to broader audiences, funding opportunities, and expertise.

3. **Collective learning and knowledge exchange:** Collaborations create spaces for collective learning and knowledge exchange. LGBTQ organizations can benefit from each other's experiences, strategies, and lessons learned, leading to continuous improvement and increased effectiveness.

4. **Amplifying marginalized voices:** Collaborations enable the inclusion and amplification of marginalized voices within the LGBTQ community. By working together, organizations can ensure that the needs and experiences of all individuals, including those at the intersections of multiple identities, are represented and centered in the fight for equality.

   Example: A collaborative effort between LGBTQ organizations and educational institutions can result in the development of LGBTQ-inclusive curriculum and policies, promoting acceptance and diversity within the education system.

Challenges and Solutions

While collaborations offer numerous benefits, they also come with challenges. Here are some common challenges and potential solutions:

1. **Differing priorities and approaches:** Organizations may have different priorities and approaches, which can sometimes hinder collaboration. Open dialogue and a commitment to finding common ground are key to overcoming these differences.

2. **Power imbalances:** Power imbalances can exist within collaborations, especially when organizations differ in size, funding, or influence. It is essential to foster an inclusive and equitable environment, ensuring that all voices are heard and given equal weight.

3. **Sustainability and resource management:** Collaborations require careful resource management and long-term sustainability planning. Developing clear agreements on resource-sharing, funding responsibilities, and decision-making helps sustain collaborative efforts.

Example: LGBTQ organizations can address the challenge of power imbalances by actively involving grassroots groups, individuals with lived experiences, and community leaders in decision-making processes.

Conclusion

Collaborating with LGBTQ organizations is a powerful strategy for advancing LGBTQ rights and creating inclusive societies. By understanding the benefits and challenges of collaboration, building strong partnerships, and maximizing impact, individuals and communities can effectively work together towards achieving equality for all.

Remember, collaboration is not about erasing differences, but rather about leveraging them to create a collective power that drives meaningful change. So, let us come together, stand united, and collaborate to build a better and more inclusive future for all LGBTQ individuals and their allies.

Resources:

1. Institute for LGBTQ Health Equity. (2021). A Guide to Successful LGBT Health Advocacy Collaboration. Retrieved from: `https://lgbt.ucsf.edu/sites/lgbt.ucsf.edu/files/wysiwyg/How%20to%20Create%20LGBT%20Networks_online.pdf`.

2. National LGBTQ Task Force. (n.d.). Tools for LGBTQ Activism: Building Alliances. Retrieved from: `https://www.thetaskforce.org/tools-lgbtq-activism-building-alliances/`.

3. Smith, D., & Johnson, S. (2019). Partnerships and Collaboration for Sustainable LGBTQ Organizations. Journal of Gay & Lesbian Social Services, 31(3), 245-259.

Intersectionality: Breaking Down Barriers

As we delve into the world of LGBTQ activism, it is essential to recognize and address the many interconnected systems of oppression that affect diverse individuals within the community. Intersectionality, a term coined by legal scholar Kimberlé Crenshaw, emphasizes the interconnectedness of multiple systems of discrimination, such as race, gender, class, ability, and sexuality. In this section, we explore the power of intersectional activism and how it can break down barriers within the LGBTQ rights movement.

Understanding Intersectionality

Intersectionality acknowledges that different social identities intersect, creating unique experiences of discrimination and privilege. By recognizing these intersecting forms of oppression, we can better understand the complex experiences of individuals within the LGBTQ community and work towards creating inclusive spaces for everyone.

One way to comprehend intersectionality is through the metaphor of an overlapping Venn diagram. Each circle represents a different social identity, such as race, gender, or sexuality. The overlapping region represents individuals who experience multiple forms of discrimination due to the intersection of these social identities. This framework highlights the need to address both the unique challenges faced by specific groups and the broader inequalities within society.

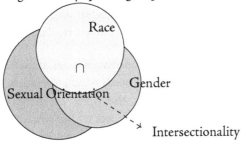

Breaking Down Barriers

Intersectionality challenges us to dismantle the barriers that prevent marginalized voices from being heard within the LGBTQ community and the broader society. Here are some strategies for breaking down these barriers:

1. **Listening and Amplifying Voices:** It is crucial to actively listen to the experiences and perspectives of individuals from marginalized communities

within the LGBTQ movement. By amplifying these voices, we center their knowledge and challenges, and ensure that diverse lived experiences are represented in decision-making processes and policy discussions.

2. **Collaboration and Coalition Building:** Intersectional activism encourages collaboration and solidarity among diverse communities. By forming alliances with other social justice movements, such as those advocating for racial equity or gender equality, we can address the interconnectedness of different forms of oppression. This coalition building can lead to collective action and more significant progress towards achieving equality.

3. **Addressing Privilege and Power Dynamics:** Recognizing privilege within the LGBTQ community is vital for dismantling barriers. Activists must critically examine their privilege and understand how it may impact their perception of the struggles faced by individuals from marginalized groups. By actively working to challenge power dynamics and advocating for the inclusion of all voices, we can create a more equitable and representative movement.

4. **Education and Awareness:** Intersectional activism necessitates a deep understanding of the histories and struggles of all communities involved. Education plays a pivotal role in raising awareness about different forms of oppression, fostering empathy, and promoting solidarity. This can be achieved through workshops, community conversations, educational campaigns, and incorporating diverse perspectives into curricula.

5. **Policy and Institutional Change:** Intersectionality calls for transforming policies and institutions to address the diverse needs of all individuals. This includes advocating for policies that protect the rights of marginalized communities and challenging discriminatory practices within structures and systems. By dismantling systemic barriers, we create a more inclusive society for everyone.

Case Study: LGBTQ+ and Disability Rights

One powerful example of intersectional activism is the fight for LGBTQ+ and disability rights. Disabled LGBTQ+ individuals face unique challenges due to the intersection of ableism, homophobia, and transphobia. By highlighting these intersections, activists have been able to advocate for broader accessibility, inclusive healthcare, and representation within the LGBTQ+ movement. This intersectional approach ensures that the specific needs and experiences of disabled LGBTQ+ individuals are addressed during policy development and advocacy efforts.

Conclusion

Intersectionality serves as a critical framework for understanding and addressing the complex challenges faced by marginalized communities within the LGBTQ rights movement. By actively incorporating intersectional perspectives into our activism, we can break down barriers, amplify diverse voices, and work towards a more inclusive and equitable society for all. Let us embrace intersectionality, recognizing that achieving true equality requires addressing the interconnected systems of discrimination that impact individuals within the LGBTQ community and beyond.

Remember: Real change occurs when the most marginalized among us are uplifted. Only with intersectional activism can we truly break down barriers and build a more inclusive world for all LGBTQ individuals.

Confronting Adversity

Facing Backlash in the Media

In the face of progress, there will always be those who resist change. As an LGBTQ activist, Zion Ellis knew this all too well. In the section "Facing Backlash in the Media," we explore the challenges and triumphs that came with combating prejudice and ignorance in the public eye.

The Media's Role in Shaping Opinions

The media is a powerful tool that can either uplift or hinder the cause of LGBTQ rights. It has the ability to shape public opinion, influence political discourse, and impact individuals' understanding of the LGBTQ community. Unfortunately, it has not always been a friend to the cause.

Misrepresentation and Stereotyping

One of the most significant challenges faced by Zion Ellis was the media's tendency to misrepresent and stereotype the LGBTQ community. This misrepresentation perpetuated harmful stereotypes and reinforced negative biases against queer individuals. By painting LGBTQ individuals in a negative light, the media fueled discrimination and hindered progress towards equality.

Responding to Biased Reporting

Zion Ellis understood the importance of countering biased reporting with accurate information. He employed various strategies to challenge the media's negative portrayal of queer individuals. One strategy was to engage with journalists and news organizations, providing them with accurate and compelling stories that debunked stereotypes.

Additionally, he leveraged social media platforms to amplify the voices of LGBTQ individuals and share authentic stories. By developing a strong online presence, Ellis was able to disseminate accurate information, counteract harmful narratives, and educate the public about the LGBTQ community.

Activism-Savvy Media Engagement

To combat media bias effectively, Zion Ellis employed an activism-savvy media engagement strategy. Instead of dismissing or boycotting media outlets, he proactively sought opportunities to collaborate with journalists who showed a genuine interest in understanding the LGBTQ experience.

By engaging with these journalists, Ellis was able to build relationships grounded in mutual respect and trust. This allowed him to effectively shape the narrative surrounding LGBTQ issues and challenge the media's biases head-on.

The Power of Truth

Zion Ellis understood that the truth was a potent weapon against media backlash. He tirelessly advocated for authenticity and transparency, encouraging LGBTQ individuals to share their personal experiences and stories.

By showcasing the diverse and vibrant lives of queer individuals, Ellis debunked harmful stereotypes and humanized the LGBTQ community. This humanization, in turn, helped to counteract the negative narratives perpetuated by the media.

Building Alliances with Media Allies

While it was essential to challenge biased reporting, Zion Ellis recognized that building alliances with media allies was equally crucial. He collaborated with journalists, editors, and news organizations that were committed to fair and accurate representation of LGBTQ issues.

Through these alliances, Ellis was able to increase LGBTQ visibility in the media and promote positive change. He worked closely with journalists who were empathetic to the cause, providing them with access to personal stories and resources to help them accurately report on LGBTQ issues.

Navigating the Online Battlefield

In today's digital era, the media landscape has expanded from traditional outlets to online platforms. Zion Ellis recognized the importance of navigating this new terrain to combat media backlash effectively.

He understood that online spaces could be hostile and prone to misinformation. To counter this, Ellis used social media to build a community of supporters, engaging with them regularly to combat hate speech and disinformation. He encouraged followers to report instances of media bias and actively challenged discriminatory narratives online.

Empowering the LGBTQ Community

Throughout his journey, Zion Ellis remained committed to empowering the LGBTQ community. He believed that by equipping individuals with the tools to combat media backlash, they could collectively challenge the status quo.

Ellis organized workshops and training sessions to help LGBTQ individuals develop media literacy skills. By teaching them how to navigate media bias and respond effectively to negative portrayals, he empowered them to reclaim their narratives and shape public opinion.

Celebrating Victories and Learning from Defeats

Facing media backlash was not an easy task, but Zion Ellis celebrated every victory, no matter how small. By highlighting positive moments and embracing progress, he inspired others to join the fight for LGBTQ rights.

At the same time, Ellis acknowledged that setbacks were inevitable. He believed that learning from defeats was crucial for growth and adaptation. By analyzing and understanding the root causes of media backlash, he developed strategies to mitigate future challenges.

In conclusion, "Facing Backlash in the Media" highlights the struggles, strategies, and triumphs of Zion Ellis as he confronted media bias and fought for LGBTQ rights. It underscores the importance of challenging stereotypes, building alliances with media allies, leveraging social media for change, and empowering the LGBTQ community. Despite the obstacles, Ellis's commitment to truth and resilience in the face of adversity laid the foundation for a more inclusive and accepting society.

Navigating Legal Challenges

Navigating legal challenges is an essential aspect of any LGBTQ activist's journey. In this section, we will explore the various obstacles that arise within the legal system and discuss strategies for overcoming them. From discriminatory laws to legal protections, we will delve into the complexities of fighting for LGBTQ rights within the legal framework.

Understanding Discriminatory Laws

Discriminatory laws can pose significant challenges to the LGBTQ community. These laws can range from restrictions on same-sex marriage to discriminatory employment practices. Understanding the legal landscape and the specific laws that target the LGBTQ community is crucial in effectively challenging them.

One example of a discriminatory law is the Defense of Marriage Act (DOMA), which denied same-sex couples federal recognition and benefits. LGBTQ activists played a pivotal role in overturning this law through advocacy and legal challenges. By leveraging the principles of equal protection and due process, they successfully argued that denying same-sex couples the right to marry was unconstitutional.

Challenging Discriminatory Laws

Challenging discriminatory laws requires a multifaceted approach that combines legal expertise, grassroots activism, and public pressure. LGBTQ activists work closely with lawyers, policymakers, and human rights organizations to identify laws that infringe upon the rights of the LGBTQ community and strategize ways to challenge them.

One strategy is to file lawsuits challenging the constitutionality of discriminatory laws. Activists can gather evidence, build strong legal arguments, and present their case to the courts. By highlighting the discriminatory nature of these laws and their impact on the lives of LGBTQ individuals, they can make a compelling case for their repeal.

Lobbying is another effective tool in challenging discriminatory laws. Activists work with lawmakers to educate them about the negative consequences of these laws and advocate for their repeal or amendment. By mobilizing support from sympathetic legislators and garnering public attention, activists can amplify their message and push for legislative change.

Securing Legal Protections

Securing legal protections for the LGBTQ community is an ongoing battle. Through advocacy, grassroots organizing, and coalition building, activists work tirelessly to develop and implement legislation that safeguards the rights of LGBTQ individuals.

One example of successful legal protection is the passage of anti-discrimination laws that prohibit employment and housing discrimination based on sexual orientation and gender identity. These laws create legal remedies for individuals who face discrimination and send a powerful message that LGBTQ rights are protected.

Legal protections can also include hate crime legislation, which enhances penalties for crimes motivated by bias against the LGBTQ community. By advocating for the inclusion of sexual orientation and gender identity in existing hate crime laws, activists ensure that these crimes are taken seriously and appropriately addressed.

Fighting for Comprehensive LGBTQ Education

Comprehensive LGBTQ education is crucial in creating a more inclusive society. Activists strive to integrate LGBTQ history, issues, and experiences into school curricula to promote understanding, empathy, and acceptance.

Advocacy efforts focus on working with education boards, teachers, and policymakers to develop guidelines and resources for LGBTQ-inclusive education. This includes promoting the inclusion of LGBTQ literature, history, and contributions in textbooks and encouraging the training of educators on LGBTQ issues.

By challenging heteronormative narratives and fostering an inclusive educational environment, activists empower future generations to combat discrimination and promote LGBTQ equality.

Advocating for LGBTQ-Inclusive Healthcare

Access to LGBTQ-inclusive healthcare is a critical aspect of achieving LGBTQ equality. LGBTQ individuals often face unique healthcare disparities and discrimination, including inadequate access to culturally competent care, discrimination from healthcare providers, and denial of gender-affirming treatments.

Activists collaborate with healthcare professionals, policymakers, and LGBTQ organizations to advocate for policies that address these disparities. This includes promoting LGBTQ-inclusive healthcare training for providers, pushing for insurance coverage for gender-affirming treatments, and working towards the removal of discriminatory barriers in the healthcare system.

Through public awareness campaigns, grassroots organizing, and lobbying efforts, activists aim to create a healthcare system that is inclusive and affirming of all individuals, regardless of their sexual orientation or gender identity.

Providing Support and Resources

Navigating legal challenges can be emotionally and mentally taxing for LGBTQ activists. It is crucial to prioritize self-care and provide support to those engaged in legal battles.

Activist organizations offer resources such as legal clinics, pro bono services, and mental health support to help individuals navigate the legal system. Additionally, community support networks provide a safe space for activists to share their experiences, seek guidance, and recharge.

In conclusion, navigating legal challenges is an integral part of LGBTQ activism. By understanding discriminatory laws, challenging them through legal means, securing legal protections, advocating for comprehensive LGBTQ education, and pushing for LGBTQ-inclusive healthcare, activists make significant strides towards achieving equality. However, this fight is ongoing, and it is essential to continue pushing boundaries and demanding justice for all members of the LGBTQ community.

Overcoming Personal Struggles

In the journey towards LGBTQ activism, Zion Ellis faced numerous personal struggles that tested his resilience and determination. This section explores how he overcame these challenges, providing inspiration for others facing similar obstacles. Ellis's ability to navigate these difficulties with grace and strength serves as a testament to the power of self-care, resilience, and finding support.

Finding Inner Strength

As an LGBTQ activist, Ellis experienced moments of self-doubt and internal turmoil. The pressure to advocate for the community while simultaneously managing personal challenges can be overwhelming. However, Ellis discovered the importance of cultivating inner strength and resilience.

To overcome personal struggles, Ellis emphasized the significance of self-reflection and self-acceptance. Taking time for introspection allowed him to understand his own emotions, fears, and limitations. By acknowledging and validating these feelings, he was able to build a strong foundation for resilience.

Seeking Support Networks

No journey is meant to be walked alone, and Ellis recognized the value of seeking support from others who shared his experiences and passions. He actively built a network of allies and friends within the LGBTQ community who provided encouragement and understanding.

Support networks played a critical role in assisting Ellis in overcoming personal struggles. These spaces provided a platform for open and honest discussions, allowing Ellis to share his challenges in a safe and non-judgmental environment. Through these connections, he found solace, advice, and validation.

Prioritizing Self-Care

To sustain his activism efforts, Ellis learned the importance of prioritizing self-care. Fighting for LGBTQ rights can be emotionally and mentally draining. Therefore, Ellis actively practiced self-care strategies to preserve his well-being.

He recognized the significance of finding balance and engaging in activities that brought joy and relaxation. This involved setting boundaries, managing stress, and allowing himself moments of rest and rejuvenation. By prioritizing self-care, Ellis was able to replenish his energy and continue tackling challenges.

Personal Growth through Adversity

Overcoming personal struggles is not always a linear process. Ellis encountered setbacks and faced challenging circumstances. However, he viewed these obstacles as opportunities for personal growth.

Instead of allowing adversity to defeat him, Ellis saw it as a chance to learn, adapt, and develop resilience. Through these experiences, he discovered his inner strength and unwavering passion for LGBTQ activism. Ellis balanced self-reflection with determination, transforming personal struggles into catalysts for change.

Leading by Example

Through his journey of overcoming personal struggles, Zion Ellis set an example for others within the LGBTQ community. His transparency about his own challenges and the strategies he employed to overcome them inspired many.

Ellis's story serves as a reminder that personal struggles do not define one's ability to make a meaningful impact. His resilience and determination ignited hope and empowered others to confront their own battles.

Unconventional Yet Relevant Story

One of the most unconventional approaches Zion Ellis took to overcome personal struggles was embracing vulnerability. In a society that often shames vulnerability, Ellis chose to share his personal challenges openly, recognizing that it strengthened his connections with others and allowed them to see him as a relatable figure.

By embracing vulnerability, Ellis demolished walls and stereotypes, creating an empowering space for others to explore their own struggles. This approach fostered a sense of community and support that transcended traditional activist narratives.

Exercises

1. Reflect on a personal struggle you have faced and identify strategies to overcome it. Consider the importance of seeking support networks, practicing self-care, and embracing vulnerability.

2. Write a short story or create a piece of art that depicts the transformation of personal struggles into sources of strength and empowerment.

3. Research the concept of self-care and its significance in maintaining mental and emotional well-being. Write a reflection on how self-care practices can support activists in their journey towards social change.

4. Explore the idea of vulnerability in activism. Discuss the potential benefits and challenges of embracing vulnerability as an activist. Provide examples of public figures or activists who have used vulnerability to create meaningful change.

5. Interview an LGBTQ activist and ask them about their personal struggles and how they have overcome them. Reflect on the insights gained from their experiences and consider how their journey can inspire and inform your own activism.

Key Takeaways

- Overcoming personal struggles is an essential part of the journey towards LGBTQ activism.

- Finding inner strength and seeking support networks are crucial in navigating personal challenges.

- Prioritizing self-care is essential for sustaining activism efforts.

- Personal struggles can lead to personal growth if approached with resilience and determination.

- Embracing vulnerability can be a powerful tool in connecting with others and fostering community.

By embracing personal struggles and developing strategies to overcome them, activists like Zion Ellis can inspire others and create lasting change in the fight for LGBTQ rights.

Dealing with Hate Crimes and Violence

In the battle for LGBTQ rights, one of the darkest aspects is the prevalence of hate crimes and violence against the community. While progress has been made in terms of legal protections and social acceptance, there is still a long way to go in eradicating hatred and bigotry. This section explores the challenges faced by LGBTQ individuals when dealing with hate crimes and violence, as well as strategies and resources to combat this pervasive issue.

Understanding Hate Crimes

Hate crimes are not mere random acts of violence. They are targeted attacks fueled by prejudice and bigotry, specifically aimed at someone's identity or perceived difference. LGBTQ individuals are particularly vulnerable to hate crimes due to pervasive homophobia, transphobia, and other forms of discrimination. These crimes can range from verbal harassment to physical assault, and in extreme cases, even murder.

To effectively combat hate crimes, it is crucial to understand the underlying causes and the impact they have on the victims and the community as a whole. By educating society about the consequences of hate crimes and the importance of acceptance and respect, we can work towards creating safer communities for LGBTQ individuals.

Support Systems and Reporting Mechanisms

One of the most important steps in dealing with hate crimes and violence is to establish robust support systems and reporting mechanisms. LGBTQ individuals need to know that they are not alone and that there are resources available to help them navigate through these challenging situations.

Community organizations, LGBTQ centers, and helplines play a crucial role in providing support to victims of hate crimes. These organizations offer counseling services, legal advice, and assistance with filing police reports. They also provide a safe space for survivors to share their experiences and find solace in the company of others who have gone through similar situations.

Reporting mechanisms, such as anonymous tip lines, online reporting platforms, and designated liaisons within law enforcement agencies, can help LGBTQ individuals feel more comfortable coming forward and reporting hate crimes. It is essential to have a clear and streamlined process for victims to report incidents, ensuring their safety and protection throughout the entire process.

Collaborative Efforts and Community Engagement

Dealing with hate crimes and violence requires a collaborative effort from various stakeholders, including law enforcement agencies, community organizations, and individuals, both within and outside the LGBTQ community. By engaging in dialogue, raising awareness, and working together, we can create a society where hate crimes are not tolerated.

Law enforcement agencies need to prioritize the investigation and prosecution of hate crimes, ensuring that LGBTQ victims receive the justice they deserve. Specialized training for police officers and other law enforcement personnel should be implemented to enhance their understanding of LGBTQ issues and improve their response to hate crimes.

Community engagement is also crucial in addressing hate crimes. LGBTQ individuals and their allies must actively participate in initiatives aimed at prevention, education, and support. This can include organizing awareness campaigns, hosting workshops on hate crime prevention, and collaborating with schools and universities to promote inclusivity and acceptance.

Empowerment and Self-Defense

In addition to collective efforts, individuals within the LGBTQ community must be empowered and educated on how to protect themselves from hate crimes and violence. Self-defense techniques and empowerment workshops can provide LGBTQ individuals with the skills and confidence to respond effectively in threatening situations.

Furthermore, educating the community at large about LGBTQ experiences and issues can help dispel stereotypes and reduce the prevalence of hate crimes. By creating a society that embraces diversity and promotes understanding, we can gradually eliminate the root causes of violence and discrimination.

Caveat: Safety First

While it is important to address hate crimes and violence, the safety and well-being of individuals should always be the top priority. The strategies outlined in this section should be implemented with caution and consideration of individual circumstances. It is crucial to assess the level of risk involved and seek professional guidance when necessary.

Conclusion

Dealing with hate crimes and violence against the LGBTQ community requires a multifaceted approach involving education, support systems, community engagement, and empowerment. By working together to create a society that values acceptance and equality, we can strive towards a future free from hate and violence. Remember, every action, no matter how small, can make a difference in the fight for LGBTQ rights. Together, we can build a world where everyone can live without fear of persecution or violence.

Mental Health Challenges in Activism

Activism is a powerful force for change, but it comes with its own set of challenges. The relentless pursuit of justice and equality can take a toll on activists, particularly when it comes to their mental well-being. In this section, we will explore the mental health challenges faced by activists and provide strategies for maintaining a healthy balance while fighting for LGBTQ rights in Cyrion.

The Psychological Impact of Activism

Engaging in activism can be emotionally draining. Activists often witness and experience various forms of discrimination, violence, and injustice, which can contribute to feelings of anger, sadness, and frustration. The constant exposure to these negative experiences can have a profound impact on an activist's mental health.

One of the most common mental health challenges faced by activists is burnout. Activism is a demanding and long-term commitment, and activists may find themselves pushing their physical and emotional limits. This can lead to exhaustion, cynicism, and a decreased sense of accomplishment. Additionally, activists may experience guilt or self-doubt, questioning whether they are doing enough or making a real difference.

Self-Care: A Vital Aspect of Activism

Taking care of one's mental health is essential for activists to sustain their energy, passion, and resilience. Building a strong foundation of self-care can help activists cope with the mental health challenges they face. Here are some strategies that activists can use to prioritize their well-being:

1. **Establish Boundaries:** Activists often have a deep sense of responsibility towards their cause, which can make it difficult to set boundaries. However, it is crucial to create boundaries between personal life and activism. This may involve scheduling time for relaxation, hobbies, and relationships, and knowing when to say no to additional commitments.

2. **Practice Mindfulness:** Mindfulness techniques, such as meditation, can help activists calm their minds, manage stress, and stay present in the moment. Taking time to focus on breathing and grounding oneself can provide a sense of balance and perspective.

3. **Seek Support:** It is important for activists to build a support network of like-minded individuals who can share the emotional weight of activism. Connecting with others who understand the challenges and frustrations can be comforting and empowering. Support can be in the form of friends, family, fellow activists, or even therapy.

4. **Practice Self-Compassion:** Activists often have high expectations of themselves and may be overly self-critical. Practicing self-compassion involves treating oneself with kindness and understanding, acknowledging limitations, and celebrating accomplishments. It is important to remember that activism is a collective effort, and no single person can carry the weight of the entire movement.

5. **Engage in Self-Reflection:** Regularly reflecting on personal values, goals, and motivations can help activists maintain their sense of purpose. Self-reflection can provide insights into the impact of their work, identify areas for growth, and serve as a reminder of why they started their activism journey in the first place.

Balancing Activism and Mental Health

Finding a balance between activism and mental health is crucial for long-term well-being. Here are some additional strategies that activists can implement to protect their mental health:

1. **Take Breaks:** Activists should allow themselves regular breaks and moments of rest. Stepping away from the constant demands of activism can rejuvenate the mind and body, improving overall mental well-being.

2. **Engage in Self-Care Rituals:** Engaging in activities that promote relaxation and self-care is essential. This can include hobbies, exercise, spending time in nature, listening to music, or engaging in creative outlets. These activities can reduce stress, increase happiness, and provide a sense of fulfillment.

3. **Educate Yourself on Mental Health:** Activists can benefit from learning about mental health, including common challenges, coping strategies, and available resources. This knowledge can help activists better understand their own mental well-being and provide informed support to others within their community.

4. **Advocate for Mental Health Services:** Recognizing the importance of mental health, activists can also advocate for improved access to mental health services for themselves and their communities. This can involve lobbying for mental health policies, increasing awareness about the intersection of mental health and activism, and collaborating with mental health organizations.

5. **Address Activist Trauma:** Activists may experience trauma as a result of their work, including witnessing or experiencing violence, discrimination, or abuse. It is important to acknowledge and address this trauma through therapy, support groups, or trauma-informed healing practices.

Cultivating a Supportive Community

Building a supportive community is vital for activists' mental health. Creating spaces for activists to come together, share experiences, and support one another can foster a sense of belonging and reduce feelings of isolation. Here are some ways to cultivate a supportive community:

1. **Organize Support Groups:** Activists can organize support groups specifically tailored to the needs of LGBTQ activists. These groups can provide a safe and understanding environment for activists to share their challenges, seek advice, and find emotional support.

2. **Collaborate with Mental Health Professionals:** Activists can collaborate with mental health professionals to provide workshops, counseling services, or training sessions focused on mental well-being. This partnership can create opportunities for activists to access professional support and develop coping strategies.

3. **Promote Peer Support:** Encouraging peer support within the activist community can strengthen solidarity and resilience. Establishing mentorship programs, support circles, or buddy systems can foster connections and provide mutual support.

4. **Normalize Mental Health Conversations:** Openly discussing mental health challenges within the activist community helps break the stigma surrounding mental health. Creating spaces where activists can have honest conversations about their mental well-being promotes a culture of support and understanding.

Remember, mental health challenges are not a sign of weakness but a natural response to the demanding nature of activism. Prioritizing mental well-being allows activists to sustain their commitment to fighting for LGBTQ rights in Cyrion effectively.

Whether you're an activist or an ally, it's important to recognize that mental health and activism are intertwined. By addressing mental health challenges and prioritizing self-care, activists can ensure their long-term well-being while continuing to drive positive change. As the fight for LGBTQ rights in Cyrion and beyond continues, let us not forget to take care of ourselves and each other.

Chapter 3: A Voice for Change

Chapter 3: A Voice for Change

Chapter 3: A Voice for Change

In this chapter, we delve into the inspiring journey of Zion Ellis as he uses his voice and influence to drive change and advocate for LGBTQ rights. Through the power of persuasion, transforming policy, and inspiring future generations, Ellis emerges as a prominent figure in the LGBTQ movement. Let's explore the strategies and challenges he faces along the way.

The Art of Persuasion

One of the most effective tools in Ellis's arsenal is the art of persuasion. He understands that changing hearts and minds is essential for societal change. Ellis harnesses the power of storytelling to connect with people on a personal level. Through personal narratives, he shares his own struggles and experiences, helping others empathize and understand the challenges faced by the LGBTQ community.

Humor also plays a significant role in Ellis's advocacy. He uses comedy and wit to break down barriers, dispel stereotypes, and promote a more inclusive society. By injecting humor into conversations about LGBTQ rights, he facilitates a more open dialogue and encourages people to challenge their preconceived notions.

Ellis recognizes the importance of turning opposition into allies. Instead of dismissing those who disagree or hold different beliefs, he engages in respectful and empathetic conversations. By finding common ground and highlighting shared values, Ellis creates opportunities for meaningful dialogue that can lead to change.

Debunking myths and misconceptions is another method Ellis employs in his quest for change. He presents verifiable facts and evidence to challenge stereotypes and biases. By providing accurate information, he aims to educate and enlighten those who may have misconceptions about the LGBTQ community.

Transforming Policy

While changing hearts and minds is crucial, Ellis understands that lasting change also requires transforming policy. He advocates for LGBTQ rights through lobbying efforts, working with lawmakers to pass legislation that protects the rights and well-being of the LGBTQ community.

Challenging discriminatory laws is an uphill battle, but Ellis remains determined. He strategically partners with other activists and organizations to amplify the collective voice for change. Through impactful campaigns and grassroots movements, he rallies support from the LGBTQ community and its allies.

Securing legal protections is another aspect of Ellis's fight for LGBTQ rights. He works tirelessly to ensure that laws are in place to safeguard against discrimination based on sexual orientation or gender identity. By advocating for comprehensive LGBTQ education, Ellis aims to create a more inclusive educational system that fosters understanding and acceptance.

Advocating for LGBTQ-inclusive healthcare is a top priority for Ellis. He pushes for policies that guarantee equal access to healthcare services for the LGBTQ community. By dismantling barriers and addressing healthcare disparities, Ellis strives to ensure that everyone, regardless of sexual orientation or gender identity, receives the care they deserve.

Inspiring Future Generations

Zion Ellis recognizes the importance of nurturing and empowering future LGBTQ activists. He believes that mentoring LGBTQ youth is essential for creating lasting change. Ellis provides guidance, support, and resources to young activists, helping them navigate the challenges they may encounter on their own journeys.

By empowering the next generation of leaders, Ellis ensures the continuation of the LGBTQ movement. He instills in them the values of resilience, compassion, and determination. Through mentorship programs and workshops, young activists gain the skills and knowledge necessary to make a difference in their communities.

Creating lasting change is another goal Ellis strives to achieve. He understands that true progress requires more than surface-level shifts in policy and public perception. Through his activism, he works to engrain LGBTQ-inclusive education as the norm, fostering a society that celebrates diversity and equality.

Youth activism plays a crucial role in amplifying LGBTQ voices. Ellis encourages young activists to use their platforms and voices to drive change. By raising awareness and demanding accountability, they can challenge systemic inequalities and pave the way for a more equitable and inclusive future.

The Importance of Self-Reflection in Activism

In the midst of his advocacy journey, Zion Ellis discovers the significance of self-reflection in activism. He realizes that true change starts from within, and to be an effective advocate, one must also address personal biases and blind spots.

Ellis encourages activists to take the time for self-care, recognizing that burnout and fatigue are prevalent challenges in the realm of activism. By balancing activism with self-care practices, individuals can sustain their energy and passion for the fight for LGBTQ rights.

Furthermore, Ellis emphasizes the importance of continuously learning and staying informed. Understanding the historical context of LGBTQ activism and the struggles faced by the community enhances the quality of advocacy. He encourages activists to engage in ongoing education and actively seek knowledge about LGBTQ culture, history, and issues.

In conclusion, Zion Ellis's journey as an LGBTQ activist showcases the power of persuasion, policy transformation, and inspiring future generations. Through a combination of personal narratives, humor, and the debunking of misconceptions, Ellis effectively advocates for LGBTQ rights. Simultaneously, his focus on transforming policy, securing legal protections, and advocating for inclusive healthcare ensures tangible change. By empowering youth activists and emphasizing self-reflection, Ellis paves the way for a more inclusive society that celebrates and supports the LGBTQ community.

The Art of Persuasion

Harnessing the Power of Storytelling

Storytelling has always been a powerful tool for communication and connection. It allows individuals to share their experiences, express emotions, and convey messages in a way that is relatable and impactful. In the context of LGBTQ activism, storytelling plays a crucial role in raising awareness, challenging misconceptions, and inspiring change.

The Importance of Personal Narratives

Personal narratives are at the heart of storytelling in LGBTQ activism. By sharing their own stories, activists can humanize the movement, making it more relatable and accessible to a wide audience. These stories provide a glimpse into the struggles, triumphs, and resilience of LGBTQ individuals, allowing others to empathize and understand their experiences.

One powerful example of harnessing the power of personal narratives is through the creation of biographical documentaries. These films not only shed light on the personal journey of LGBTQ activists but also highlight the broader systemic challenges faced by the community. By showcasing individual stories of resilience, these documentaries ignite compassion and motivate people to take action.

Example: *An inspiring documentary titled "Pride Unleashed" follows the life of Alex Martinez, a transgender activist fighting for transgender rights in their conservative hometown. Through intimate interviews, the film explores Alex's journey of self-discovery, the discrimination they faced, and their tireless efforts to create a more inclusive society. The film empowers audiences to challenge their own biases and stand up for transgender rights.*

Creating Emotional Connections

Storytelling has the power to evoke emotions and create lasting connections with the audience. By incorporating emotionally powerful narratives, LGBTQ activists can elicit empathy, compassion, and understanding from others. These emotional connections are key to breaking down barriers and building bridges of support.

Example: *In a public speech, renowned LGBTQ activist Sarah Adams shares her personal experience of coming out to her conservative family. She recounts the fear, rejection, and subsequent journey to self-acceptance. Through her emotional storytelling, Sarah connects with the audience on a deeply personal level and challenges societal norms, ultimately inspiring others to embrace diversity and equality.*

Changing Hearts and Minds

Storytelling has the remarkable ability to challenge stereotypes, debunk misconceptions, and change hearts and minds. By presenting diverse narratives that defy societal expectations, LGBTQ activists can dismantle harmful beliefs and promote a more inclusive understanding of gender and sexuality.

One effective technique in storytelling for LGBTQ activism is using allegories and metaphors. By framing the experiences of LGBTQ individuals in relatable and universal terms, activists can bridge the gap between different communities and foster understanding.

Example: *In a TED Talk, LGBTQ activist and author Jamie Cooper compares the journey of self-discovery as an LGBTQ individual to the metaphor of a caterpillar transforming into a butterfly. By using this allegory, Jamie enables the audience to grasp the beauty and transformative nature of embracing one's true identity and challenges preconceived notions about gender and sexuality.*

Fostering Empathy and Solidarity

Storytelling not only helps create empathy but also fosters a sense of solidarity within and beyond the LGBTQ community. By listening to and sharing stories, individuals can find common ground, recognize shared struggles, and unite in the fight for equality.

Online platforms, such as social media and digital storytelling campaigns, greatly amplify the voices of LGBTQ individuals, allowing their stories to reach a wider audience. Through the power of hashtags, online activism brings together diverse narratives and creates a sense of community and support.

Example: *The hashtag campaign #OurStoriesMatter floods social media with personal stories of LGBTQ individuals from around the world. By sharing their experiences, activists foster a global network of support, breaking down geographical boundaries and inspiring others to join the fight for LGBTQ rights.*

Unconventional Methods: Storytelling through Art

Artistic mediums offer unique opportunities for storytelling in LGBTQ activism. Visual art, poetry, music, and performance can evoke emotions, challenge stereotypes, and convey powerful messages of inclusivity and acceptance.

An unconventional yet effective method of storytelling in LGBTQ activism is through drag performances. Drag artists use the power of performance to challenge societal norms and push boundaries. Their colorful, creative, and bold expressions of gender and identity challenge audiences to question and reconsider their own beliefs.

Example: *In a captivating performance piece titled "Breaking the Mold," drag performer Leo Madison uses their flamboyant personality and extravagant costumes to celebrate queer identity and challenge societal expectations. Through their art, Leo inspires others to embrace their authentic selves and confront the limitations imposed by traditional gender norms.*

In conclusion, storytelling is an indispensable tool in LGBTQ activism. By harnessing the power of personal narratives, creating emotional connections, changing hearts and minds, fostering empathy and solidarity, and exploring unconventional methods such as art, activists can cultivate understanding, challenge societal norms, and inspire lasting change. The art of storytelling amplifies diverse voices and creates a platform for diverse experiences, ultimately paving the way towards a more inclusive and equal society.

Using Humor to Break Barriers

Humor has always been a powerful tool for social change, and the LGBTQ rights movement is no exception. Zion Ellis understood the importance of using humor to break down barriers and challenge societal norms. In this section, we will explore how humor can be a catalyst for change and discuss various strategies that Zion Ellis employed to tackle discrimination through laughter.

The Power of Laughter

Laughter is a universal language that has the ability to unite people and dissolve tension. It can bridge the gap between different perspectives and create a shared experience. In the context of the LGBTQ rights movement, humor serves as a means to engage with the audience, challenge stereotypes, and ultimately change hearts and minds.

By using humor, activists like Zion Ellis were able to convey serious messages in a non-threatening and accessible way. Whether through stand-up comedy, satirical sketches, or clever one-liners, humor brings a level of relatability to the struggles faced by the LGBTQ community. It helps to humanize the issues and create empathy among those who may not have previously understood or supported LGBTQ rights.

Satire as a Weapon

Satire is a powerful form of humor that Zion Ellis effectively utilized to confront prejudice and challenge the status quo. Through satire, he could highlight the absurdity of discriminatory attitudes and practices. By exaggerating these absurdities, Zion Ellis brought attention to the underlying injustices.

One of his popular tactics was to create fictional characters or scenarios that mirrored real-life situations. By presenting these situations in a humorous and exaggerated way, he forced the audience to confront the irrationality of their own biases. This approach allowed people to reflect on their own beliefs in a non-confrontational manner, opening the door for deeper conversations and change.

Subversive Comedy

Subversive comedy takes the traditional form of comedy and twists it to challenge societal norms. Zion Ellis employed this strategy to expose the hypocrisy and double standards faced by the LGBTQ community. Through clever wordplay, irony, and sarcasm, he flipped common stereotypes on their head and subverted expectations.

For example, he would use self-deprecating humor to playfully challenge stereotypes about gay men. By embracing and exaggerating these stereotypes, Zion Ellis effectively defused their power and prompted the audience to question their own assumptions. This subversion of expectations encouraged critical thinking and ultimately helped break down barriers.

The Role of Internet Memes

In the digital age, internet memes have become a powerful tool for social commentary, and Zion Ellis recognized their potential in the fight for LGBTQ rights. Memes combine humor and visual content to deliver poignant messages in a format that is easily shareable and relatable.

Zion Ellis and his team created a series of LGBTQ-themed memes that spread like wildfire across social media platforms. These memes not only entertained but also helped educate and raise awareness about LGBTQ issues. By leveraging popular internet culture, Zion Ellis reached a wider audience and engaged with younger generations in a way that traditional methods might struggle to achieve.

Using Humor Responsibly

While humor can be an effective weapon for change, it is crucial to use it responsibly and ethically. Zion Ellis understood the importance of punching up rather than punching down with his jokes. He directed his humor towards those in positions of power or privilege, aiming to challenge systemic oppression rather than perpetuate harm towards marginalized groups.

Additionally, he recognized that humor should never be used to mock or belittle individuals within the LGBTQ community. The intention should always be to empower, uplift, and create a sense of belonging. Inclusive humor that celebrates diversity and unity is a powerful tool that can foster positive change.

Conclusion

Humor has the ability to break down barriers, challenge stereotypes, and engage audiences in conversations that may otherwise be difficult or uncomfortable. Zion

Ellis understood the power of humor to drive social change and effectively used it as a tool in the fight for LGBTQ rights. Whether through satire, subversive comedy, or internet memes, he harnessed the universal language of laughter to dismantle prejudice and create space for understanding and acceptance. But, like any tool, humor must be used responsibly and ethically, with the intention to uplift and empower. Zion Ellis's use of humor serves as a valuable lesson for future activists seeking to create a more inclusive and accepting world through laughter.

Turning Opposition to Allies

In the ongoing fight for LGBTQ rights, one of the most crucial challenges is turning opposition into allies. It is not enough to simply fight against discrimination and prejudice; we must also work towards changing hearts and minds. In this section, we explore strategies and tactics that can be employed to effectively persuade and convert individuals who may initially be opposed to LGBTQ issues.

Understanding the Opposition

To effectively turn opposition to allies, it is essential to understand the underlying reasons for their stance. Opposition to LGBTQ rights often stems from a variety of sources, including religious or cultural beliefs, misconceptions, and fears. By taking the time to grasp the motivations behind the opposition, we can tailor our approach to effectively counter their arguments.

Example: Consider a religious conservative who opposes same-sex marriage due to their belief in traditional marriage as defined by their faith. Instead of dismissing their stance outright, it is important to approach the conversation with respect and empathy. By engaging in a genuine dialogue, we can address their concerns and provide alternative perspectives that align with LGBTQ rights.

Empathy and Active Listening

One of the most effective tools in turning opposition into allies is empathy. By actively listening and acknowledging the concerns and fears of the opposition, we demonstrate that we value their perspective and are willing to engage in a respectful conversation. This allows for a deeper understanding of their objections and opens the door for meaningful dialogue.

Example: Imagine a parent who is concerned about their child being exposed to LGBTQ education in schools. Instead of dismissing their worries, we can empathize with their desire for the best education for their child. By acknowledging their concerns and sharing our own experiences and knowledge, we can address their fears and provide reassurance that LGBTQ education is crucial for fostering inclusivity and understanding.

Education and Awareness

Another key strategy in turning opposition to allies is education and awareness. By providing accurate information and dispelling misconceptions, we can challenge the opposition's preconceived notions and promote understanding. This involves sharing personal stories, statistics, and research that highlight the positive impact of LGBTQ rights.

Example: When confronted with the misconception that being LGBTQ is a choice, we can provide scientific evidence that supports the understanding of sexual orientation and gender identity as innate traits. By explaining the complexities of human sexuality and drawing on personal experiences, we can humanize the LGBTQ experience and debunk harmful stereotypes.

Appealing to Shared Values

To effectively persuade the opposition, it is crucial to find common ground and appeal to shared values. By highlighting the values of love, equality, and acceptance, we can demonstrate how supporting LGBTQ rights aligns with these core principles.

Example: When engaging with a political conservative who prioritizes small government and personal freedom, we can frame LGBTQ rights as an issue of individual liberty and the right to pursue happiness. By emphasizing the importance of respecting personal choices and autonomy, we can bridge the gap between seemingly opposing ideologies.

Building Bridges through Collaboration

Collaboration with individuals or groups who are not directly part of the LGBTQ community but share similar goals can be a powerful way to turn opposition into allies. By forming alliances and working together towards common objectives, we can break down barriers and foster a sense of unity.

Example: Consider partnering with organizations advocating for women's rights or racial equality. By joining forces and highlighting the intersectionality between different social justice movements, we can emphasize the broader fight for equality and justice, which includes LGBTQ rights.

The Power of Personal Stories

One of the most compelling ways to turn opposition into allies is through personal storytelling. By sharing our own experiences or those of LGBTQ individuals, we can humanize the struggle for acceptance and equality. Personal stories have the power to evoke empathy and challenge preconceived notions, making it an effective tool for persuasion.

Example: Rather than relying solely on statistics and facts, sharing personal stories of LGBTQ individuals who have faced discrimination or experienced personal growth can have a profound impact on the opposition. By highlighting the shared humanity and emotions, we can create a connection that fosters understanding and acceptance.

Exercises

1. Imagine you are engaged in a conversation with someone who is opposed to LGBTQ rights due to religious beliefs. How would you approach the conversation to turn their opposition into allyship? Provide a step-by-step strategy.

2. Research a case study of a public figure who was initially opposed to LGBTQ rights but became an ally. Analyze their transformation and identify the strategies used to change their viewpoint.

3. Create a persuasive campaign aimed at turning celebrities and public figures into LGBTQ allies. Develop key messages, storytelling techniques, and a comprehensive plan for mobilizing public support.

Resources

- Human Rights Campaign: https://www.hrc.org

- LGBTQ Task Force: https://www.thetaskforce.org

- It Gets Better Project: https://itgetsbetter.org

- PFLAG: https://pflag.org

Remember, turning opposition into allies is a gradual process that requires patience, empathy, and persistence. By employing these strategies and cultivating meaningful connections, we can continue to expand the network of support for LGBTQ rights and create a more inclusive and accepting society. **Together, we can make a difference!**

Debunking Myths and Misconceptions

In the fight for LGBTQ rights, one of the biggest challenges activists face is the widespread ignorance and perpetuation of myths and misconceptions about the community. To create a more inclusive and accepting society, it is crucial to debunk these myths and replace them with accurate information. In this section, we will explore some of the common myths and misconceptions surrounding the LGBTQ community and provide evidence-based explanations to counter them.

Myth: Being LGBTQ is a Choice

One of the most persistent myths about the LGBTQ community is that being LGBTQ is a choice. This belief often stems from a lack of understanding of sexual orientation and gender identity. Contrary to this misconception, scientific research consistently shows that sexual orientation and gender identity are innate traits that individuals discover about themselves.

Multiple studies in the fields of psychology and neuroscience have found evidence supporting the biological basis of sexual orientation. For example, a study published in the Journal of Homosexuality in 2014 found that homosexuality is influenced by a combination of genetic and environmental factors. Similarly, research on gender identity suggests that it is determined by a complex interaction of biological, genetic, and environmental factors.

It is essential to emphasize that being LGBTQ is not a choice but rather a fundamental aspect of an individual's identity. By debunking this myth, we can combat prejudice and discrimination faced by the LGBTQ community.

Misconception: LGBTQ Rights Threaten Religious Freedom

Another misconception often used to oppose LGBTQ rights is the belief that recognizing and protecting the rights of LGBTQ individuals infringes upon religious freedom. This argument often arises in the context of discussions surrounding marriage equality or transgender rights.

In reality, there is no inherent conflict between LGBTQ rights and religious freedom. Many religious institutions and leaders have embraced and supported LGBTQ individuals, advocating for equality and inclusivity. Furthermore, LGBTQ individuals can hold religious beliefs and engage in spiritual practices, just like anyone else.

It is crucial to recognize that protecting LGBTQ rights does not require individuals or religious institutions to change their beliefs or practices. Instead, it aims to ensure that LGBTQ individuals have the same rights and opportunities as everyone else, regardless of their sexual orientation or gender identity.

Myth: LGBTQ inclusive education promotes a "gay agenda"

Another myth often used to oppose LGBTQ-inclusive education is the claim that it promotes a so-called "gay agenda" or tries to influence students' sexual orientation or gender identity. This argument is not only unfounded but also harmful.

LGBTQ-inclusive education does not aim to change students' sexual orientation or gender identity. Instead, it seeks to create a safe and supportive learning environment for all students, including LGBTQ individuals. It provides accurate information about sexual orientation, gender identity, and the history of LGBTQ rights, fostering understanding, empathy, and respect among students.

Numerous studies have shown that LGBTQ-inclusive education reduces bullying, supports mental health, and improves overall well-being for both LGBTQ and non-LGBTQ students. By debunking this myth, we can ensure that all students receive a comprehensive education that celebrates diversity and promotes inclusivity.

Misconception: LGBTQ individuals are a threat to children

One of the most harmful and baseless misconceptions about the LGBTQ community is the belief that LGBTQ individuals are a threat to children. This misconception reinforces harmful stereotypes and leads to discrimination and prejudice.

Research consistently shows that there is no correlation between an individual's sexual orientation or gender identity and their ability to be responsible and loving parents. Major professional organizations, such as the American Psychological Association, have affirmed that LGBTQ individuals can and do form healthy and nurturing family relationships.

Denying LGBTQ individuals the right to become parents or limiting their parental rights based on their sexual orientation or gender identity only serves to harm children by depriving them of loving and caring families.

By challenging this misconception and promoting inclusivity in family and parenting policies, we can ensure that all children, regardless of their parents' sexual orientation or gender identity, have the same rights and opportunities to thrive.

In conclusion, debunking myths and misconceptions about the LGBTQ community is crucial in the fight for equality. By providing evidence-based explanations and promoting accurate information, we can challenge prejudice, discrimination, and ignorance. Through education and compassion, we can create a more inclusive and accepting society for all individuals, regardless of their sexual orientation or gender identity.

The Power of Personal Narratives

In the world of LGBTQ activism, personal narratives have proven to be a powerful tool for driving social change. It is through these stories that individuals find the courage to share their experiences, challenge stereotypes, and inspire others to join the fight for equality. In this section, we will delve into the significance of personal narratives in the LGBTQ movement, explore the different ways they can be used, and highlight their impact on promoting understanding and acceptance.

The Importance of Authenticity

Authenticity lies at the heart of personal narratives. In order for these stories to resonate with others, they must be genuine and reflect the lived experiences of the individuals sharing them. By expressing their true selves, activists can debunk misconceptions and stereotypes that often perpetuate discrimination and prejudice. Authentic personal narratives become a catalyst for empathy, as others can see themselves in the stories being told and develop a deeper understanding of the challenges faced by the LGBTQ community.

Building Connections through Storytelling

Storytelling has always played a fundamental role in human culture. It is a powerful means of communication, capable of transcending barriers and connecting people from diverse backgrounds. LGBTQ activists have harnessed the power of storytelling to create a common ground, bridging the gap between the community and society at large. By sharing personal narratives, activists can create emotional connections with individuals who may have previously held biases or misconceptions about LGBTQ individuals. These stories have the ability to evoke empathy and drive a shift in perspective.

Challenging Stereotypes

Personal narratives have the unique ability to challenge societal stereotypes surrounding gender identity and sexual orientation. By sharing their experiences and struggles, LGBTQ activists can create a counter-narrative that defies limiting notions of what it means to be queer. They expose the diversity within the community and break down the confines of societal norms. Through personal narratives, activists debunk the notion that there is only one "correct" way to be LGBTQ, effectively eradicating harmful stereotypes and fostering a more inclusive society.

Empowering Change

Personal narratives serve as a powerful tool for empowering individuals and communities. By sharing their stories, LGBTQ activists show others that change is possible and that their voices matter. Personal narratives provide hope to individuals who may be struggling with their own identity or facing discrimination. They empower LGBTQ individuals to embrace and celebrate their authentic selves, inspiring them to advocate for their rights and become agents of change.

Exercising Agency

Personal narratives also allow LGBTQ individuals to exercise agency over their own stories. Historically, the experiences of LGBTQ individuals have been silenced or misrepresented, perpetuating systemic oppression. By reclaiming their narratives, activists challenge the dominant discourse and assert their right to be heard. In doing so, they not only reclaim their agency but also create space for others to do the same. Personal narratives become a tool for liberation and a catalyst for dismantling heteronormative structures.

Breaking the Silence

Personal narratives have the capacity to break the silence that surrounds issues affecting the LGBTQ community. By sharing stories of discrimination, harassment, and marginalization, activists confront the uncomfortable realities faced by LGBTQ individuals on a daily basis. Through storytelling, activists shed light on the often hidden or ignored struggles of the community, compelling society to acknowledge and address these issues. By breaking the silence, personal narratives become a call to action, urging individuals and institutions to work towards a more inclusive and equitable society.

Practical Tips for Sharing Personal Narratives

Sharing personal narratives can be a vulnerable and empowering experience. Here are a few practical tips for individuals who wish to share their stories:

1. Start with self-reflection: Take the time to reflect on your own experiences and identify key themes or messages you want to convey. Consider the impact you hope to achieve.

2. Find a supportive community: Seek out safe, supportive spaces where you can share your story without fear of judgment or discrimination. This could be in LGBTQ organizations, support groups, or online platforms.

3. Practice active listening: Attend storytelling events and listen to the narratives of others. Learn from their experiences and find inspiration in their stories.

4. Craft your narrative: Develop your story with intention, focusing on the key messages you want to convey. Consider the emotions and impact you want to evoke in your audience.

5. Share responsibly: Be mindful of your own boundaries and the potential impact sharing your story may have on your well-being. Take breaks if needed and seek support when necessary.

Remember, personal narratives have the power to change hearts and minds. By sharing our stories, we can create lasting change and bring us closer to a world where everyone is embraced and celebrated for who they are.

Now, let's dive into an example of how a personal narrative can be used to challenge stereotypes and inspire change.

Example: Breaking the Binary

Meet Alex, a 23-year-old non-binary individual who has embraced their gender identity and wants to create a more inclusive society. Alex grew up in a small town where gender norms were strictly enforced. Their personal narrative focuses on their journey of self-discovery and acceptance, shedding light on the struggles they faced as they navigated a world that only recognized traditional gender roles.

Through their personal narrative, Alex challenges the binary understanding of gender and highlights the need for a more diverse and inclusive understanding of identity. Their story resonates with individuals who may have never considered the existence of non-binary or gender-inclusive people. Through sharing their experiences, Alex confronts stereotypes, promotes acceptance, and inspires change.

By embracing the power of personal narratives, individuals like Alex are reshaping societal understanding and paving the way for a more inclusive future. Through their stories, they challenge us to question the limitations of traditional norms and to celebrate the vast spectrum of human identity.

Exercises

1. Reflect on your own experiences and explore the key messages you would like to convey through your personal narrative. How can your story challenge stereotypes

and promote understanding?

2. Find a supportive community or platform where you can share your personal narrative. Engage in discussions with others who have similar experiences and learn from their stories.

3. Attend a storytelling event or listen to personal narratives shared online. Reflect on the impact these stories have on your own understanding and empathy towards the LGBTQ community.

4. Take the time to craft your personal narrative with intention and purpose. Consider the emotions and impact you wish to evoke in your audience.

5. Practice active listening and engage in conversations with individuals whose experiences differ from your own. Seek to learn from their stories and expand your understanding of LGBTQ issues.

Remember, the power of personal narratives lies not only in the act of sharing but also in actively listening and empathizing with the stories of others. Each narrative, whether shared or heard, contributes to the collective movement towards equality and acceptance.

Transforming Policy

Lobbying for LGBTQ Rights

In the fight for LGBTQ rights, lobbying plays a crucial role in creating social change and promoting equality. Lobbying involves strategically advocating for laws and policies that protect the rights and well-being of the LGBTQ community. It requires building strong relationships with lawmakers, organizing grassroots campaigns, and using persuasive techniques to influence decision-makers. In this section, we will explore the principles and strategies behind effective lobbying for LGBTQ rights and examine its impact on achieving equality.

Understanding the Legislative Process

To effectively lobby for LGBTQ rights, it is essential to have a solid understanding of the legislative process. Laws and policies are not created in a vacuum. They go through a series of steps and stages that lobbying efforts can target to shape or stop legislation.

1. **Introduction of Legislation:** The process begins when a lawmaker proposes a bill, which is then introduced in the legislative body. Lobbyists need to closely monitor legislative calendars and stay informed about bills relevant to LGBTQ rights.

2. **Committee Review:** Once a bill is introduced, it is assigned to a committee or multiple committees related to its subject matter. Lobbyists should engage with committee members, present research, and offer expert testimony to influence the committee's decision-making process.

3. **Floor Debate and Voting:** If a bill passes through committee review, it moves to the floor for debate and voting. Lobbyists must work to build support among legislators and ensure that they understand the importance and impact of the proposed legislation.

4. **Conference Committee:** If different versions of a bill are passed by each legislative chamber, a conference committee is formed to reconcile the differences. Lobbyists can engage with conference committee members to advocate for LGBTQ-inclusive provisions.

5. **Governor's Approval:** Once a bill is passed by both chambers, it is sent to the governor for approval. Lobbyists can apply pressure on the governor through public campaigns, media engagement, and coalition-building.

Building Relationships with Lawmakers

Effective lobbying relies on building strong relationships with lawmakers, as they are the ones who can create change through legislation. Here are some principles and strategies for building positive relationships with lawmakers:

1. **Research and Targeting:** Identify lawmakers who have shown support for LGBTQ rights or have the potential to become allies. Research their voting records, policy positions, and personal backgrounds to tailor your lobbying approach.

2. **Establishing Personal Connections:** Schedule meetings with lawmakers to introduce yourself and present your case for LGBTQ rights. Share personal stories and experiences that illustrate the impact of discriminatory policies. Building a personal connection can make a significant difference in changing hearts and minds.

3. **Coalition-Building:** Lobbying efforts are more effective when multiple organizations and individuals come together. Identify like-minded organizations and individuals who share your goals and form coalitions to amplify your voice and influence.

4. **Engaging with Legislative Staff:** Legislative staff members play a crucial role in shaping lawmakers' opinions. Establish relationships with key staff members, provide them with educational resources, and be responsive to their inquiries. They can be valuable allies in advocating for LGBTQ rights.

5. **Follow-Up and Relationship Maintenance:** Lobbying is an ongoing process, and relationships with lawmakers should be nurtured over time. Follow up with

legislators after meetings, provide them with updates on relevant issues, and offer assistance in drafting LGBTQ-inclusive legislation.

Crafting Persuasive Messages

To effectively lobby for LGBTQ rights, it is important to develop persuasive messages that resonate with lawmakers and the general public. Here are some strategies for crafting compelling messages:

1. **Storytelling:** Personal stories have the power to humanize the issues and create empathy. Share stories of LGBTQ individuals who have faced discrimination and highlight the importance of protecting their rights.

2. **Framing the Issue:** Frame LGBTQ rights as a matter of equality, fairness, and human dignity. Emphasize that protecting LGBTQ rights benefits society as a whole and aligns with the values of justice and inclusivity.

3. **Research and Data:** Use concrete data and research to support your arguments. Highlight the economic, social, and psychological benefits of LGBTQ-inclusive policies and laws.

4. **Messaging for Different Audiences:** Tailor your messages to different audiences, including conservative lawmakers, religious leaders, and the general public. Understand their concerns and values and address them in a way that aligns with LGBTQ rights.

5. **Collaboration with Grassroots Activists:** Work closely with grassroots activists to amplify your messages. Encourage supporters to contact their representatives, write letters, make phone calls, and attend legislative hearings to show widespread support for LGBTQ rights.

Challenges and Strategies

Lobbying for LGBTQ rights is not without its challenges. Here are some common challenges and strategies to overcome them:

1. **Opposition and Misinformation:** Lobbyists often face opposition from individuals and groups that propagate misinformation and perpetuate stereotypes about the LGBTQ community. Combat this by providing accurate information, dispelling myths, and engaging in respectful debates.

2. **Conservative Backlash:** Some lawmakers may be hesitant to support LGBTQ rights due to fear of conservative backlash. Build relationships with conservative lawmakers, focus on shared values, and showcase the growing public support for LGBTQ rights.

3. **Lack of Awareness:** Some lawmakers may not fully understand the challenges faced by the LGBTQ community. Educate them about the disparities and discrimination LGBTQ individuals face, and the importance of legal protections to ensure their well-being.

4. **Incremental Change vs. Sweeping Reforms:** Achieving progress in LGBTQ rights often requires patience, as incremental change is more attainable than sweeping reforms. Celebrate victories, no matter how small, and highlight their importance in the broader fight for equality.

5. **Political and Legal Barriers:** Lobbyists must be aware of political and legal barriers that may limit progress on LGBTQ rights. Develop strategies to navigate these barriers, including coalition-building, public campaigns, and legal challenges.

Case Study: The Fight for Marriage Equality

The fight for marriage equality in the United States serves as a powerful example of effective lobbying efforts. Lobbying organizations like Human Rights Campaign (HRC) worked tirelessly to build relationships with lawmakers, educate the public, and challenge discriminatory laws in court.

By engaging with lawmakers and providing research-backed arguments, lobbying organizations gained support for marriage equality. They coordinated grassroots campaigns to create public pressure and used strategic lawsuits to challenge the constitutionality of discriminatory laws.

The lobbying efforts culminated in the Supreme Court case of Obergefell v. Hodges in 2015, where the court legalized same-sex marriage across the United States. This landmark decision was a result of years of dedicated lobbying work and demonstrates the power of persistence and strategic advocacy.

Additional Resources and Tips

To enhance your understanding of lobbying for LGBTQ rights, here are some additional resources and tips:

1. **Organizations:** Connect with organizations like the Human Rights Campaign, LGBTQ Victory Fund, and National LGBTQ Task Force for resources, guidance, and opportunities to get involved.

2. **Lobbying Workshops and Trainings:** Attend lobbying workshops and trainings organized by LGBTQ advocacy organizations to learn effective strategies and techniques for lobbying.

3. **Legislative Internships:** Consider internships with legislators or lobbying organizations to gain first-hand experience in the legislative process and build networks within the LGBTQ advocacy community.

4. **Advocacy Toolkits:** Utilize advocacy toolkits and online resources provided by LGBTQ organizations to gain in-depth knowledge on advocacy techniques, lobbying best practices, and relevant policy issues.

5. **Current Events:** Stay informed about current events related to LGBTQ rights. Follow news outlets, social media accounts of LGBTQ organizations, and legislative updates to be aware of new opportunities and challenges.

Remember, lobbying is a continuous effort, and it requires collaboration, perseverance, and dedication. By employing effective strategies, building relationships, and crafting persuasive messages, we can continue to make substantial progress in achieving LGBTQ rights and equality. Let's embrace the power of advocacy to create a more inclusive and just society for all.

Challenging Discriminatory Laws

In the fight for LGBTQ rights, one of the most critical aspects is challenging discriminatory laws that hinder equality and perpetuate marginalization. Discriminatory laws not only infringe upon the basic human rights of LGBTQ individuals, but they also create a hostile environment that fuels inequality and prejudice. In this section, we will explore the strategies and tactics used by activists like Zion Ellis to challenge discriminatory laws and initiate lasting change.

Understanding Discriminatory Laws

Discriminatory laws can manifest in various forms, such as laws that criminalize same-sex relationships, deny LGBTQ individuals the right to marry, or allow discrimination based on sexual orientation and gender identity in areas like employment, housing, and public accommodations. The first step in challenging these laws is to understand their origins, implications, and impact on the LGBTQ community.

Activists like Zion Ellis dive deep into the legal framework to identify specific laws that perpetuate discrimination. They analyze the historical context, legislative intent, and social attitudes that underpin these laws. This understanding helps in formulating effective strategies to dismantle discriminatory laws.

Litigation and Legal Advocacy

One of the primary methods employed by activists to challenge discriminatory laws is litigation and legal advocacy. By using the court system, they seek to challenge the constitutionality of these laws and have them struck down. This approach is particularly effective in systems where the judiciary is impartial and upholds the principles of equality and justice.

Zion Ellis and other LGBTQ activists collaborate with legal experts to build strong cases that highlight the discriminatory nature of these laws. They strategically select plaintiffs who have been directly affected by the laws, allowing the court to witness the personal hardships faced by LGBTQ individuals and their families. By presenting compelling arguments backed by legal precedents and constitutional principles, they aim to convince judges to rule in favor of equality.

It is important to note that the process of challenging discriminatory laws through litigation can be slow and cumbersome. It requires extensive research, thorough legal analysis, and financial resources to sustain a prolonged legal battle. However, successful outcomes not only lead to the repeal of discriminatory laws but also set legal precedents that protect LGBTQ rights for generations to come.

Community Mobilization and Grassroots Advocacy

While litigation plays a crucial role in challenging discriminatory laws, it is equally important to mobilize the community and build grassroots support for change. Activists like Zion Ellis recognize that sustained pressure from the LGBTQ community and its allies can significantly influence policymakers and legislators.

Community mobilization involves organizing protests, demonstrations, and public awareness campaigns to shed light on the impact of discriminatory laws. By bringing the LGBTQ community and its supporters together, activists create a powerful voice for change. They employ various tactics, such as rallies, marches, and social media campaigns, to raise awareness, educate the public, and exert pressure on lawmakers to rethink discriminatory legislation.

Grassroots advocacy complements community mobilization by engaging individuals at the local level. Activists encourage LGBTQ individuals and their allies to write letters, make phone calls, and meet with their elected representatives to express their concerns and demand action. This collective effort amplifies the voices of those affected by discriminatory laws and emphasizes the urgency for change.

Educational Initiatives

Challenging discriminatory laws also involves educational initiatives aimed at debunking myths, dispelling stereotypes, and fostering understanding among the general population. Zion Ellis recognizes that ignorance and prejudice often underlie support for discriminatory laws. By providing accurate information and personal narratives, activists can gradually change hearts and minds.

Educational initiatives may include workshops, training sessions, and public forums that cover topics such as LGBTQ history, culture, and rights. By engaging schools, universities, and other educational institutions, activists create opportunities to educate the younger generation and equip them with the knowledge to challenge discriminatory beliefs and practices.

Additionally, activists collaborate with LGBTQ organizations and allies to develop educational resources, such as pamphlets, brochures, and online content, that are accessible to the public. These resources not only provide information on the harms of discriminatory laws but also offer guidance on how individuals can support the movement for equality.

International Advocacy

Discriminatory laws are not confined to a single country or region. To create meaningful and lasting change, activists like Zion Ellis extend their efforts beyond national borders and engage in international advocacy. They collaborate with LGBTQ organizations and activists from around the world to address global challenges and work towards a common goal of LGBTQ equality.

International advocacy involves participating in conferences, summits, and forums to share experiences, strategies, and best practices. Activists leverage international human rights mechanisms, such as the United Nations and regional human rights bodies, to draw attention to discriminatory laws and hold governments accountable for their actions.

By building alliances across borders, activists can exert collective pressure on governments and foster international solidarity in the fight against discriminatory laws. This global approach not only amplifies the voices of marginalized communities but also creates a network of support that can achieve significant advances in LGBTQ rights.

Conclusion

Challenging discriminatory laws is a complex and multifaceted endeavor that requires a combination of legal expertise, community mobilization, educational initiatives, and international advocacy. Activists like Zion Ellis embody the spirit of resilience and determination needed to take on this monumental task. Through their efforts, discriminatory laws are being challenged and dismantled, paving the way for a more inclusive and equal world for the LGBTQ community. As we continue to confront such laws, let us draw inspiration from these activists and join forces to create lasting change.

Securing Legal Protections

In this chapter, we explore the crucial role that legal protections play in the fight for LGBTQ rights. Securing legal rights and protections is essential to ensuring equality and fairness for the LGBTQ community. Throughout history, LGBTQ individuals have faced discrimination, persecution, and marginalization, but through the tireless efforts of activists like Zion Ellis, progress has been made in securing legal rights and protections.

The Need for Legal Protections

LGBTQ individuals have faced various forms of discrimination, both overt and systemic, throughout history. They have often been denied basic rights and freedoms enjoyed by the majority of the population. Legal protections are necessary to address this discrimination and ensure that LGBTQ individuals are treated fairly and equally. Without legal protections, LGBTQ individuals may face discrimination in areas such as employment, housing, healthcare, and public accommodations. They may also face barriers to adopting children, obtaining proper identification documents, and accessing other rights and benefits.

Challenges Faced

Securing legal protections for the LGBTQ community has not been an easy task. Activists like Zion Ellis have faced numerous challenges along the way. Some of the key challenges include:

+ **Political Resistance:** Legislation to protect LGBTQ rights has often faced significant political resistance. Some lawmakers and influential individuals hold discriminatory views or misunderstand the needs of the LGBTQ community. Overcoming these challenges requires strong advocacy and strategic engagement with policymakers.

+ **Prejudice and Bias:** Discrimination and bias against LGBTQ individuals can be deeply ingrained in society. Overcoming deeply rooted prejudices requires education, awareness campaigns, and constantly challenging misconceptions.

+ **Legal Limitations:** Existing legal systems may not provide adequate protections for the LGBTQ community. Changing and expanding laws to be more inclusive may require significant legal battles and advocacy efforts.

+ **Changing Public Opinion:** Achieving legal protections often requires changing public opinion. Building public support through awareness campaigns, storytelling, and highlighting the importance of LGBTQ rights is crucial.

Advocacy Strategies

To secure legal protections for the LGBTQ community, activists like Zion Ellis have employed various advocacy strategies. The following are some effective strategies used in the fight for LGBTQ rights:

+ **Lobbying:** Activists engage with lawmakers to advocate for the passage of laws that protect LGBTQ rights. This involves building relationships with politicians, providing expert testimony, and utilizing grassroots movements to demonstrate public support.

+ **Litigation:** Challenging discriminatory laws and policies through the legal system is another key strategy. Activists work with lawyers to file lawsuits and argue cases that aim to establish legal precedents protecting LGBTQ rights.

+ **Education and Awareness:** Education is a powerful tool in changing public opinion. Activists engage in outreach programs, public speaking engagements, and media campaigns to raise awareness about LGBTQ issues, dispel myths, and foster understanding.

+ **Coalition Building:** Collaborating with other social justice movements and organizations can amplify the impact of LGBTQ advocacy efforts. Building coalitions allows for the sharing of resources, strategies, and collective action.

+ **Public Demonstrations:** Protests, rallies, and marches are effective ways to raise awareness and show the strength and unity of the LGBTQ community. These actions help to put pressure on lawmakers and make LGBTQ rights a prominent public issue.

Successes and Ongoing Work

Through the relentless efforts of activists like Zion Ellis, significant progress has been made in securing legal protections for the LGBTQ community. Some notable successes include:

- **Marriage Equality:** The fight for marriage equality has resulted in landmark legal victories across many countries. Same-sex couples can now legally marry and enjoy the same benefits and protections as heterosexual couples.

- **Anti-Discrimination Laws:** Many jurisdictions have enacted laws that prohibit discrimination based on sexual orientation and gender identity in various areas, including employment, housing, and public accommodations.

- **Adoption and Parental Rights:** LGBTQ individuals and couples have made significant strides in securing adoption and parental rights, allowing them to form families and provide loving homes for children.

- **Healthcare Rights:** Advocacy efforts have led to improvements in access to healthcare for the LGBTQ community, including ensuring access to gender-affirming treatments and ending discriminatory practices.

- **Transgender Rights:** In recent years, there has been increased recognition of transgender rights, including legal protections against gender identity discrimination and the right to change gender markers on identification documents.

While substantial progress has been made, there is still much work to be done in securing legal protections for the LGBTQ community. Ongoing work includes:

- **Comprehensive Equality Laws:** Advocates continue to push for the enactment of comprehensive equality laws that protect LGBTQ individuals in all aspects of life, leaving no room for discrimination or prejudice.

- **Transgender and Non-Binary Rights:** The fight for transgender and non-binary rights remains ongoing, with a focus on securing legal protections in areas such as healthcare, education, and employment.

- **Intersectional Advocacy:** Recognizing the intersecting identities and experiences of LGBTQ individuals is crucial. Advocacy efforts aim to address the specific challenges faced by LGBTQ individuals who also belong to other marginalized communities.

+ **Global LGBTQ Rights:** Activists work to promote LGBTQ rights on a global scale, advocating for legal protections and challenging discrimination and violence faced by LGBTQ individuals worldwide.

In conclusion, securing legal protections is a vital component of the fight for LGBTQ rights. Activists like Zion Ellis have made significant progress, but the work continues. Through strategic advocacy, coalition building, and raising public awareness, legal systems can be transformed to ensure equality and justice for all members of the LGBTQ community. It is a journey that requires perseverance, resilience, and a collective commitment to creating a more inclusive and equitable world.

Fighting for Comprehensive LGBTQ Education

Education plays a crucial role in promoting understanding, acceptance, and equality for the LGBTQ community. In this section, we will explore the importance of comprehensive LGBTQ education and how it can contribute to a more inclusive and tolerant society.

The Need for LGBTQ-Inclusive Education

Education is not just about acquiring knowledge; it is also about shaping attitudes and beliefs. LGBTQ-inclusive education is essential because:

+ LGBTQ youth face unique challenges: LGBTQ students often encounter bullying, discrimination, and isolation in schools. Comprehensive education can help create safe and supportive environments where they can thrive.

+ Breaking down stereotypes and bias: By providing accurate information about different sexual orientations and gender identities, LGBTQ-inclusive education challenges harmful stereotypes, misconceptions, and prejudices.

+ Promoting empathy and understanding: When students learn about LGBTQ history, culture, and experiences, they develop empathy and understanding, which are crucial for building inclusive communities.

+ Fostering mental health and well-being: Comprehensive LGBTQ education can boost the mental health and well-being of LGBTQ students by validating their identities and reducing the stigma associated with being LGBTQ.

Challenges to LGBTQ-Inclusive Education

Despite its importance, LGBTQ-inclusive education faces several challenges:

+ Resistance from conservative groups: Some conservative groups argue that LGBTQ-inclusive education promotes a so-called "gay agenda" and goes against their religious beliefs. These groups often put pressure on policymakers and school administrators to limit or exclude LGBTQ-related content.

+ Lack of teacher training and resources: Many educators feel ill-equipped or uncomfortable addressing LGBTQ issues in the classroom due to a lack of training and resources. This can hinder the implementation of comprehensive LGBTQ education.

+ Legal restrictions and inconsistent policies: In certain regions, legal restrictions and inconsistent policies impede LGBTQ-inclusive education. Without clear guidelines and support from policymakers, schools may hesitate to introduce LGBTQ-related content.

Strategies for Implementing Comprehensive LGBTQ Education

To overcome these challenges and promote LGBTQ-inclusive education, several strategies can be employed:

+ Policy advocacy: LGBTQ activists and organizations can advocate for comprehensive LGBTQ education policies at the local, regional, and national levels. These policies can provide clear guidelines and resources for schools to implement LGBTQ-inclusive curricula.

+ Teacher training and professional development: Providing educators with adequate training and professional development opportunities on LGBTQ issues is crucial. This training can help them create inclusive and affirming classroom environments and handle sensitive topics effectively.

+ LGBTQ-inclusive curricula: Schools should integrate LGBTQ-related content into existing curricula across various subjects, such as history, literature, and social sciences. This approach helps normalize LGBTQ topics and fosters understanding among all students.

+ Guest speakers and community involvement: Inviting LGBTQ individuals and activists to speak at schools can offer firsthand perspectives and personal stories. Additionally, involving LGBTQ community organizations in the development of educational programs can enhance their relevance and effectiveness.

+ Creating safe spaces: Establishing LGBTQ-inclusive student clubs, safe spaces, and support groups can provide a sense of belonging for LGBTQ students. These spaces can also serve as platforms for dialogue, education, and peer support.

The Benefits of Comprehensive LGBTQ Education

Comprehensive LGBTQ education yields several benefits for students and society as a whole:

+ Foster a culture of respect and tolerance: LGBTQ-inclusive education promotes respect, tolerance, and acceptance of diversity among students. This creates a more inclusive and supportive school environment for all.

+ Reduce bullying and discrimination: By educating students about the experiences and challenges faced by LGBTQ individuals, comprehensive education can help reduce bullying and discrimination against LGBTQ students.

+ Improve mental health outcomes: LGBTQ-inclusive education can contribute to improved mental health outcomes for LGBTQ students. By reducing stigma and providing support, comprehensive education can enhance their overall well-being.

+ Prepare students for the diverse world: In an increasingly diverse society, comprehensive LGBTQ education equips students with the knowledge and skills needed to navigate and thrive in a world characterized by various sexual orientations and gender identities.

+ Promote social justice and equality: Education plays a vital role in promoting social justice and equality. LGBTQ-inclusive education helps break down barriers and fosters a more just and equitable society for LGBTQ individuals.

Conclusion

Fighting for comprehensive LGBTQ education is an essential part of the broader LGBTQ rights movement. By promoting understanding, empathy, and acceptance, this education can contribute to building a more inclusive and tolerant society. Through policy advocacy, teacher training, LGBTQ-inclusive curricula, and creating safe spaces, we can pave the way for a future where LGBTQ individuals are fully valued and included. Let us continue to fight for comprehensive LGBTQ education, one classroom at a time.

Advocating for LGBTQ-Inclusive Healthcare

The fight for LGBTQ rights extends far beyond social acceptance and legal protections. It also encompasses the struggle to ensure that healthcare systems are inclusive and responsive to the unique needs of LGBTQ individuals. In this chapter, we delve into the challenges faced by the LGBTQ community in accessing healthcare and explore the strategies employed by activists like Zion Ellis to advocate for LGBTQ-inclusive healthcare.

Understanding the Disparities

LGBTQ individuals often encounter significant disparities in healthcare compared to their cisgender and heterosexual counterparts. These disparities result from a combination of factors, including societal stigma, discrimination, and lack of cultural competence within the healthcare system.

One particular area of concern relates to mental health. LGBTQ individuals are at a higher risk of experiencing mental health issues, such as depression, anxiety, and suicidality, due to the challenges they face in a heteronormative society. However, they often encounter barriers in accessing LGBTQ-affirming mental healthcare services.

Moreover, transgender and gender-nonconforming individuals face obstacles in accessing gender-affirming healthcare, including hormone replacement therapy and gender-affirming surgeries. Limited insurance coverage, lack of knowledgeable providers, and cisnormative healthcare guidelines contribute to these disparities.

Advocacy Strategies

To combat the disparities in LGBTQ healthcare, activists like Zion Ellis employ various advocacy strategies and work towards creating a more inclusive healthcare system. Let's explore some of these strategies:

1. Raising Awareness: Activists play a crucial role in educating the public and healthcare providers about the unique healthcare needs of LGBTQ individuals. They conduct workshops, seminars, and awareness campaigns to promote understanding and sensitivity towards LGBTQ health issues.

2. Collaboration with Healthcare Providers: Building partnerships with healthcare providers is crucial for effecting change. Activists work closely with healthcare organizations to develop LGBTQ-inclusive policies and guidelines, provide training to staff, and ensure that LGBTQ individuals feel welcome and respected in healthcare settings.

3. Policy Advocacy: LGBTQ activists engage in policy advocacy to create legal frameworks that protect the rights of LGBTQ individuals in healthcare. They lobby for nondiscrimination laws, expanded insurance coverage for gender-affirming procedures, and guidelines promoting LGBTQ-inclusive healthcare practices.

4. Fostering LGBTQ Medical Professionals: To improve LGBTQ healthcare, it is essential to increase the representation of LGBTQ professionals in the medical field. Activists support and encourage LGBTQ individuals to pursue careers in healthcare, ensuring that there are providers who can better understand and address the unique needs of the community.

5. Empowering LGBTQ Patients: Activists work towards empowering LGBTQ individuals to become informed consumers of healthcare. They provide resources, organize support groups, and facilitate access to LGBTQ-friendly healthcare providers. By empowering individuals to advocate for themselves, activists promote self-advocacy and help LGBTQ patients navigate the healthcare system effectively.

Case Study: The Push for LGBTQ-Inclusive Healthcare Policies

Zion Ellis's activism includes a significant focus on advocating for LGBTQ-inclusive healthcare policies. One notable accomplishment was his involvement in the campaign for the passage of the Healthcare Equality Index (HEI) in Cyrion.

The HEI is a benchmarking tool developed by the Human Rights Campaign Foundation to assess healthcare organizations' policies and practices for LGBTQ inclusion. It evaluates factors such as patient non-discrimination policies, staff training, and patient and community engagement.

Through intensive lobbying efforts, public awareness campaigns, and collaboration with LGBTQ organizations, Zion Ellis and his allies successfully advocated for the adoption of HEI as a standard in Cyrion's healthcare system.

This achievement led to significant improvements in LGBTQ healthcare accessibility, cultural competence, and sensitivity.

Unconventional Approach: Queer Health Festivals

In addition to traditional advocacy strategies, Zion Ellis also spearheaded the organization of Queer Health Festivals. These festivals serve as platforms to educate the LGBTQ community about their healthcare rights, promote dialogue between healthcare providers and community members, and provide free or low-cost health screenings and services.

The festivals feature a dynamic mix of informative booths, interactive workshops, panel discussions, and cultural performances. They provide a safe and inclusive space for LGBTQ individuals to engage with healthcare professionals, become more informed about their health options, and find support within their community.

By combining education, activism, and celebration, Queer Health Festivals aim to break down the barriers to LGBTQ healthcare and foster a sense of empowerment and resilience within the community.

Conclusion

Advocating for LGBTQ-inclusive healthcare encompasses a multidimensional approach that addresses the disparities and challenges faced by the LGBTQ community in accessing quality healthcare. Through awareness-raising, collaboration with healthcare providers, policy advocacy, empowerment of LGBTQ patients, and unconventional approaches like Queer Health Festivals, activists like Zion Ellis strive to create a healthcare system that is truly inclusive and responsive to the diverse needs of LGBTQ individuals.

Inspiring Future Generations

Mentoring LGBTQ Youth

Mentoring LGBTQ youth is a crucial aspect of creating lasting change and fostering a sense of empowerment within the community. By providing guidance, support, and resources, mentors play a vital role in helping young individuals navigate the challenges they may face due to their sexual orientation or gender identity. In this section, we will explore the importance of mentoring LGBTQ youth and discuss various strategies and principles that mentors can employ to make a positive impact.

Understanding the Needs of LGBTQ Youth

To effectively mentor LGBTQ youth, it is essential to have a deep understanding of their unique needs and experiences. LGBTQ youth often face higher rates of bullying, discrimination, rejection, and mental health issues compared to their heterosexual and cisgender peers. By recognizing these challenges, mentors can provide tailored support and guidance to help LGBTQ youth thrive.

Creating a Safe and Inclusive Environment   Mentors should prioritize creating safe and inclusive spaces for LGBTQ youth. This includes fostering an environment where youth can freely express their identities without fear of judgment or discrimination. By actively listening and validating their experiences, mentors can help LGBTQ youth develop a sense of self-acceptance and belonging.

Addressing Mental Health Challenges   Mental health is a significant concern for many LGBTQ youth. Mentors should be equipped with knowledge about LGBTQ-specific mental health issues and be attuned to signs of distress or psychological struggles. By providing resources, referrals, and emotional support, mentors can help LGBTQ youth navigate these challenges and access appropriate mental health care.

Empowering Self-Advocacy   Empowering LGBTQ youth to advocate for themselves is a crucial aspect of mentoring. Mentors should provide guidance on self-advocacy skills, such as assertive communication, understanding legal rights, and accessing LGBTQ-affirming resources. By equipping youth with the tools to navigate systems and institutions, mentors can help empower them to effect positive change in their own lives.

Creating Meaningful Mentor-Mentee Relationships

Building strong and meaningful relationships is at the core of effective mentoring. When working with LGBTQ youth, mentors should employ strategies that foster trust, understanding, and open communication.

Active Listening and Validation   Listening attentively and validating the experiences, feelings, and concerns of LGBTQ youth is essential in building trust and rapport. Mentors should create a non-judgmental space where youth feel heard, understood, and supported. This validation can go a long way in helping LGBTQ youth develop self-esteem and confidence.

Role Modeling and Sharing Personal Narratives   Mentors can serve as positive role models by openly sharing their personal narratives and experiences.   By demonstrating resilience, self-acceptance, and success despite adversity, mentors can inspire and motivate LGBTQ youth.   Sharing personal stories can also help LGBTQ youth feel seen, validated, and connected to a larger community.

Supporting Identity Exploration and Development   Identity exploration is a crucial part of LGBTQ youth's journey.   Mentors can support this process by encouraging self-reflection, providing resources on LGBTQ history and culture, and facilitating access to queer spaces and events.   By helping youth explore their identities, mentors can contribute to their overall personal growth and self-acceptance.

Building Skills and Resilience

In addition to providing emotional support and guidance, mentors can also help LGBTQ youth build essential life skills and foster resilience.

Educational and Career Guidance   Mentors can provide support and guidance regarding educational and career pathways for LGBTQ youth.   This can include sharing information about LGBTQ-inclusive colleges and universities, scholarship opportunities, networking events, and mentorship programs.   By helping LGBTQ youth navigate educational and career choices, mentors can contribute to their long-term success and fulfillment.

Building Healthy Relationships   Understanding healthy relationship dynamics is crucial for LGBTQ youth.   Mentors can provide guidance on building and maintaining healthy relationships, emphasizing communication skills, consent, and boundaries.   By fostering healthy relationship dynamics, mentors can contribute to LGBTQ youth's overall well-being and happiness.

Resilience and Self-Care   Resilience is essential when facing challenges in life. Mentors can teach LGBTQ youth resilience strategies, such as stress management techniques, self-care practices, and building a support network.   By equipping youth with these skills, mentors can help them navigate adversity and develop a strong sense of self.

Challenges and Caveats

Mentoring LGBTQ youth may come with its own set of challenges and caveats that mentors should be aware of and address.

Cultural Sensitivity and Intersectionality Mentors should acknowledge and respect the diverse identities and experiences within the LGBTQ community. Cultural sensitivity is crucial when mentoring youth who may face unique challenges based on their race, ethnicity, religion, or socioeconomic background. Mentors should be educated about intersectionality and work to create inclusive spaces that honor the complexity of identities.

Confidentiality and Safety Concerns Mentoring LGBTQ youth requires maintaining confidentiality and ensuring their safety. Mentors should respect and uphold the trust placed in them by youth, as well as follow legal and ethical guidelines. It is essential to be aware of reporting obligations for any cases involving abuse, self-harm, or harm to others.

Ongoing Learning and Self-Reflection Mentors should commit to ongoing learning and self-reflection to stay informed about current LGBTQ issues, advancements, and best practices. This includes keeping up with the latest research, attending professional development workshops, and engaging in dialogue with other mentors and LGBTQ community members. Continuous learning ensures mentors provide accurate and relevant support.

Conclusion

Mentoring LGBTQ youth is a powerful way to make a lasting impact on their lives and contribute to the broader LGBTQ movement. By understanding their unique needs, building strong relationships, fostering resilience, and addressing challenges, mentors can empower LGBTQ youth to navigate their journeys with confidence and pride. Remember, being a mentor is not just about guiding the way; it's about instilling hope, advocating for change, and creating a brighter future for LGBTQ youth.

Empowering the Next Activist Leaders

Empowering the next generation of activist leaders is crucial for the continued progress of the LGBTQ rights movement. As an experienced activist and leader in the community, Zion Ellis understands the importance of nurturing and supporting young individuals who are passionate about creating social change. In this section, we will explore the strategies and approaches that Zion Ellis has employed to empower and inspire the next wave of LGBTQ activists.

Mentoring LGBTQ Youth

Zion Ellis recognizes the significance of mentoring LGBTQ youth and providing them with guidance and support as they navigate their own journeys of self-discovery and activism. Through his work, he has established mentorship programs that pair experienced activists with young individuals who are eager to make a difference.

One example of empowering LGBTQ youth through mentorship is the "Activist Mentorship Program," where Zion Ellis assigns mentors to youth based on their specific interests and goals. These mentors offer guidance, share personal experiences, and provide resources to help young activists develop their leadership skills and navigate the challenges that come with advocacy work.

Additionally, empowering LGBTQ youth also involves creating safe spaces for them to express themselves, share their stories, and connect with like-minded individuals. Zion Ellis has been instrumental in establishing LGBTQ youth centers and support networks, providing a platform for young activists to build relationships, gain knowledge, and receive mentorship from experienced leaders.

Empowering through Education

Education plays a vital role in empowering the next generation of activist leaders. Zion Ellis believes in the power of comprehensive LGBTQ education, both within formal educational settings and through grassroots initiatives. By educating young individuals about LGBTQ history, culture, and the ongoing fight for equality, Zion Ellis aims to inspire them to join the movement and become change-makers themselves.

To support LGBTQ-inclusive education, Zion Ellis has collaborated with educational institutions, policymakers, and LGBTQ organizations to develop curriculum guidelines that ensure accurate and diverse representation of LGBTQ individuals and issues. These guidelines promote understanding, empathy, and acceptance, fostering a future generation that is knowledgeable and equipped to advocate for LGBTQ rights.

Furthermore, empowering the next activist leaders also involves providing them with the tools and resources they need to succeed. Zion Ellis has been involved in the creation of online platforms and digital resources that offer educational content, training modules, and networking opportunities for young activists. By leveraging the power of technology, he ensures that educational resources are accessible to a wider audience and bridging the gap between different communities.

Amplifying Diverse Voices

In his efforts to empower the next generation of activist leaders, Zion Ellis places a strong emphasis on amplifying diverse voices within the LGBTQ community. He acknowledges that representation matters and that every individual's experience is unique and valuable to the movement.

To achieve this, Zion Ellis spearheads initiatives that encourage intersectionality and embrace diverse identities. By creating spaces for people of color, transgender individuals, non-binary individuals, and other underrepresented groups, he ensures their voices are heard, their experiences are validated, and their leadership potential is recognized.

Zion Ellis actively collaborates with LGBTQ organizations that focus on intersectionality, inviting their members to share their stories and perspectives. In doing so, he promotes inclusivity, fosters collaborations, and empowers activists at the intersections of various identities to build solidarity and unity within the movement.

Inspiring Action

Empowering the next generation of activist leaders ultimately comes down to inspiring them to take action. Zion Ellis believes in the power of storytelling to instill passion and create a sense of urgency for change. He encourages young activists to share their personal narratives, highlighting the impact of discrimination and inequality on their lives and communities.

Through powerful storytelling, young activists are inspired to use their voices and experiences to advocate for their rights and challenge societal norms. Zion Ellis emphasizes the importance of authenticity and vulnerability, urging young activists to be true to themselves and to take pride in their identities.

Moreover, Zion Ellis organizes events and campaigns that showcase the achievements of LGBTQ activists and the progress made in the fight for equality. By celebrating success stories and highlighting the positive impact of activism, he inspires the next generation to believe in their ability to make a difference.

In conclusion, empowering the next generation of activist leaders is a critical aspect of creating sustainable change within the LGBTQ rights movement. Through mentorship, education, representation, and inspiration, Zion Ellis has successfully paved the way for young activists to rise and take up the mantle of advocacy. By investing in the potential of the youth, he ensures that the fight for LGBTQ rights continues to evolve and thrive in the hands of capable and passionate leaders.

Creating Lasting Change

Creating lasting change is the goal of any social movement, and the fight for LGBTQ rights is no exception. In this section, we will explore strategies and approaches that can help activists and organizations in their quest to make a significant and lasting impact on society. From policy reform to cultural shifts, we will examine the various avenues through which change can be achieved.

Understanding the Power of Education

Education is a powerful tool in creating lasting change. By promoting LGBTQ-inclusive education, we can help challenge harmful stereotypes, reduce discrimination, and foster a more inclusive society. It is crucial to advocate for comprehensive LGBTQ education that goes beyond simply acknowledging the existence of queer individuals.

To achieve this, activists can work with educational institutions and policymakers to develop curriculum guidelines that include LGBTQ history, contributions, and experiences. By providing accurate and affirming information, we can help dispel myths, promote understanding, and create a more inclusive learning environment.

Example: One effective approach is to create LGBTQ-inclusive literature lists for schools. By incorporating books that feature diverse LGBTQ characters and experiences, we can foster empathy and understanding among students. Additionally, organizing workshops and seminars for teachers can help equip them with the knowledge and tools to create safe spaces for LGBTQ youth.

Advocating for Equal Opportunities

Another powerful way to create lasting change is by advocating for equal opportunities for all LGBTQ individuals. Discrimination in areas such as employment, housing, healthcare, and public services is still prevalent in many parts of the world. Activists can work towards implementing legal protections that ensure equal treatment and opportunities for queer individuals.

It is crucial to collaborate with lawmakers, employers, and organizations to push for policies that prohibit discrimination based on sexual orientation and gender identity. By securing legal protections, we can empower LGBTQ individuals to live authentically without fear of being denied access to essential services or facing unfair treatment.

Example: A successful initiative undertaken by activists is the push for LGBTQ-inclusive workplace policies. By working with human resources departments and corporate leaders, activists can advocate for policies that protect LGBTQ employees from discrimination, provide equitable benefits, and promote an inclusive work environment. This can lead to tangible improvements in the lives of LGBTQ individuals and create lasting change within organizations.

Promoting Cultural Change

Creating lasting change also requires challenging societal norms and promoting cultural shifts. By actively engaging with media, entertainment, and popular culture, activists can work towards dismantling stereotypes, increasing visibility, and changing public perceptions of the LGBTQ community.

Supporting and promoting diverse LGBTQ artists, filmmakers, writers, and creators is essential in ensuring authentic representation in mainstream media. By amplifying queer voices and stories, we can help shape a culture that celebrates diversity and challenges heteronormative expectations.

Example: An innovative approach to promoting cultural change is the use of social media influencers. Partnering with LGBTQ influencers who have a broad reach and impact can help spread awareness, challenge stigma, and promote acceptance. By encouraging influencers to share personal stories and experiences, we can humanize the queer experience and foster empathy among their followers.

Engaging Allies

Building strong alliances and engaging allies is crucial for creating lasting change. LGBTQ activists can collaborate with other social justice movements and organizations to amplify their impact and advocate for intersectional equality.

Recognizing the interconnected nature of various forms of oppression is key to building meaningful alliances. By working together with organizations fighting against racism, sexism, ableism, and other forms of discrimination, activists can generate a more powerful collective voice for change.

Example: One effective way to engage allies is through joint events and campaigns. By organizing intersectional rallies, conferences, and workshops, activists can bring together diverse groups of people and foster cross-movement solidarity. This not only strengthens the work being done but also creates a broader understanding of the LGBTQ struggle and its connections to other social justice causes.

Sustaining the Momentum

Creating lasting change requires sustained efforts and a long-term vision. Activists must prioritize self-care and well-being to ensure their continued capacity for advocacy. Burnout and compassion fatigue are common challenges faced by activists, so it is essential to establish support networks, practice self-reflection, and engage in self-care activities.

Activists can also work towards mentorship and leadership development programs to ensure the future sustainability of the movement. By empowering and inspiring the next generation of LGBTQ activists, we can ensure that the fight for equality continues for years to come.

Example: A creative approach to sustaining momentum is the establishment of LGBTQ-led community centers. These centers can serve as safe spaces for LGBTQ individuals, providing resources, support, and opportunities for community engagement. They can also offer mentorship programs, workshops, and events that empower and educate individuals, strengthening the movement from within.

Conclusion

Creating lasting change in the fight for LGBTQ rights requires a multi-faceted and holistic approach. By advocating for comprehensive education, equal opportunities, cultural change, engaging allies, and sustaining the momentum, activists can make a significant impact on society. It is through these efforts that we can continue to challenge discrimination, promote acceptance, and create a future that is truly inclusive for all.

LGBTQ-Inclusive Education: The Path to Equality

In the fight for LGBTQ rights, education plays a crucial role in promoting understanding, acceptance, and equality. LGBTQ-inclusive education is a powerful tool that not only empowers LGBTQ individuals but also creates a more inclusive and supportive environment for all students. In this section, we will explore why LGBTQ-inclusive education is essential, the challenges it faces, and the strategies to achieve a more inclusive education system.

The Importance of LGBTQ-Inclusive Education

LGBTQ-inclusive education is a key component of creating a safe and inclusive learning environment for all students. It aims to address the historical marginalization and erasure of LGBTQ individuals and their experiences in educational settings. By incorporating LGBTQ issues and perspectives into the curriculum, schools can foster a more accepting and inclusive atmosphere, free from discrimination and prejudice.

One primary goal of LGBTQ-inclusive education is to prevent bullying and harassment faced by LGBTQ students. According to studies, LGBTQ individuals are more likely to experience verbal and physical bullying, leading to lower self-esteem, higher rates of mental health issues, and even increased risk of suicide. By educating students about LGBTQ history, identities, and experiences, we can challenge stereotypes, reduce prejudice, and create a positive and supportive school climate.

Additionally, LGBTQ-inclusive education benefits all students, not just those who identify as LGBTQ. It promotes empathy, respect, and understanding, fostering a culture of diversity, inclusion, and social justice. By teaching students about different sexual orientations and gender identities, we can help them develop critical thinking skills, challenge heteronormative assumptions, and embrace diversity in all its forms.

Challenges and Solutions

Despite the importance of LGBTQ-inclusive education, several challenges hinder its implementation. Some educators may lack the knowledge, training, or resources to effectively teach LGBTQ-inclusive content. Others may face resistance from parents, community members, or even school administrators who hold biased beliefs or fear controversy.

To address these challenges, it is crucial to provide comprehensive training and professional development opportunities for educators. This can include workshops, online courses, and resources that enhance their understanding of LGBTQ identities, history, and issues. By equipping educators with the knowledge and skills necessary to create LGBTQ-inclusive classrooms, we can overcome the barriers to effective implementation.

Another key solution is to establish supportive policies and guidelines at the school and district levels. Schools should adopt anti-discrimination policies that explicitly protect LGBTQ students and staff. They should also create safe spaces, such as LGBTQ student organizations or support groups, where students feel comfortable expressing their identities and seeking support.

Furthermore, collaboration with LGBTQ organizations, community leaders, and families can help build strong alliances and generate support for LGBTQ-inclusive education. Engaging parents and caregivers in discussions about LGBTQ issues and dispelling myths or misconceptions can alleviate concerns and foster a more inclusive educational environment.

Examples and Resources

Numerous examples and resources exist to help educators incorporate LGBTQ-inclusive education into their curriculum. The following are just a few examples:

1. The Trevor Project: This organization provides resources and training for educators, including webinars and lesson plans that address LGBTQ issues and mental health.

2. GLSEN (Gay, Lesbian, and Straight Education Network): GLSEN offers a variety of resources, including toolkits, research-based reports, and professional development opportunities, to support LGBTQ-inclusive education.

3. LGBTQ History Month: Celebrated in October, LGBTQ History Month provides an opportunity to teach students about LGBTQ historical figures, events, and contributions.

4. Queer Kid Stuff: An accessible online resource that uses videos and educational materials to introduce young children to LGBTQ issues and concepts.

5. LGBTQ-inclusive literature: Incorporating LGBTQ-themed books into the curriculum is an effective way to normalize LGBTQ identities and experiences. Books such as "Heather Has Two Mommies" by Lesléa Newman or "George" by Alex Gino can be used in elementary classrooms to promote inclusivity.

These resources, along with others tailored to specific grade levels and subjects, provide educators with the tools they need to create LGBTQ-inclusive lessons and activities.

Unconventional Idea: LGBTQ-Inclusive Education in STEM

One area where LGBTQ-inclusive education can be particularly impactful is in STEM (Science, Technology, Engineering, and Mathematics) fields. Often seen as lacking diversity and inclusive practices, STEM education can benefit greatly from incorporating LGBTQ perspectives.

For example, educators can highlight the contributions of LGBTQ scientists and mathematicians throughout history. By including LGBTQ role models and narratives in STEM curriculum, we can challenge stereotypes and broaden students' understanding of who can excel in these fields.

Additionally, embracing LGBTQ-inclusive education in STEM can provide opportunities for students to explore the intersections between their LGBTQ identities and their interests in science or math. Encouraging students to investigate LGBTQ-related research questions, such as the impact of LGBTQ-inclusive policies on mental health outcomes, can foster curiosity and critical thinking.

By integrating LGBTQ content and perspectives into STEM education, we can create a more diverse, inclusive, and equitable learning environment that prepares students for the modern world.

Exercises

1. Research the policies and guidelines regarding LGBTQ-inclusive education in your local school district or region. What recommendations or requirements exist? Are there any areas where improvement is needed?

2. Design a lesson plan for a specific subject area that incorporates LGBTQ-inclusive content. Outline the learning objectives, activities, and resources you would use to ensure a comprehensive and engaging learning experience.

3. Identify an LGBTQ scientist, mathematician, or inventor who has made significant contributions to their field. Create a presentation or poster that highlights their achievements and the impact of their work.

4. Imagine you are an LGBTQ student who faces bullying or harassment due to your sexual orientation or gender identity. Write a letter to your school administration outlining the importance of LGBTQ-inclusive education and requesting additional support and resources.

5. Explore the LGBTQ-inclusive literature section of your local library or bookstore. Choose a book that you believe would be valuable in promoting inclusivity and understanding. Write a short review explaining why you selected this book and how it could be used in an educational setting.

Remember, LGBTQ-inclusive education is a continuous process that requires ongoing effort and commitment. By engaging in these exercises and promoting dialogue around LGBTQ issues, we can move closer to achieving a more inclusive and equitable educational system for all.

Youth Activism: Amplifying LGBTQ Voices

In the realm of LGBTQ activism, young people have always played a significant role in driving social change and challenging the status quo. With their passion, energy, and determination, they have the power to amplify LGBTQ voices and make a lasting impact on society. This section explores the importance of youth activism in the fight for LGBTQ rights and provides valuable insights for young activists to inspire and mobilize their communities effectively.

The Power of Youth Activism

Youth activism is a force to be reckoned with, capable of transforming societal norms and attitudes towards LGBTQ individuals. The energy and enthusiasm that young activists bring to the table can inspire others and create a ripple effect of change.

One of the key elements of youth activism is its ability to disrupt and challenge established narratives and systems of oppression. By questioning the status quo, young activists can expose societal injustices and push for inclusivity, equality, and acceptance.

Methods for Amplifying LGBTQ Voices

1. **Education Campaigns:** Knowledge is power, and education is a critical tool in the fight for LGBTQ rights. Youth activists can organize workshops, seminars, and awareness campaigns within their communities to promote understanding and empathy towards LGBTQ individuals. By providing accurate information and dispelling myths and misconceptions, they can foster a more inclusive environment that values diversity.

2. **Social Media Activism:** In the digital age, social media platforms have become powerful tools for activism. Young activists can leverage social media platforms like Facebook, Twitter, and Instagram to amplify LGBTQ voices, raise awareness, and mobilize support. Engaging in online discussions, sharing personal stories, and promoting LGBTQ-friendly initiatives can have a far-reaching impact and reach a wider audience.

3. **Artistic Expression:** Art has always been a means of self-expression and a powerful tool for social change. Youth activists can use mediums such as music,

poetry, theater, and visual arts to convey the LGBTQ experience and challenge societal norms. Art can ignite emotions, spark conversations, and challenge ingrained prejudices, ultimately paving the way for a more inclusive society.

4. Coalition Building: Collaboration is crucial in any activist movement. Youth activists can reach out to other organizations and groups that promote social justice and human rights to form powerful alliances. By working together, they can amplify their voices, share resources, and create a united front against discrimination and inequality.

Challenges and Solutions

While youth activism can be empowering, it also comes with its fair share of challenges. Here are some common hurdles young activists may face and potential solutions to overcome them:

1. Opposition and Resistance: Young activists may encounter opposition from those who resist change or hold discriminatory views. To address this challenge, it is crucial to develop effective communication and negotiation skills. Engaging in respectful dialogue and presenting evidence-based arguments can help change hearts and minds.

2. Burnout and Self-Care: Engaging in activism can be emotionally and mentally demanding. Young activists must prioritize self-care to avoid burnout. This involves setting boundaries, practicing self-reflection, seeking support from like-minded individuals, and engaging in activities that promote personal well-being.

3. Safety and Security: Fighting for LGBTQ rights can sometimes expose activists to physical harm or discrimination. Ensuring personal safety should be a top priority. Establishing support networks, learning self-defense techniques, and working with established LGBTQ organizations can help create a safer environment for activists.

Examples of Youth Activism

1. Greta Thunberg: While not directly associated with LGBTQ activism, Greta Thunberg's environmental activism serves as a powerful example of how a young person's voice can make a significant impact on global issues. Her activism has mobilized millions of people worldwide to demand action on climate change.

2. Marsha P. Johnson: Marsha P. Johnson, a key figure in the Stonewall Riots of 1969, was a transgender woman of color who fought tirelessly for LGBTQ rights.

Her activism played a crucial role in inspiring future generations of LGBTQ activists to advocate for their rights.

Resources and Next Steps

For young activists looking to get involved in LGBTQ advocacy, here are some resources and next steps to consider:

1. **Get Educated:** Familiarize yourself with the history of LGBTQ activism, current issues facing the community, and LGBTQ rights laws in your region.

2. **Connect with LGBTQ Organizations:** Seek out local LGBTQ organizations or youth groups that focus on activism. Collaborating with established organizations can provide guidance, resources, and a sense of community.

3. **Start Small:** Begin by raising awareness in your immediate community. Organize educational events, share informative posts about LGBTQ issues on social media, and engage in conversations that challenge stereotypes and biases.

4. **Listen and Learn:** Actively listen to the experiences and stories of LGBTQ individuals to gain a deeper understanding of the challenges they face. Use this knowledge to inform your advocacy work and amplify their voices.

5. **Advocate for Inclusive Policies:** Lobby your local government or educational institutions to ensure the implementation of LGBTQ-inclusive policies and initiatives. Write letters, attend meetings, and collaborate with other activists to push for change.

Remember, youth activism is a journey that requires patience, resilience, and continual learning. By harnessing your passion, collaborating with others, and amplifying LGBTQ voices, you have the power to create a more inclusive world for all.

Chapter 4: Breaking Boundaries

Chapter 4: Breaking Boundaries

Chapter 4: Breaking Boundaries

In this chapter, we delve into the inspiring journey of Zion Ellis as he breaks boundaries and revolutionizes the LGBTQ movement in Cyrion. Fueled by passion and a vision for a more inclusive society, Ellis sets out to challenge social norms, redefine relationships, and advocate for LGBTQ rights on a global scale.

Redefined Relationships and Love

Love has always been a powerful force, capable of transcending boundaries and breaking down barriers. Ellis firmly believes in the importance of redefining relationships and love in a changing world. He understands that love is not limited by gender or sexual orientation, and it is essential to celebrate queer love in all its forms.

To illustrate this point, Ellis shares stories of diverse relationships within the LGBTQ community. He highlights relationships that challenge traditional norms and showcases the beauty of queer love. By embracing individuality and breaking free from societal expectations, Ellis encourages his readers to find happiness and fulfillment in authentic and loving relationships.

Problem-solving in Relationships:

One common challenge faced by LGBTQ individuals in relationships is the impact of toxic masculinity. This societal construct often places pressure on individuals to conform to traditional gender roles, leading to power imbalances and unhealthy dynamics. Ellis addresses this issue by advocating for open communication, mutual respect, and the rejection of toxic masculinity in relationships.

Example: Jo and Pat, a queer couple who have been together for years, find themselves struggling with the expectations imposed by society. Jo, who identifies as non-binary, often feels invalidated and overlooked in their relationship. Through the support and guidance of Ellis, Jo and Pat learn to confront toxic masculinity together and embrace a more equal and loving partnership.

Spreading the Movement Globally

The fight for LGBTQ rights knows no borders, and Ellis recognizes the importance of spreading the movement globally. He believes that every individual, regardless of their geographic location, should have the right to love and live authentically. Thus, Ellis becomes a vocal advocate for LGBTQ rights worldwide.

Building International Networks:

Ellis understands that creating change on a global scale requires building international networks and alliances. He actively seeks partnerships with LGBTQ activists and organizations from different countries to share knowledge, resources, and strategies. Through collaboration, he aims to amplify the voices of LGBTQ individuals and drive progress in societies that are still resistant to change.

Problem-solving in Global Activism:

One challenge faced by global LGBTQ activism is the lack of cultural sensitivity. Different regions and countries have unique sociopolitical contexts and cultural practices, making it essential to approach activism with cultural nuance. Ellis emphasizes the need for deep understanding, respect, and cooperation with local activists to ensure that LGBTQ movements are tailored to fit diverse cultural landscapes.

Example: When working with LGBTQ activists in a conservative country, Ellis learns about the cultural and religious sensitivities that shape the narrative around LGBTQ rights. Through respectful dialogue and empathy, he helps local activists navigate societal challenges while still advocating for fundamental LGBTQ rights.

Ensuring Long-Term Sustainability

As Ellis continues to make strides in the LGBTQ movement, he also contemplates the long-term sustainability of his activism. He seeks to leave a lasting legacy that will continue to uplift LGBTQ voices and bring about societal change even after he has passed the torch to the next generation.

Passing the Torch to the Next Generation:

Ellis believes in the power of youth activism and recognizes that the next generation will be at the forefront of the fight for LGBTQ rights. He dedicates his time and resources to mentoring LGBTQ youth, empowering them to become effective leaders and activists in their own right. By fostering mentorship and providing opportunities for growth, he ensures that the movement will continue to thrive long into the future.

Problem-solving in Activism:

One challenge faced by LGBTQ activists is the need for self-care and balance. Activism can be emotionally and mentally draining, leading to burnout. Ellis offers insights on the importance of self-reflection, self-care practices, and setting boundaries to maintain personal well-being while continuing to fight for the cause.

Example: Maya, a young LGBTQ activist, finds herself deeply affected by the constant battles and setbacks in the fight for equality. Through Ellis's mentorship, Maya learns the significance of self-care and develops strategies to mitigate burnout. This enables her to sustain her activism in the long run and make a lasting impact.

Breaking boundaries is not an easy task, but Zion Ellis's relentless dedication to the LGBTQ movement in Cyrion proves that change is possible. Through redefining relationships, spreading the movement globally, and ensuring long-term sustainability, Ellis leaves an indelible mark on the LGBTQ community and inspires generations to come. As we conclude this chapter, let's reflect on the journey of breaking boundaries and look forward to the infinite possibilities that lie ahead.

Love in a Changing World

Founding Cyrion's First LGBTQ Center

In this section, we delve into the inspiring story of Zion Ellis as he takes on the monumental task of founding Cyrion's first LGBTQ Center. This endeavor represents a pivotal moment in the fight for LGBTQ rights and serves as a beacon of hope for the queer community in Cyrion.

The Need for a Safe Space

As Zion became more involved in LGBTQ activism, he noticed a common concern among queer individuals in Cyrion – the lack of a safe and inclusive space where they could freely express their identities and find support. Many LGBTQ individuals faced discrimination, prejudice, and sometimes even violence in their daily lives. This highlighted the urgent need for a dedicated LGBTQ Center.

Building a Vision

Zion understood that a successful LGBTQ Center would require careful planning and collaboration. He began by identifying key stakeholders within the queer community, including activists, artists, educators, and community leaders. Bringing them together, Zion initiated a series of meetings to discuss the vision, purpose, and structure of the center.

Creating a Welcoming Environment

One of the primary goals of the LGBTQ Center was to create a space that would be welcoming and inclusive to everyone, regardless of their gender identity or sexual orientation. Zion and his team ensured that the center's physical layout was designed with this in mind. They incorporated gender-neutral restrooms, comfortable common areas, and accessible resources.

Providing Support Services

Recognizing the myriad of challenges faced by LGBTQ individuals, Zion knew that the LGBTQ Center needed to offer a wide range of support services. These services included mental health counseling, legal assistance, healthcare referrals, and support groups. Additionally, the center became a hub for educational workshops on topics such as LGBTQ history, allyship, and navigating discrimination.

Funding and Sustainability

Securing funding for the LGBTQ Center was a significant challenge. Zion and his team approached local businesses, community organizations, and individuals who were passionate about LGBTQ rights to contribute. They also organized fundraising events, including art exhibitions and performances, to generate income. To ensure long-term sustainability, they established partnerships with corporate sponsors and implemented a membership program.

Forging Community Partnerships

Zion understood the importance of building alliances with other organizations and community groups in order to maximize impact. He collaborated with grassroots LGBTQ organizations, feminist groups, racial justice activists, and social service providers. These partnerships allowed for the exchange of knowledge, resources, and a stronger collective voice.

Empowerment and Education

The LGBTQ Center became a catalyst for empowerment and education. It offered a platform for queer individuals to share their stories and experiences, providing inspiration and hope to others. Zion also organized training programs and workshops to equip community members with the tools and knowledge to advocate for LGBTQ rights, resulting in an engaged and well-informed community.

Creating Lasting Change

Zion's vision for the LGBTQ Center extended beyond immediate impact. He aimed to create lasting change by working towards systemic shifts in laws, policies, and societal attitudes. The center became a hub for activism, rallying support for LGBTQ-inclusive legislation and advocating for comprehensive sex education in schools. By challenging heteronormative structures, the LGBTQ Center played a pivotal role in transforming Cyrion's social landscape.

Lessons from Cyrion's First LGBTQ Center

The journey of founding Cyrion's first LGBTQ Center was not without its hurdles. Zion Ellis and his team faced opposition, funding challenges, and bureaucratic hurdles. However, their unwavering commitment and perseverance prevailed. The impact of the center on the lives of LGBTQ individuals in Cyrion was immeasurable, proving the importance of dedicated spaces for marginalized communities.

As future activists and changemakers, we can learn from Zion's experience and apply these lessons to our own endeavors. By recognizing the need for safe spaces, fostering collaboration, providing comprehensive support services, and forging strong community partnerships, we can create real and lasting change in our societies. Let us be inspired by the example set by Cyrion's first LGBTQ Center and continue the fight for LGBTQ rights and equality worldwide.

Redefining Relationships and Love

In this chapter, we explore how Zion Ellis has played a pivotal role in redefining relationships and love within the LGBTQ community. Through his activism and personal experiences, Zion has challenged societal norms, broken down barriers, and fostered a more inclusive and accepting environment for all individuals.

Love Beyond Boundaries

One of Zion's key contributions to the LGBTQ movement has been his advocacy for love beyond boundaries. He believes that love knows no gender, no sexual orientation, and no societal constructs. Zion encourages individuals to embrace their authenticity and form relationships based on mutual respect and emotional connection.

Zion's work has shed light on the diversity of relationships within the LGBTQ community. He has highlighted the importance of recognizing and celebrating various relationship dynamics, including same-sex relationships, non-binary relationships, polyamorous relationships, and more. By challenging the traditional understanding of romantic partnerships, Zion has encouraged people to explore and embrace different forms of love.

Navigating Intersectionality in Relationships

Zion Ellis understands that relationships are not isolated from the social issues that impact the LGBTQ community. In his advocacy work, he has emphasized the significance of intersectionality in relationships. Intersectionality recognizes that individuals may hold multiple marginalized identities, such as being both LGBTQ and a person of color or LGBTQ and disabled.

Zion encourages individuals in relationships to consider how their identities intersect and how they can support and uplift one another. He emphasizes the importance of listening, learning, and engaging in conversations about privilege, power dynamics, and social justice within relationships. By fostering dialogue and understanding, Zion aims to create relationships that are not only loving and supportive but also socially conscious and inclusive.

Challenging Toxic Masculinity in Relationships

Toxic masculinity is a deeply ingrained societal issue that affects relationships and individuals within the LGBTQ community. Zion Ellis has been at the forefront of challenging and dismantling toxic masculinity to create healthier, more equitable relationships.

He believes that relationships should be built on communication, consent, and emotional vulnerability. By challenging traditional notions of masculinity and promoting feminist ideals, Zion encourages individuals to embrace their emotions, express themselves authentically, and cultivate empathetic and nurturing characteristics.

Zion's advocacy work includes organizing workshops and discussions that address toxic masculinity within relationships. These initiatives aim to educate individuals about the harmful effects of toxic masculinity while empowering them to create relationships rooted in respect, consent, and equity.

Supporting Healthy Relationship Practices

In addition to challenging societal norms and promoting inclusivity, Zion Ellis emphasizes the importance of healthy relationship practices within the LGBTQ community. He believes that relationships should be based on trust, communication, and consent to create a safe and supportive environment for all involved.

Zion encourages individuals to prioritize emotional well-being and mental health in their relationships. He promotes self-care practices, such as setting boundaries, practicing active listening, and seeking professional help when needed. By fostering healthy relationship practices, Zion aims to create spaces where individuals feel respected, valued, and loved.

A Personal Journey

Zion's advocacy for redefining relationships and love is deeply personal. Through his own experiences, he has navigated the complexities of love, faced societal challenges, and found strength in embracing his authentic self.

His journey serves as an inspiration to others in the LGBTQ community who may be struggling with their own relationships and identities. Zion's message of love, acceptance, and inclusivity resonates with individuals who seek to redefine relationships based on their own terms, free from societal expectations.

Unconventional Wisdom: The Love Language of the LGBTQ Community

Within the LGBTQ community, love languages can take on a unique and diverse range of expressions. While many people are familiar with the five love languages explored by Gary Chapman - Acts of Service, Words of Affirmation, Receiving Gifts, Quality Time, and Physical Touch, Zion Ellis unveils an unconventional sixth love language exclusive to the LGBTQ community: Acts of Resistance.

Acts of Resistance encompass the various ways individuals in the LGBTQ community navigate and challenge societal norms and prejudices. It can manifest through political activism, art, fashion, storytelling, or any form of self-expression that seeks to dismantle heteronormativity, cisnormativity, and other oppressive systems.

Zion Ellis encourages individuals to recognize Acts of Resistance as an expression of love and solidarity within their relationships. By embracing this unconventional love language, individuals can create powerful connections based on shared values, dreams, and aspirations for a more inclusive and equitable world.

Exercises

1. Reflect on your own understanding of relationships and love. How have societal norms influenced your perception, and how can you challenge and redefine these norms?

2. Engage in conversations with your partner or friends about intersectionality within relationships. Discuss how your intersecting identities influence your experiences, and explore ways to support each other in navigating societal barriers.

3. Research and learn about different relationship dynamics within the LGBTQ community, such as polyamory, non-monogamy, or non-binary relationships. Reflect on your own beliefs and biases, and consider how you can promote inclusivity and acceptance of these diverse relationship forms.

4. Explore your understanding of masculinity and femininity. How have societal expectations shaped your views? Challenge toxic masculinity by engaging in activities that promote emotional vulnerability, such as journaling or participating in support groups.

5. Familiarize yourself with self-care practices for healthy relationships, such as setting boundaries, practicing active listening, and prioritizing mental health. Implement these practices in your own relationships, and encourage your partner or friends to do the same.

6. Research local LGBTQ organizations or support groups that provide resources for healthy relationships. Connect with these communities to learn from their experiences and contribute to the collective effort of redefining relationships and love.

Resources

1. Lambda Legal – LGBTQ Legal Advocacy organization: https://www.lambdalegal.org/

2. GLAAD – LGBTQ Media Advocacy organization: `https://www.glaad.org/`

3. The Trevor Project – LGBTQ Youth Support organization: `https://www.thetrevorproject.org/`

4. PFLAG – Support for LGBTQ Individuals and their Families: `https://pflag.org/`

5. "The 5 Love Languages" by Gary Chapman

Remember, love and relationships should always be approached with empathy, respect, and consent. Embrace the power of love beyond boundaries and join the movement to redefine relationships and create a more inclusive world for everyone.

Celebrating Queer Love in all its Forms

Love is a universal language that transcends boundaries and defies societal norms. In this chapter, we explore the power of celebrating queer love in all its beautiful and diverse forms. From same-sex relationships to polyamory and everything in between, we delve into the challenges faced by queer individuals in their quest for love and acceptance.

Breaking Stereotypes

Queer love challenges traditional notions of romance and partnership, often breaking free from the confines of heteronormative expectations. It is important to debunk stereotypes and misconceptions surrounding queer relationships, as they hinder acceptance and understanding.

For example, the idea that all queer relationships are purely sexual or temporary is a harmful stereotype that erases the depth and emotional connection present in these partnerships. Through education and dialogue, we can challenge these assumptions and foster a more inclusive understanding of queer love.

The Spectrum of Love

Queer love exists on a beautiful spectrum, encompassing a wide range of identities and orientations. It is not limited to binary concepts of gender or monogamy. From lesbian and gay relationships to bisexual, pansexual, and asexual partnerships, the spectrum of queer love is rich and diverse.

By celebrating this spectrum, we can create space for individuals to explore their authentic selves and form relationships that align with their personal identities. Recognizing the validity of all expressions of queer love is vital in creating a more inclusive and accepting society.

Polyamory: Rewriting the Script

Polyamory, the practice of having multiple consensual and ethical romantic or sexual relationships simultaneously, challenges the idea that love can only exist between two people. It is important to acknowledge and celebrate polyamorous relationships as a valid expression of queer love.

While polyamory is not exclusive to the LGBTQ+ community, it speaks to the broader concept of reimagining love beyond societal conventions. By embracing polyamory, we open up discussions about the autonomy, communication, and consent necessary for healthy relationships, regardless of their structure.

Intersectionality in Love

Queer love intersects with other identities, such as race, ethnicity, and social class. It is crucial to recognize and celebrate the diversity within the LGBTQ+ community and how it shapes queer love experiences.

For example, queer love for people of color may face unique challenges due to systemic racism and discrimination. Celebrating and amplifying the voices of queer people of color in conversations about love and relationships is a powerful way to promote inclusivity and solidarity.

Challenging Gender Norms

Queer love has the potential to challenge and redefine traditional gender roles and expectations. By celebrating relationships that transcend gender boundaries, we disrupt cisnormativity and create space for individuals to express their true selves.

For example, queer love can include relationships where one or both partners identify as non-binary or genderqueer. These relationships allow for a reimagining of love that is not bound by societal expectations of masculinity or femininity.

Promoting Self-Love and Acceptance

Celebrating queer love starts with promoting self-love and acceptance within the LGBTQ+ community. It is important to highlight stories of resilience, self-discovery, and self-acceptance as a means of inspiring others on their own journeys.

By nurturing a culture of self-love, we empower individuals to seek and cultivate healthy relationships based on mutual respect, consent, and support. This not only strengthens the individual but also fosters a community that celebrates and uplifts queer love in all its forms.

Conclusion

Celebrating queer love in all its forms is a powerful way to challenge heteronormativity and foster acceptance and inclusivity. By breaking stereotypes, recognizing the spectrum of love, embracing polyamory, highlighting intersectionality, challenging gender norms, and promoting self-love, we create a world where queer individuals can freely express their love and be celebrated for who they are.

Love knows no boundaries, and by celebrating queer love, we take a step closer to creating a society that is truly accepting and inclusive for all.

Navigating Intersectionality in Queer Relationships

Intersectionality plays a crucial role in understanding the complexities of queer relationships. It acknowledges that individuals can experience multiple forms of oppression or privilege based on their intersecting identities such as race, gender, class, and ability. In this section, we will explore how navigating intersectionality in queer relationships can lead to greater inclusivity, understanding, and support.

Recognizing Privilege and Oppression

In any relationship, it is important to recognize and acknowledge the privileges and oppressions that each partner brings to the table. Intersectionality reminds us that identities are not mutually exclusive, and individuals can hold different levels of privilege or experience varying forms of oppression simultaneously. For example, a white queer person may experience privilege based on their race while also facing oppression based on their sexual orientation or gender identity.

By recognizing and discussing these dynamics within a relationship, partners can better understand each other's experiences and work together to challenge systems of oppression and promote equality.

Embracing Different Perspectives

Intersectionality invites us to embrace and value the diverse perspectives and experiences that each partner brings to the relationship. It encourages partners to actively listen and learn from one another, recognizing that no single experience can represent the entire queer community.

Through open and respectful communication, partners can challenge their assumptions, broaden their understanding of different identities, and foster empathy and compassion within the relationship. This will create a safe and inclusive space where both partners can truly be themselves.

Challenging Power Dynamics

Intersectionality also requires us to examine power dynamics within queer relationships. It recognizes that power can manifest in various ways, such as through gender roles, cultural expectations, and societal norms. Partners must be mindful of how these power imbalances can impact their relationship dynamic.

By questioning and challenging traditional gender roles and norms, partners can create a relationship that is based on equality and mutual respect. This involves actively dismantling toxic masculinity and embracing diverse expressions of gender identity, as well as supporting each other in navigating societal expectations.

Exploring Unique Challenges

Navigating intersectionality in queer relationships means acknowledging and addressing the unique challenges faced by individuals with multiple marginalized identities. For example, queer people of color may face racism within the LGBTQ+ community, while disabled queer individuals may encounter ableism and accessibility issues.

Partners must actively educate themselves on the specific challenges faced by their loved ones and engage in advocacy and allyship. This can include supporting LGBTQ+ organizations that center the experiences of marginalized communities, amplifying their voices, and advocating for inclusive policies and spaces.

Promoting Inclusivity and Support

Creating an inclusive and supportive environment within a queer relationship requires ongoing effort. Partners should actively seek out resources and support networks that address the intersectional needs of both themselves and their loved ones.

This can involve participating in intersectional LGBTQ+ organizations, attending workshops and events that focus on inclusive practices, and building relationships with individuals who share similar experiences. By fostering a sense of community and support, partners can navigate the complexities of intersectionality more effectively and create a relationship that celebrates diversity.

Conclusion

Navigating intersectionality in queer relationships is an ongoing process that requires open-mindedness, compassion, and a commitment to challenging systems of oppression. By recognizing privilege, embracing different perspectives, challenging power dynamics, addressing unique challenges, and promoting inclusivity and support, partners can foster a relationship that values and uplifts all identities. Ultimately, embracing intersectionality in queer relationships leads to greater understanding, empathy, and a stronger foundation for love and advocacy.

Challenging Toxic Masculinity in Relationships

In this chapter, we delve into the complex topic of toxic masculinity in relationships, exploring how it affects individuals and relationships within the LGBTQ community. Toxic masculinity refers to harmful stereotypes and behaviors associated with traditional masculinity, including aggression, emotional suppression, dominance, and homophobia. We will explore the ways in which toxic masculinity manifests in relationships and discuss strategies for challenging and dismantling these harmful patterns.

Understanding the Impact

Toxic masculinity not only harms individuals but also impacts relationships within the LGBTQ community. It perpetuates harmful power dynamics, restricts emotional expression, and reinforces gender stereotypes. Understanding the impact of toxic masculinity is the first step towards challenging and transforming these harmful behaviors.

Example: Imagine a same-sex couple, Alex and Ryan. Alex, influenced by toxic masculinity, may feel the need to exert dominance and control over Ryan. This behavior can lead to power struggles, emotional distance, and a lack of communication in their relationship.

Breaking Free from Traditional Gender Roles

Challenging toxic masculinity in relationships requires breaking free from the constraints of traditional gender roles. This involves embracing diverse forms of masculinity, femininity, and gender identities within relationships. By challenging rigid gender roles, individuals can create healthier, more equitable dynamics.

Example: In a same-sex relationship, both partners have the opportunity to redefine standard gender roles. They can distribute household responsibilities based on personal preferences and skills, rather than subscribing to traditional expectations. This not only challenges toxic masculinity but also promotes gender equality within the relationship.

Promoting Emotional Vulnerability

Toxic masculinity often discourages emotional expression, perpetuating the notion that vulnerability is a sign of weakness. Challenging this belief involves promoting emotional vulnerability within relationships. By creating a safe space for emotional sharing, individuals can break free from the expectations of toxic masculinity and foster emotional connection.

Example: In a healthy LGBTQ relationship, partners actively encourage and support each other in expressing emotions. They communicate openly, listen non-judgmentally, and validate each other's feelings. Through this process, they challenge the toxic masculine narrative that emotions should be suppressed or avoided.

Consent and Boundaries

Toxic masculinity can also manifest in disregard for consent and boundaries within relationships. Challenging this behavior involves fostering a culture of consent, respect, and open communication. It is essential to establish clear boundaries and engage in ongoing conversations about consent to ensure a healthy and empowering relationship.

Example: A trans man, Sean, is in a relationship with a cisgender gay man, Tyler. They navigate the intersection of their identities and actively discuss consent and boundaries. By proactively communicating about their comfort levels, desires, and limits, they challenge toxic masculine norms that may prioritize one partner's needs over the other.

Seeking Support and Education

Challenging toxic masculinity requires ongoing learning and support. Engaging in dialogue with other LGBTQ individuals and seeking resources on healthy relationships can provide valuable insights and guidance. Education about gender, power dynamics, and healthy communication can empower individuals to challenge toxic masculine norms.

Example: Zara and Taylor, a non-binary couple, actively seek support from LGBTQ community centers and attend workshops on healthy relationships. They engage in conversations with other LGBTQ individuals, sharing experiences and strategies for challenging toxic masculinity. Through continued education and support, they work towards dismantling harmful stereotypes and behaviors within their relationship.

Embracing Intersectionality

It is crucial to acknowledge the intersectionality of experiences when challenging toxic masculinity in relationships. Intersectionality recognizes that individuals may face multiple oppressions and privileges based on their gender, race, sexuality, and other social identities. By acknowledging these intersecting identities, we can challenge toxic masculine behaviors within a broader context and work towards more inclusive and equitable relationships.

Example: In a relationship between a black gay man and an Asian transgender woman, they grapple with the effects of toxic masculinity and racism. They support each other in navigating these intersecting identities and challenging harmful stereotypes. By embracing intersectionality, they work towards creating a relationship that is free from the harmful effects of toxic masculinity and other forms of oppression.

In conclusion, challenging toxic masculinity in relationships is essential for creating healthier, more equitable dynamics within the LGBTQ community. By breaking free from traditional gender roles, promoting emotional vulnerability, establishing consent and boundaries, seeking support and education, and embracing intersectionality, individuals can challenge harmful stereotypes and behaviors, ultimately creating stronger, more fulfilling relationships. Remember, redefining masculinity is not about diminishing it, but rather expanding it to create space for diverse expressions and experiences.

Beyond Borders

Spreading the Movement Globally

In this section, we delve into the importance of spreading the LGBTQ rights movement globally and the steps taken by Zion Ellis to advocate for LGBTQ rights beyond the borders of Cyrion. While Zion's activism began at a local level, his impact and vision extended far beyond the confines of his hometown. Through international advocacy and collaboration, he aimed to create a global network that would work towards achieving LGBTQ equality worldwide.

The Global Fight for LGBTQ Equality

Zion understood that achieving true equality required a global effort. While progress had been made in some countries, many nations still had oppressive laws and policies that targeted LGBTQ individuals. In this interconnected world, it was crucial to address human rights abuses against the LGBTQ community on an international level.

Zion actively sought to raise awareness about the state of LGBTQ rights worldwide. He emphasized the need to challenge discriminatory laws, promote LGBTQ inclusivity, and protect the human rights of individuals irrespective of their sexual orientation or gender identity.

Advocating for LGBTQ Rights Worldwide

Zion's journey to advocate for LGBTQ rights globally began by understanding the unique challenges faced by different regions and cultures. He recognized that cultural, religious, and political factors influenced the level of acceptance and equality for LGBTQ individuals in different parts of the world.

With this understanding, Zion teamed up with local activists, organizations, and policymakers in various countries to advocate for change. He engaged in dialogue, offered support and guidance, and worked collaboratively to develop strategies tailored to each context.

Through public speaking engagements, media interviews, and social media campaigns, Zion highlighted the importance of LGBTQ rights and the transformational impact they could have on individuals, communities, and society as a whole. He used his platform to share stories of individuals facing discrimination, shining a light on the urgent need for change.

Building International Networks

Recognizing the power of collaboration, Zion worked tirelessly to build strong international networks of LGBTQ activists, human rights organizations, and allies. He understood that by joining forces, they could amplify their voices and exert more pressure on governments and institutions.

Zion established connections and partnerships with organizations that shared his vision for global LGBTQ equality. Together, they organized conferences, workshops, and events that brought together activists from around the world. These gatherings provided a space for knowledge sharing, skill development, and the formulation of joint advocacy strategies.

Zion also utilized digital platforms and social media to connect LGBTQ activists globally. He created online communities where individuals could exchange ideas, seek support, and share resources. These digital networks played a crucial role in fostering solidarity and empowering activists, regardless of geographical limitations.

The Importance of Cultural Sensitivity in Global Activism

As Zion embarked on international activism, he recognized the importance of cultural sensitivity and respect for local traditions and customs. He acknowledged that while the goal was universal equality, the approach had to be adapted to the cultural and social context of each region.

Zion engaged in dialogue with representatives from different cultures, religions, and political systems. He listened attentively, seeking to understand perspectives that may differ from his own. This approach allowed him to build bridges and find common ground with individuals and communities who were initially skeptical or resistant to LGBTQ rights.

Zion's commitment to cultural sensitivity was instrumental in overcoming barriers and creating a more inclusive and accepting global movement. He believed that understanding and respecting diverse cultures was essential for effecting lasting change.

Raising LGBTQ Awareness and Empathy

Beyond advocating for policy and legal changes, Zion saw the importance of raising awareness and empathy within communities around the world. He embarked on educational initiatives that aimed to dispel myths, challenge stereotypes, and foster greater understanding of LGBTQ individuals.

Zion collaborated with local educational institutions to develop LGBTQ-inclusive curricula. He believed that educating young minds about the existence and experiences of LGBTQ individuals would promote acceptance and inclusion from an early age.

Additionally, he used storytelling and media campaigns to humanize the experiences of LGBTQ individuals and foster empathy among the general public. Zion recognized that personal narratives were powerful tools for creating connection and promoting understanding.

Creating Lasting Change

Zion's work to spread the LGBTQ rights movement globally was driven by a desire to create lasting change. He understood that progress required more than short-term victories; it necessitated a shift in societal attitudes, institutional practices, and legal frameworks.

To achieve this, Zion focused on sustainable strategies, emphasizing the importance of engaging with local communities and influencing the next generation of leaders. He mentored young activists, empowering them to continue the fight for LGBTQ rights within their own countries and communities.

Zion's legacy lies not only in the policy changes he helped institute but also in the transformative impact he had on individuals and communities around the world. Through his global activism, he paved the way for a more inclusive and accepting future, where LGBTQ individuals could live authentically and free from discrimination.

Unconventional yet Relevant: The Power of Mass Protests

While diplomacy and dialogue played vital roles in Zion's international advocacy, he also recognized the power of mass protests as an unconventional yet relevant tool for effecting change.

Zion understood that peaceful demonstrations could capture the attention of the global community, putting pressure on governments and institutions to address LGBTQ rights. He coordinated and participated in mass protests that brought together thousands of LGBTQ individuals and allies, calling for equality and an end to discrimination.

These protests not only created a public forum for the LGBTQ movement but also provided a space for participants to find strength and solidarity in their shared experiences. The collective voice was amplified through these displays of unity, captivating the attention of media outlets worldwide and generating widespread support for the LGBTQ cause.

In summary, spreading the LGBTQ rights movement globally was a key focus of Zion Ellis's activism. Through advocacy, collaboration, and global networking, he worked towards creating a more inclusive and equal world for LGBTQ individuals. By raising awareness, fostering empathy, and engaging in cultural sensitivity, Zion laid the groundwork for lasting change on a global scale. Ultimately, his legacy continues to inspire activists and allies around the world to fight for LGBTQ rights.

Advocating for LGBTQ Rights Worldwide

In this chapter, we delve into the global fight for LGBTQ rights, exploring the challenges, successes, and strategies employed by activists like Zion Ellis to advocate for equality on an international scale. From inspiring policy changes to fostering cultural sensitivity, this section highlights the importance of global LGBTQ activism and its impact on communities around the world.

Understanding the Global Landscape

Advocating for LGBTQ rights worldwide requires a deep understanding of the diverse cultural, political, and social contexts in which the fight takes place. It is crucial to have a comprehensive understanding of local laws, customs, and attitudes toward LGBTQ individuals. By recognizing the unique challenges faced by different communities, activists can tailor their strategies to make a lasting impact.

For instance, in some countries, homosexuality is criminalized, and LGBTQ individuals face significant discrimination and violence. Understanding the legal and social obstacles faced by individuals in such regions is essential in order to provide support and create effective advocacy strategies.

Building International Networks

To create lasting change, LGBTQ activists must build strong networks and alliances across borders. This collaboration allows for the exchange of ideas, experiences, and best practices. By amplifying the collective voice of the global LGBTQ community, activists can pressure governments and international organizations to prioritize and protect LGBTQ rights.

Organizing LGBTQ conferences, forums, and summits brings together activists, experts, and policymakers from around the world. These platforms provide opportunities for networking, knowledge sharing, and coordinated efforts to address global challenges.

Example: One notable example of international collaboration is the formation of the Global LGBTQ Advocacy Alliance. This alliance brings together LGBTQ organizations from different countries to create a unified front in the fight for equality. By coordinating advocacy efforts and leveraging their collective influence, the alliance has successfully influenced policy changes and improved the legal status of LGBTQ individuals in several countries.

Engaging with International Institutions

Engaging with international institutions and organizations is another crucial aspect of advocating for LGBTQ rights worldwide. Institutions like the United Nations and regional bodies such as the European Union play a vital role in promoting human rights and can be powerful allies in the fight for LGBTQ equality.

By actively participating in human rights mechanisms, such as the Universal Periodic Review, activists can hold governments accountable for their treatment of LGBTQ individuals. This involves submitting reports, attending sessions, and engaging in advocacy efforts to ensure that LGBTQ rights are included in the international human rights agenda.

Example: The International LGBTQ Rights Commission (ILGRC) works closely with the United Nations to advance LGBTQ rights globally. Through strategic partnerships and collaboration, ILGRC has successfully mobilized support within the UN system, resulting in the adoption of resolutions and policies that promote and protect LGBTQ rights.

Addressing Cultural Sensitivity

Advocating for LGBTQ rights worldwide requires a nuanced understanding of cultural sensitivity. While challenging discriminatory laws and practices is necessary, it must be done in a way that respects and considers the cultural and religious beliefs of different communities. Sensitivity to local customs and traditions is essential to effectively engage and gain support from diverse populations.

Cultural sensitivity can be achieved through dialogue, education, and fostering cross-cultural understanding. By promoting LGBTQ-inclusive education and awareness campaigns, activists can challenge stereotypes and misconceptions about LGBTQ individuals, helping to break down barriers and build acceptance within communities.

Tips for Addressing Cultural Sensitivity: 1. Engage in dialogue: Create spaces for respectful conversations that allow for different perspectives to be shared and understood. 2. Collaborate with local organizations: Partnering with local LGBTQ organizations can provide valuable insights and guidance on cultural norms and sensitivities. 3. Utilize storytelling: Share personal narratives and experiences to foster empathy and understanding, creating a connection between diverse cultures and the LGBTQ community.

Promoting LGBTQ Rights through Diplomacy

Diplomacy can be a powerful tool in advocating for LGBTQ rights worldwide. Activists can work with diplomats, ambassadors, and political leaders to promote LGBTQ-inclusive policies and mobilize international pressure. By building relationships with key decision-makers, activists can influence legislative and policy changes at a global level.

Example: The LGBTQI+ Rights Caucus, a coalition of LGBTQ activists and diplomats, actively engages with governments and international organizations to promote LGBTQ rights globally. Their diplomatic efforts have resulted in the adoption of LGBTQ-inclusive policies, including the decriminalization of homosexuality and the protection of LGBTQ individuals from discrimination.

Challenges and Future Directions

Advocating for LGBTQ rights worldwide is not without its challenges. Deep-seated cultural, religious, and legal barriers can impede progress. Moreover, backlash, discrimination, and violence against LGBTQ individuals and activists remain significant obstacles.

Moving forward, the global LGBTQ movement must continue to address intersectionality and recognize that the fight for equality extends beyond sexual orientation and gender identity. Advocacy efforts must include the voices and experiences of marginalized communities within the LGBTQ community, such as transgender and non-binary individuals.

Exercise: Research a country where homosexuality is criminalized and create an advocacy plan to promote LGBTQ rights in that country. Consider the legal, social, and cultural challenges in your plan.

Additional Resource: The International Lesbian, Gay, Bisexual, Trans and Intersex Association (ILGA) provides comprehensive resources and reports on LGBTQ rights worldwide. Their publications can serve as a valuable reference for activists and researchers alike.

Building International Networks

In the global fight for LGBTQ equality, building international networks is crucial. It allows activists to connect, collaborate, and share resources and strategies. By coming together, they can amplify their voices and create a unified force to challenge discriminatory practices and advocate for LGBTQ rights worldwide.

Understanding the Power of International Networks

Building international networks provides a powerful platform for activists to exchange ideas and experiences. It helps them gain insights into the different challenges faced by LGBTQ communities in various parts of the world. This understanding is crucial in developing effective strategies that can be adapted to different cultural and political contexts.

By fostering connections with activists from diverse backgrounds, advocates can learn from each other's successes and failures. They can explore innovative approaches to address common problems and find inspiration in the resilience and courage demonstrated by activists worldwide.

Identifying Partnerships and Collaborations

Establishing international networks requires identifying potential partners and collaborations. LGBTQ organizations, advocacy groups, and social justice movements from different countries can come together to promote LGBTQ rights globally.

By partnering with well-established organizations, activists can leverage existing networks, resources, and expertise. For example, collaborating with international human rights organizations can provide a broader platform to advocate for LGBTQ rights at the United Nations and other global forums.

Engaging with other social justice movements, such as feminist groups or racial equality organizations, can create synergies and strengthen intersectional activism. Recognizing the interconnectedness of different oppressions helps build solidarity and amplifies the collective voice for change.

Utilizing Technology for Global Connectivity

In today's digital age, technology plays a crucial role in connecting activists across borders. Online platforms, social media, and digital communication tools allow for instant and continuous communication, breaking down barriers of distance and time zones.

Virtual conferences and webinars provide opportunities for activists to share knowledge and exchange ideas without the need for expensive travel. Online collaboration platforms facilitate the coordination of joint initiatives and campaigns.

Digital activism campaigns, such as online petitions or social media awareness initiatives, can reach a global audience and generate support for LGBTQ rights. Utilizing online platforms effectively enables activists to mobilize people from all corners of the world, making the fight for LGBTQ equality a truly global movement.

Addressing Cultural Sensitivity and Contextual Challenges

When building international networks, it is essential to recognize the importance of cultural sensitivity and the contextual challenges faced by LGBTQ communities in different countries.

Understanding local customs, traditions, and laws is crucial to develop strategies that resonate with the specific cultural and political context. Issues such as religion, traditional gender norms, and societal attitudes towards sexuality can significantly impact the LGBTQ rights movement.

By actively engaging with local activists and organizations, international networks can provide support while respecting the leadership of those directly affected by local struggles. This approach ensures that initiatives are rooted in the lived experiences and priorities of LGBTQ individuals, as opposed to imposing external agendas.

Promoting Global Solidarity and Intersectionality

Building international networks fosters global solidarity and intersectionality within the LGBTQ rights movement. Recognizing the interconnections of different struggles and advocating for social justice as a whole strengthens the fight against all forms of oppression.

By actively engaging with other marginalized communities and social justice movements, LGBTQ activists can amplify their impact. Collaborating with organizations focused on racial justice, gender equality, and disability rights, among others, helps build stronger alliances and create platforms for lasting change.

Promoting intersectionality within international networks ensures that the experiences of LGBTQ individuals at the intersections of multiple marginalized identities are uplifted and centered. By addressing the complex ways intersecting oppressions manifest, activists can work towards a more inclusive and equitable world for all.

Case Study: The Global LGBTQ Coalition

The Global LGBTQ Coalition is a prime example of an international network built to fight for LGBTQ rights. It brings together activists, organizations, and allies from different regions to advocate for legal protections, equal rights, and social acceptance.

This coalition employs a multi-pronged approach to create change, including lobbying governments, influencing international organizations, and mobilizing grassroots campaigns. Through its network, the coalition has successfully supported activists in countries where LGBTQ rights are under threat, amplifying their voices and providing resources and support.

The Global LGBTQ Coalition also prioritizes intersectionality, recognizing that LGBTQ rights are interconnected with other social justice issues. By collaborating with organizations focused on gender equality, racial justice, and disability rights, the coalition ensures a holistic and comprehensive approach to fighting for LGBTQ rights worldwide.

Key Takeaways

Building international networks is essential for LGBTQ activists to create meaningful change on a global scale. It allows for the exchange of ideas, collaboration, and solidarity, amplifying the collective voice for LGBTQ rights.

Key takeaways for building international networks include:

+ Understanding the power of international connections in developing effective strategies.

+ Identifying partnerships and collaborations with LGBTQ organizations, advocacy groups, and social justice movements.

+ Utilizing technology for global connectivity and digital activism.

+ Addressing cultural sensitivity and contextual challenges specific to different countries.

+ Promoting global solidarity and intersectionality within the LGBTQ movement.

+ Learning from successful examples like the Global LGBTQ Coalition.

By building international networks, LGBTQ activists can join forces and work towards a world where every individual, regardless of their sexual orientation or gender identity, can live with dignity, equality, and respect.

The Global Fight for LGBTQ Equality

The fight for LGBTQ equality extends far beyond national borders, as activists like Zion Ellis work tirelessly to advocate for the rights and well-being of LGBTQ individuals around the world. In this section, we will explore the challenges faced by the global LGBTQ community and the strategies employed to address them.

The Landscape of LGBTQ Rights Worldwide

The state of LGBTQ rights varies widely across different countries and regions. In some progressive nations, LGBTQ individuals enjoy legal protections against discrimination, marriage equality, and comprehensive healthcare. However, in many parts of the world, LGBTQ people face significant barriers to equality and justice.

In some countries, same-sex relationships are criminalized, and LGBTQ individuals are subject to violence, persecution, and even death. Homophobia, transphobia, and stigma create hostile environments that negatively impact the lives of LGBTQ people, limiting their opportunities for education, employment, and advancement.

Advocating for Change on the Global Stage

To address the global challenges faced by LGBTQ individuals, activists like Zion Ellis recognize the importance of engaging in international advocacy efforts. By working collectively and forming alliances with local activists, organizations, and governments, the fight for global LGBTQ equality becomes stronger and more effective.

One strategy employed by activists is lobbying at international institutions such as the United Nations and the European Union. By leveraging their platform and engaging with diplomats and policymakers, activists can push for changes in policies and attitudes towards LGBTQ individuals. This includes advocating for the decriminalization of homosexuality, the protection of LGBTQ rights, and the inclusion of LGBTQ issues in broader human rights discussions.

Building International Networks

In the global fight for LGBTQ equality, building international networks is crucial. Activists like Zion Ellis work to establish connections with LGBTQ organizations and allies across different regions, sharing knowledge, resources, and experiences. This collaborative approach allows for the exchange of best practices and strategies that can be adapted to local contexts.

One example of successful international networking is the formation of the International Lesbian, Gay, Bisexual, Trans and Intersex Association (ILGA). ILGA works to advance LGBTQ rights through research, advocacy, and support for local organizations. By bringing together activists from around the world, ILGA strengthens the global LGBTQ movement and facilitates solidarity among its members.

Addressing Cultural Sensitivity

Fighting for LGBTQ equality on a global scale requires an understanding of diverse cultural contexts. Cultural sensitivity is essential in crafting strategies that respect and resonate with the specific cultural norms and beliefs of different regions.

Activists like Zion Ellis collaborate with local LGBTQ activists to ensure that efforts are culturally appropriate and sustainable. They engage in dialogue and education to challenge prejudices and foster acceptance within communities. By framing LGBTQ rights within the framework of human rights and emphasizing shared values of fairness, dignity, and equality, activists can effectively gain support and understanding, even in traditionally conservative societies.

Challenging Colonial Legacies

A significant aspect of the global fight for LGBTQ equality involves addressing the legacy of colonial-era laws and attitudes that still persist in many countries. In some cases, anti-LGBTQ legislation was introduced during the colonial period and remains in place today.

Activists work to challenge and repeal these laws, highlighting their discriminatory nature and their infringement upon the rights and dignity of LGBTQ individuals. They emphasize the importance of decolonization in the fight for global LGBTQ equality, recognizing that dismantling systems of oppression is a crucial step towards achieving justice and equality for all.

The Role of the Media

In the fight for global LGBTQ equality, the media plays a vital role in shaping public opinion and challenging societal norms. Activists like Zion Ellis leverage media platforms to raise awareness about LGBTQ rights, share personal narratives, and challenge stereotypes and misconceptions.

By telling compelling stories and humanizing the experiences of LGBTQ individuals, the media can help create empathy and understanding among wider audiences. Documentaries, films, and TV shows that highlight LGBTQ issues and experiences serve as powerful tools for advocacy and education.

Promoting LGBTQ-Inclusive Education

Education is key to achieving lasting change and promoting LGBTQ equality on a global scale. Activists advocate for LGBTQ-inclusive education systems that teach students about diversity, tolerance, and acceptance.

Through curriculum reforms, training programs, and awareness campaigns, activists work to address the erasure of LGBTQ history and identities within educational institutions. They stress the importance of providing LGBTQ-inclusive resources, promoting inclusive language and creating safe spaces for LGBTQ students.

Conclusion

The global fight for LGBTQ equality is an ongoing battle that requires strategic and collaborative efforts. Activists like Zion Ellis, through international advocacy, networking, cultural sensitivity, and media engagement, work towards promoting legal protections, challenging discriminatory practices, and fostering acceptance in all corners of the world. By continuing to fight for LGBTQ rights globally, we inch closer to a world that embraces diversity, inclusivity, and equality for all.

Cultural Sensitivity in Global Activism

In the fight for LGBTQ rights around the world, it is crucial to recognize the importance of cultural sensitivity in global activism. Cultural sensitivity refers to the awareness and respect for different cultural practices, beliefs, and values, which influences the ways in which we approach activism in different regions and communities. It requires navigating the delicate balance between promoting LGBTQ equality and respecting cultural diversity.

Understanding Cultural Context

One of the fundamental principles of cultural sensitivity in global activism is understanding the cultural context within which we are advocating for change. Each country, region, or community has unique cultural, religious, and historical backgrounds that shape people's attitudes towards LGBTQ rights. It is essential to invest time and effort into learning about these nuances and understanding the local context.

For example, in some cultures, conversations about sexuality and gender identity may be considered taboo or not openly discussed. Approaching LGBTQ activism in such contexts requires finesse and an understanding of culturally appropriate ways to engage in dialogue and education. This might involve partnering with local organizations or individuals who are well-versed in local customs, traditions, and sensitivities.

Respecting Local Customs and Traditions

Cultural sensitivity in global activism also means respecting and acknowledging local customs and traditions. It is essential to recognize that different communities may have varying views and perspectives on LGBTQ rights based on their cultural heritage.

While we fight for equality and challenge discriminatory practices, it is crucial to do so in a manner that does not impose Western ideals or values onto other cultures. The goal is to promote understanding, empathy, and dialogue rather than imposing one's own beliefs.

For example, in some traditional communities, gender roles may be deeply ingrained, and concepts such as non-binary or gender fluid identities may be unfamiliar. In such cases, it is important to approach advocacy in a way that respects local gender norms while still advocating for inclusivity and understanding. This might involve highlighting historical examples of diverse gender roles within the community or focusing on the harmful consequences of rigid gender expectations.

Building Local Partnerships

To achieve true cultural sensitivity in global activism, it is essential to build local partnerships and collaborations. Working with local LGBTQ organizations, activists, and community leaders can help ensure that the activism is rooted in the local context and tailored to the specific needs of the community.

By partnering with local stakeholders, activists can gain valuable insights and guidance on the most effective and culturally appropriate strategies for advocacy. These partnerships can also help foster a sense of ownership and empowerment within the community itself, which is crucial for driving sustainable change.

Education and Awareness

Education and awareness are powerful tools in promoting cultural sensitivity in global activism. By providing information on LGBTQ rights, dispelling myths and misconceptions, and fostering dialogue, activists can help bridge the gap between cultures and promote understanding.

Educational initiatives should be tailored to the specific cultural context and delivered in a way that is accessible and relatable. This might involve using culturally relevant examples, storytelling, or multimedia approaches to engage diverse audiences.

Challenges and Pitfalls

Cultural sensitivity in global activism is not without its challenges and pitfalls. One of the main challenges is navigating the tension between respecting local customs and challenging discriminatory practices. Striking the right balance requires careful consideration and a deep understanding of the cultural nuances.

There is also a risk of unintentionally perpetuating harmful stereotypes or reinforcing negative attitudes by relying on tropes or generalizations about certain cultures. It is essential to avoid these pitfalls by ensuring that activism is based on accurate information, respectful engagement, and a commitment to dismantling prejudice and discrimination.

Unconventional Approach: Storytelling as a Bridge

One unconventional yet powerful approach to promoting cultural sensitivity in global activism is through the art of storytelling. Stories have the ability to transcend cultural boundaries, evoke empathy, and bridge gaps in understanding.

By sharing personal narratives and stories of LGBTQ individuals within specific cultural contexts, activists can humanize the struggle for equality and challenge stereotypes. This approach allows for the exploration of shared values and experiences, fostering a sense of empathy and connection that can help break down barriers.

For example, sharing stories of LGBTQ individuals who have made significant contributions to their communities or highlighting the experiences of LGBTQ individuals who have faced discrimination and overcome adversity can create a platform for dialogue and understanding.

Conclusion

Cultural sensitivity in global activism is essential for effectively advocating for LGBTQ rights around the world. It involves understanding cultural context, respecting local customs, building partnerships, promoting education and awareness, and being mindful of potential challenges and pitfalls.

By navigating cultural sensitivities with respect and empathy, activists can foster meaningful dialogue, challenge discriminatory practices, and work towards a more inclusive and accepting world for everyone, regardless of their sexual orientation or gender identity.

Leaving a Legacy

Ensuring Long-Term Sustainability

In the ever-changing landscape of LGBTQ activism, one of the paramount challenges is ensuring the long-term sustainability of the movement. As the fight for equality continues, it becomes imperative to establish strategies and frameworks that will guarantee the progress achieved thus far will be maintained and built upon for future generations. In this section, we will explore key considerations for ensuring the long-term sustainability of LGBTQ activism.

Building Strong Organizational Structures

A crucial element of long-term sustainability lies in establishing strong organizational structures within the LGBTQ movement. Robust organizations provide the foundation for effective coordination, resource management, and strategic planning. By fostering collaboration and inclusivity, these structures can harness the collective power of activists, maximizing their impact.

One avenue to achieve this is through the establishment of LGBTQ centers, which serve as physical spaces for community engagement, advocacy, and support. These centers can house various services ranging from counseling and legal assistance to educational programs and social events. By creating an inclusive and welcoming environment, these centers play a vital role in fostering community resilience and long-term sustainability.

Fostering Collaboration and Partnership

The fight for LGBTQ rights requires collaboration not only within the movement but also with external stakeholders. By forging partnerships with allied organizations, universities, corporations, and government entities, the LGBTQ movement can expand its influence and leverage shared resources.

Collaboration can take various forms, from joint advocacy campaigns to co-organizing events and initiatives. By pooling together expertise and resources, activists can amplify their impact and create lasting change. Moreover, forging partnerships with diverse communities and social movements facilitates the exploration of intersectionality, a critical aspect of modern activism that considers the interconnected nature of various forms of oppression.

Financial Sustainability

Financial sustainability is at the heart of long-term planning for any movement. Securing adequate funding is crucial for maintaining organizational infrastructure, sustaining operational costs, and initiating impactful projects.

Diversifying funding sources is key to financial sustainability. Beyond individual donations, grant funding, and corporate sponsorships, the LGBTQ movement can explore innovative approaches such as social enterprises or crowdfunding campaigns. By embracing evolving technological platforms, activists can engage wider audiences and generate sustained financial support.

Equally important is building financial literacy and strategic financial management within LGBTQ organizations. By acquiring financial skills and knowledge, activists can ensure efficient and transparent allocation of resources, maximizing the impact of funding received.

Leadership Development and Succession Planning

To secure the long-term sustainability of the movement, leadership development and succession planning are paramount. Cultivating the next generation of LGBTQ activists and leaders fosters continuity and ensures the transmission of knowledge, experience, and values.

Organizations can establish mentorship programs, internships, and leadership training initiatives to provide opportunities for emerging leaders to develop their skills. This not only empowers individuals but also strengthens the movement as a whole by ensuring a diverse and inclusive leadership pipeline.

Succession planning involves actively identifying and preparing potential leaders to step into key roles when the time comes. By strategizing and implementing succession plans, organizations can mitigate the risk of losing institutional knowledge and momentum.

Global Solidarity and Cultural Sensitivity

In an increasingly interconnected world, global solidarity is crucial for the long-term sustainability of the LGBTQ movement. Recognizing and supporting LGBTQ communities across borders fosters collaboration and learning, helping to address shared challenges and shape international norms.

However, cultural sensitivity is paramount when engaging in global advocacy. The LGBTQ movement must strive to understand the specific contexts, struggles, and nuances of different regions and cultures. Engaging in respectful dialogue, cultural exchange, and cross-cultural training can help avoid inadvertently imposing Western-centric approaches and ensure that advocacy efforts are tailored to local circumstances.

Balancing Activism with Self-Care

In the pursuit of long-term sustainability, it is vital to prioritize the well-being of activists. Advocacy work can be emotionally and mentally demanding, often resulting in burnout, compassion fatigue, or vicarious trauma. Balancing activism with self-care is essential for individual sustainability and ultimately for the movement as a whole.

Promoting mental health policies within organizations, providing access to counseling services, and fostering a culture of self-care are critical steps. Additionally, creating spaces for activists to decompress, reflect, and rejuvenate can help combat the toll of continuous activism.

Training on stress management, mindfulness techniques, and boundary setting can equip activists with the necessary tools to sustain themselves over the long term. By prioritizing self-care, activists can continue to fight for LGBTQ rights with resilience and passion.

Conclusion

Ensuring the long-term sustainability of LGBTQ activism requires a multi-faceted approach. Building strong organizational structures, fostering collaboration, securing financial sustainability, investing in leadership development, cultivating global solidarity, and prioritizing self-care are all crucial elements. By implementing these strategies, the LGBTQ movement can continue to make progress, create change, and build a more inclusive and equitable future for generations to come.

Passing the Torch to the Next Generation

As the fight for LGBTQ rights continues, it is important to ensure the sustainability of the movement by passing the torch to the next generation of activists. Zion Ellis, in all his wisdom and experience, understands the significance of nurturing and empowering young leaders who will carry the legacy forward. In this section, we explore the strategies and principles behind this endeavor.

Mentoring LGBTQ Youth

One of the critical aspects of passing the torch is providing guidance and mentorship to LGBTQ youth. Young individuals who are grappling with their sexual orientation or gender identity often face unique challenges and require support from those who have walked the same path. Zion Ellis believes in the power of mentorship to help navigate the complexities of their journey.

Example: Zion Ellis shares his own story of being mentored by an older queer activist when he was just starting his journey. This mentor became a guiding light, offering invaluable advice, sharing personal experiences, and empowering him to confidently step into his role as an LGBTQ activist. The mentor-mentee relationship forged a deep connection, cementing Zion's commitment to ensuring that future generations benefit from the same source of support and guidance.

Empowering the Next Activist Leaders

To ensure the long-lasting impact of the LGBTQ movement, it is essential to empower and equip the next generation of activists with the necessary skills, knowledge, and resources. Zion Ellis recognizes the importance of nurturing future leaders and empowering them to be agents of change.

Principles and Strategies:

- **Education and Training:** Providing comprehensive education and training on LGBTQ history, advocacy, and organizing. Workshops, seminars, and online resources can be utilized to build a solid foundation of knowledge.

- **Skill Development:** Offering opportunities for developing critical skills like public speaking, community organizing, policy analysis, and media relations. Workshops focused on effective communication, strategic planning, and leadership can help shape the next leaders.

+ **Building Networks:** Facilitating connections between new activists and established LGBTQ organizations, community groups, and other social justice movements. Networking events, conferences, and mentorship programs can help establish valuable connections and foster collaboration.

+ **Encouraging Initiative:** Inspiring young activists to take initiative and create change in their own communities. Encouraging them to identify issues that are important to them, develop their campaigns, and provide ongoing support throughout the process.

+ **Celebrating Diversity:** Emphasizing the importance of intersectionality and inclusivity within the LGBTQ movement. Creating spaces where activists from diverse backgrounds feel welcome and valued, and encouraging dialogue and collaboration across various identities.

+ **Recognizing Achievements:** Acknowledging and celebrating the contributions of young activists. Highlighting their successes and providing platforms for them to share their experiences, insights, and stories of resilience.

Creating Lasting Change

The ultimate goal of passing the torch is to create lasting change within society. By nurturing the next generation of activists, Zion Ellis envisions a future where LGBTQ rights are fully recognized and protected.

Approaches for Creating Lasting Change:

+ **Policy Advocacy:** Equipping future activists with the skills to engage in policy advocacy. This includes understanding the legislative process, the importance of grassroots mobilization, and the power of coalition building.

+ **Community Organizing:** Fostering a sense of community and empowering young activists to organize at the grassroots level. Encouraging them to identify local issues, mobilize support, and work towards systemic change.

+ **Cultural Shifts:** Recognizing the significance of cultural shifts in transforming societal attitudes towards the LGBTQ community. Encouraging young activists to use art, media, and storytelling as powerful tools to challenge stereotypes, break down barriers, and foster empathy.

+ **International Solidarity:** Promoting international solidarity and collaboration to address global LGBTQ rights. Supporting young activists in building connections and exchanging ideas with activists from different countries and regions.

+ **Continued Education:** Emphasizing the importance of ongoing education and awareness about LGBTQ issues. Encouraging young activists to stay informed, update their knowledge, and remain open to evolving conversations within the movement.

Balancing Activism with Self-Care

Zion Ellis understands the toll that activism can take on individuals, particularly those who are on the frontlines of the fight for equality. It is crucial to instill a culture of self-care and well-being within the next generation of activists.

Strategies for Self-Care:

+ **Boundary Setting:** Encouraging young activists to set boundaries and prioritize their mental and emotional well-being. Teaching them that self-care is not selfish, but a necessary aspect of sustaining their activism in the long run.

+ **Cultivating Support Systems:** Emphasizing the importance of building strong support systems within the LGBTQ community and beyond. Encouraging activists to lean on one another, seek guidance, and share experiences to mitigate burnout.

+ **Recharging Activities:** Highlighting the significance of engaging in activities that bring joy and fulfillment outside of activism. Encouraging hobbies, exercise, nature, and other forms of self-expression to restore energy and maintain a healthy work-life balance.

+ **Mental Health Support:** Promoting access to mental health resources and encouraging activists to seek professional help when needed. Creating safe spaces for open dialogue about mental health challenges and addressing the stigma associated with seeking support.

+ **Celebrating Milestones:** Taking the time to celebrate milestones and achievements, both big and small. Recognizing the resilience, dedication, and impact of young activists to boost morale and encourage a sense of accomplishment.

The Impact of Zion Ellis's Activism

Zion Ellis's commitment to passing the torch ensures that the legacy of LGBTQ activism remains strong and progresses into the future. By mentoring and empowering young activists, he paves the way for a more inclusive and just society, where LGBTQ rights are not only protected but celebrated.

Caveats: Passing the torch does not mean abdicating responsibility. It is crucial for established activists like Zion Ellis to continuously support and collaborate with the next generation, while allowing space for their fresh perspectives and ideas. It is a delicate balance that requires mutual respect, learning, and adaptation.

Unconventional Tip: Zion Ellis encourages young activists to explore unconventional means of advocacy, such as utilizing social media, digital storytelling, and creative forms of resistance. Embracing innovative approaches and technology can amplify voices, reach broader audiences, and inspire change in unexpected ways.

By passing the torch to the next generation, Zion Ellis ensures that the LGBTQ movement remains resilient, vibrant, and sustained. The torch burns bright, illuminating the path towards equality, justice, and liberation for all.

Reflections on a Life Well Lived

As Zion Ellis reflects on his journey of LGBTQ activism, he can't help but marvel at the incredible impact he has had on the world. His tireless efforts and unwavering dedication have transformed the lives of countless individuals, and his legacy will continue to inspire generations to come. In this final chapter, Zion shares his reflections on a life well lived, offering invaluable insights and lessons that have shaped his activism.

One of the key lessons Zion has learned throughout his journey is the importance of balancing activism with self-care. As an activist, it is easy to get caught up in the constant battle for change and neglect one's own well-being. Zion emphasizes the need for self-reflection and nurturing one's mental, emotional, and physical health. He reminds us that taking care of ourselves is not selfish; it is essential for sustaining long-term activism. Zion encourages activists to find healthy outlets, such as hobbies or mindfulness practices, that replenish their energy and prevent burnout.

Another vital reflection Zion shares is the power of collaboration and building a strong network of allies. He believes that while individual activism is important, collective action is what truly drives systemic change. Through collaborating with other activists, communities, and organizations, Zion has witnessed the incredible strength that comes from unified voices. He emphasizes the importance of finding common ground and uniting diverse movements to create a more inclusive and just society.

Zion also reflects on the significance of intersectionality in his activism. He acknowledges that the fight for LGBTQ rights cannot be divorced from other social justice issues. Recognizing the experiences and struggles of marginalized groups, Zion aims to amplify their voices and work towards intersectional equality. By embracing diverse perspectives and embracing the diversity within the LGBTQ community, Zion ensures that his activism is inclusive and comprehensive.

Throughout his journey, Zion has come to understand that change is not achieved overnight. It requires patience, perseverance, and a long-term vision. He encourages future activists to celebrate the small victories along the way and to maintain a sense of hope even in the face of adversity. Zion believes that even the smallest acts of resistance can ignite a spark of change that ripples through society.

In the digital age, Zion recognizes the immense power of social media and technology in amplifying LGBTQ voices and organizing movements. He encourages activists to utilize these tools to reach a wider audience, share stories, educate, and mobilize for change. However, he also cautions about the pitfalls of the online world, urging activists to stay vigilant against online harassment and misinformation. Staying true to oneself and maintaining authenticity in the digital realm is crucial for impactful activism.

Zion's reflections on a life well lived extend beyond his own accomplishments. He ponders his role in inspiring future generations of activists and fostering a legacy of LGBTQ rights advocacy. He stresses the importance of mentorship and nurturing young LGBTQ leaders, empowering them to carry the torch and continue the fight for equality. Zion believes that the most significant measure of his success will be the lasting impact he leaves behind.

As Zion concludes his reflections, he urges readers to never underestimate the power of a single individual to effect change. He reminds us that each person has the ability to challenge norms, dismantle oppressive systems, and inspire others to join the fight for justice. Zion's story serves as a poignant reminder that one person's passionate commitment to creating a more inclusive world can truly make a difference.

Throughout his journey, Zion Ellis has faced challenges, celebrated victories, and inspired countless individuals through his unwavering dedication to LGBTQ activism. His reflections on a life well lived offer valuable insights for current and future activists, reminding them of the importance of self-care, collaboration, intersectionality, and perseverance. As Zion's journey continues, the fight for LGBTQ rights endures, carried forward by a new generation of passionate advocates.

Balancing Activism with Self-Care

Activism can be an all-consuming passion, driving individuals to channel their energy towards creating positive change for the LGBTQ community. While the work is undoubtedly important, it can also take a toll on activists' physical and mental well-being. In this section, we will explore the concept of balancing activism with self-care and why it is essential for the longevity and effectiveness of any activist's journey.

Understanding the Importance of Self-Care

When we're deeply committed to a cause, it's easy to prioritize the needs of the community over our own. However, the truth is that self-care is not a selfish act, but a necessary one. Taking care of ourselves is crucial for maintaining the energy, resilience, and clarity needed to continue fighting for LGBTQ rights.

Recognizing the Signs of Burnout

Burnout is a common struggle for activists who dedicate themselves relentlessly to their cause. It manifests as physical, emotional, and mental exhaustion, leading to reduced effectiveness and even health issues. It's important to recognize the warning signs to prevent burnout from taking control. Some signs include:

+ Fatigue and lack of energy

+ Increased irritability and impatience

+ Difficulty focusing or making decisions

+ Withdrawal from social activities

+ Physical symptoms such as headaches or stomachaches

Prioritizing Self-Care Techniques

To maintain a healthy balance between activism and self-care, it's necessary to incorporate specific techniques into our daily lives. Here are some practical strategies that activists can adopt:

1. **Setting Boundaries:** Establishing clear boundaries between work and personal life is crucial. Designate specific times for activism-related activities and commit to disconnecting during personal time.

2. **Physical Well-being:** Engage in regular physical activities such as exercise, yoga, or meditation to reduce stress and maintain physical well-being. Also, prioritize healthy eating habits and ensure an adequate amount of sleep.

3. **Emotional Support:** Seek support from friends, family, or mental health professionals to process emotions and share the burdens of activism. Consider joining support groups or connecting with like-minded individuals to foster a sense of community.

4. **Time for Rest and Relaxation:** Incorporate regular moments of rest and relaxation into your schedule. Engage in activities that bring joy and help you unwind, such as reading, listening to music, or engaging in hobbies.

5. **Reflection and Self-Reflection:** Regularly reflect on your purpose, motivations, and achievements as an activist. Engage in self-reflection to understand your emotions, triggers, and areas where you may need support or improvement.

Challenges and Strategies

Finding a balance between activism and self-care can be challenging, given the demands and urgency of the work. However, acknowledging these challenges is the first step towards overcoming them. Let's explore some common challenges and strategies to address them:

- **Guilt and Prioritization:** Activists may feel guilty for prioritizing their own well-being over the cause. Remember, taking care of yourself allows you to show up fully for others. Establish clear priorities and allocate time for self-care without guilt.

- **Time Management:** Activism often requires dedication beyond regular working hours. Efficient time management techniques, such as setting specific goals, delegating tasks, and practicing mindful multitasking, can help create more time for self-care.

- **Burnout Prevention:** Recognize the signs of burnout early on and take proactive steps to prevent it. Regularly assess your energy levels, limit exposure to triggering content, and take breaks when needed.

+ **Building a Support System:** Surround yourself with a supportive network of individuals who understand the challenges of activism. Lean on them for emotional support, guidance, and accountability in maintaining a healthy work-life balance.

Unconventional Yet Relevant: The Power of Radical Self-Care

Radical self-care pushes the boundaries of traditional self-care practices. It emphasizes the importance of indulging in activities that nourish your soul and cater to your individual needs. Engaging in activities that bring you joy, exploring your creativity, or embarking on new adventures outside the realm of activism can revitalize your spirit and enhance your effectiveness as an activist.

Exercises for Self-Reflection

Self-reflection is an essential practice in maintaining the balance between activism and self-care. Here are some exercises that can help you reflect on your journey:

+ **Journaling:** Set aside time regularly to write about your experiences, emotions, and personal growth as an activist. Use these reflections as a guide to identify areas where you need self-care and areas where you excel.

+ **Mindfulness Practice:** Engage in mindfulness exercises such as meditation or deep breathing. This will help you develop a greater awareness of your thoughts, emotions, and physical sensations, enabling better self-care decisions.

+ **Collaborative Reflection:** Engage in conversations with fellow activists or mentors to discuss the challenges and rewards of balancing activism and self-care. Share strategies, insights, and experiences to learn from one another.

Conclusion

Activism is a lifelong commitment that requires sustained energy and dedication. Balancing activism with self-care is not a luxury but a necessity for activists to thrive and continue making a difference. By prioritizing self-care and adopting strategies to find equilibrium, activists can maintain their passion and effectiveness in creating a more inclusive and equitable world for the LGBTQ community and beyond.

Remember, the journey towards equality begins within ourselves, and by taking care of ourselves, we not only nourish our own well-being but also empower ourselves to create lasting change in the world.

As Zion Ellis once said, "We must remember that self-care is an act of revolution, for it is through self-care that we can sustain the fight for a better future."

The Impact of Zion Ellis's Activism

Zion Ellis's activism has had a profound impact on the LGBTQ community and beyond. Through his unwavering dedication and tireless efforts, he has successfully raised awareness, fought for equal rights, and inspired countless individuals to embrace their authentic selves. Let's explore the lasting impact of Zion Ellis's activism.

Creating Visibility and Representation

One of the key impacts of Zion's activism has been his ability to bring visibility to the LGBTQ community. By stepping into the spotlight and unapologetically embracing his identity, Zion has shattered stereotypes and challenged societal norms. His presence has given a voice to those who have been silenced, showing the world that LGBTQ individuals are just as diverse, talented, and deserving of respect and equal rights as anyone else.

Moreover, Zion's commitment to authentic representation has been transformative. By breaking barriers and redefining beauty standards, he has empowered LGBTQ individuals to embrace their unique identities and express themselves freely. Zion's fearless fashion choices and use of style as a political statement have not only turned heads but also sparked conversations about the importance of self-expression in creating a more inclusive society.

Building Bridges and Allies

Zion's impact extends beyond the LGBTQ community, as he has successfully built alliances with individuals and organizations from diverse backgrounds. By creating safe spaces and fostering dialogue, Zion has initiated meaningful conversations about LGBTQ rights and built bridges between different social movements. Through collaboration and mutual support, he has demonstrated that the struggle for equality is interconnected with issues of race, gender, and class.

His advocacy for intersectionality has allowed him to unite different communities and strengthen the fight for social justice as a whole. By nurturing these alliances, Zion has created powerful networks of change-makers, amplifying the voices of marginalized individuals and driving systemic transformation.

Challenging Legal and Social Barriers

Zion's activism has also been instrumental in challenging discriminatory laws and societal norms. He has fearlessly confronted legal barriers, lobbying for LGBTQ rights and advocating for comprehensive LGBTQ education. Through his advocacy efforts, Zion has played a crucial role in securing legal protections for the LGBTQ community, fostering a more inclusive legal landscape.

Beyond the legal realm, Zion has been a relentless force in dismantling societal prejudices. By debunking myths and misconceptions, he has fostered understanding and empathy, helping to chip away at deeply ingrained biases. Through the power of personal narratives, Zion has humanized the LGBTQ experience and fostered empathy, creating an environment that promotes acceptance and respect.

Inspiring and Mentoring Future Activists

Zion's impact transcends his own generation, as he dedicatedly mentors and inspires future LGBTQ activists. By nurturing LGBTQ youth, he ensures the continuity of the movement and empowers the next generation to carry the torch forward. Through mentorship programs and educational initiatives, Zion provides guidance, support, and inspiration to young activists, enabling them to navigate the challenges they face as they advocate for LGBTQ rights.

Moreover, Zion's activism has paved the way for LGBTQ-inclusive education, driving change within educational institutions and challenging heteronormative expectations. By advocating for comprehensive LGBTQ history and education, Zion promotes understanding, empathy, and inclusivity, creating a society that is more accepting and respectful of LGBTQ individuals.

Balancing Activism with Self-Care

In addition to all his achievements, Zion has also emphasized the importance of self-care in the activist journey. He recognizes that burnout and emotional exhaustion can hinder progress and sustainability. By sharing his personal experiences and strategies for self-care, Zion encourages activists to prioritize their well-being, fostering resilience and long-term commitment to the cause.

Zion Ellis's activism has been nothing short of life-changing. Through his visibility, ability to build alliances, challenge legal and social barriers, inspire future activists, and promote self-care, he has made a significant impact in the fight for

LGBTQ rights. As we reflect on his journey, we are reminded that the fight continues, and Zion's legacy serves as a beacon of hope and inspiration for all those striving for a more inclusive and just world.

Chapter 5: The Fight Continues

Chapter 5: The Fight Continues

Chapter 5: The Fight Continues

In this chapter, we delve deeper into the ongoing battle for LGBTQ rights and equality. Zion Ellis, our fearless advocate, remains at the forefront, challenging the status quo and uncovering hidden truths. As the fight evolves, so too does the need for a deeper understanding of the struggles faced by the LGBTQ community. In this section, we explore the importance of unmasking false allies and reclaiming LGBTQ narratives.

Exposing Hidden Oppression

As society progresses, it is crucial to unveil the subtle forms of oppression that continue to persist. Zion Ellis realizes that oppression can sometimes take on a covert nature, making it harder to identify and address. Discrimination, prejudice, and microaggressions persist in workplaces, educational institutions, and even within LGBTQ communities themselves.

To expose hidden oppression, we must encourage open conversations and empower individuals to share their experiences. Zion Ellis creates a platform where people can freely discuss their encounters with systemic prejudice and discrimination. By shedding light on these experiences, we can challenge and dismantle the structures that perpetuate hidden oppressions.

Unmasking False Allies

False allies pose a significant challenge to the LGBTQ movement. They claim to support equality and inclusivity while simultaneously perpetuating harmful beliefs or perpetrating discriminatory acts. Identifying false allies becomes crucial to maintain the integrity and forward momentum of the movement.

Zion Ellis teaches us to critically evaluate individuals and organizations claiming to be allies. We must analyze their actions, challenge their motives, and investigate their track records. By doing so, we can identify those who merely pay lip service to the cause rather than actively working towards positive change.

Unmasking false allies is a delicate task that requires diplomacy and careful discernment. Zion Ellis provides guidance on navigating these situations, emphasizing the importance of evidence-based judgment and seeking diverse perspectives to corroborate or challenge one's findings.

Reclaiming LGBTQ Narratives

Throughout history, LGBTQ narratives have often been silenced or distorted, leading to misrepresentation and erasure. It is crucial to reclaim these narratives, ensuring that the stories of LGBTQ individuals are told accurately and with the respect they deserve.

Zion Ellis emphasizes the significance of sharing personal stories and experiences. By providing a platform for individuals to share their narratives, we can challenge stereotypes and misconceptions. Through personal narratives, we can humanize the struggles, triumphs, and diversity within the LGBTQ community, leading to greater understanding and empathy.

Reclaiming LGBTQ narratives also involves revitalizing historical accounts of queer individuals and communities. We must highlight their contributions and the challenges they faced, helping to shape and inspire future generations of activists. This chapter explores Zion Ellis's efforts to reclaim LGBTQ narratives and the profound impact such storytelling has on societal perceptions.

Intersectionality: Uniting Social Movements

The fight for LGBTQ rights does not exist in isolation but intersects with various social justice movements. Zion Ellis recognizes the importance of building alliances and working collaboratively toward shared goals.

Intersectionality, a concept coined by Kimberlé Crenshaw, signifies the interconnected nature of social identities and how they intersect with systems of oppression. Zion Ellis advocates for an inclusive approach, highlighting the interconnectedness of gender, race, class, and other forms of identity. By incorporating intersectionality into activism, the LGBTQ movement becomes more resilient, inclusive, and impactful.

In this chapter, we explore how Zion Ellis forges alliances with other social justice movements, such as racial equality, gender equity, and disability rights. By learning from the struggles and successes of these other movements, Zion Ellis and the LGBTQ community gain valuable insights into fighting for justice and equality across all intersections.

The Importance of LGBTQ History and Education

Understanding LGBTQ history is key to contextualizing the present and informing future advocacy efforts. Zion Ellis recognizes that a lack of knowledge about LGBTQ history perpetuates the cycle of discrimination and erasure.

This chapter emphasizes the significance of LGBTQ-inclusive education. By incorporating LGBTQ history and narratives into school curricula, we can foster understanding, empathy, and acceptance from an early age. Zion Ellis advocates for comprehensive education that dispels stereotypes and challenges heteronormative expectations.

Through engaging storytelling and thought-provoking examples, this chapter aims to educate readers about the importance of LGBTQ history and its impact on the ongoing fight for equality and justice.

In the ever-evolving struggle for LGBTQ rights, Zion Ellis maintains unwavering dedication to dismantling hidden oppressions, unmasking false allies, reclaiming narratives, promoting intersectionality, and advocating for comprehensive education. This chapter serves as a testament to Zion Ellis's tireless work and inspires readers to continue the fight for a more inclusive and equitable world.

Unraveling the Truth

Exposing Hidden Oppression

In this section, we delve into the important task of exposing hidden oppression faced by the LGBTQ community. Despite growing acceptance and legal protections in many parts of the world, there are still numerous forms of oppression that persist in silence. As LGBTQ activists continue to fight for equality, it becomes crucial to shed light on these hidden forms of discrimination.

The First Step: Recognizing Hidden Oppression

The journey to exposing hidden oppression begins with recognition. In many cases, oppression faced by LGBTQ individuals may not be immediately apparent or easily identifiable. This can make it challenging for mainstream society to understand the true extent of the discrimination faced by the community.

One example of hidden oppression is heteronormativity, a social framework that assumes heterosexuality as the norm and invalidates non-heterosexual identities. Heteronormative beliefs and practices reinforce the notion that heterosexual relationships are superior, resulting in the marginalization of queer relationships and identities.

Another form of hidden oppression is cisnormativity, which refers to the assumption that cisgender identities are superior and normal. This erases the experiences of transgender and non-binary individuals and perpetuates harmful stereotypes and biases.

Unveiling the Mask: Techniques to Expose Hidden Oppression

Exposing hidden oppression requires strategic and creative techniques. LGBTQ activists employ several approaches to unveil the mask of discrimination and bring attention to marginalized experiences. Let's explore some effective strategies:

1. **Storytelling and Personal Narratives:** Sharing personal stories and experiences can be a powerful tool to expose hidden oppression. By telling their stories, LGBTQ individuals humanize their struggles and provide insights into the everyday challenges they face. Through personal narratives, society can gain a deeper understanding and empathy for the experiences of the LGBTQ community.

2. **Intersectional Analysis:**   Intersectionality recognizes that individuals' identities do not exist in isolation, but rather are shaped by their multiple social identities. By using an intersectional lens, activists highlight how LGBTQ oppression intersects with other forms of discrimination, such as racism, sexism, ableism, and classism. This perspective unveils the interconnections between different systems of power and reveals the complex web of oppression faced by marginalized communities.

3. **Research and Data Collection:** Utilizing research and data collection techniques is vital in exposing hidden oppression. By conducting surveys, interviews, and case studies, activists are able to gather evidence of discrimination

and its impact on LGBTQ individuals. The empirical data can be used to challenge societal misconceptions and push for policy changes.

4. Media Advocacy: Harnessing the power of media is another effective way to expose hidden oppression. LGBTQ activists collaborate with journalists, filmmakers, and social media influencers to amplify marginalized voices and bring attention to pressing issues. Documentaries, articles, and social media campaigns play an instrumental role in raising awareness and sparking public discussions.

5. Challenging Stereotypes: Exposing hidden oppression requires breaking down stereotypes and challenging societal norms. LGBTQ activists employ various strategies to challenge heteronormative and cisnormative beliefs. They highlight the diversity within the LGBTQ community, showcase positive queer role models, and debunk myths and misconceptions that perpetuate discrimination.

Examples of Hidden Oppression

To understand the impact of hidden oppression, let's examine a few real-world examples:

1. Employment Discrimination: LGBTQ individuals often face discrimination in the workplace, which may go unnoticed by their colleagues or employers. This can manifest through being denied promotions, experiencing workplace harassment, or being subjected to unequal treatment based on their sexual orientation or gender identity.

2. Conversion Therapy: Conversion therapy, also known as "reparative therapy," is a harmful practice that attempts to change an individual's sexual orientation or gender identity. It is often done in secrecy, behind closed doors, and can have devastating psychological and emotional effects on LGBTQ individuals.

3. Familial Rejection: Many LGBTQ individuals face familial rejection due to their sexual orientation or gender identity. This hidden oppression can lead to strained relationships, loss of support systems, and increased mental health challenges.

4. **Violence and Hate Crimes:** LGBTQ individuals disproportionately face higher rates of violence and hate crimes. These acts of oppression often occur in hidden spaces, such as dark alleys or private settings, making them challenging to address and eradicate.

Resources for Exposing Hidden Oppression

Educating oneself about hidden oppression faced by the LGBTQ community is crucial for effective activism. Here are some resources to learn more about this topic:

1. **Books:** "Queer, There, and Everywhere: 23 People Who Changed the World" by Sarah Prager, "This Book is Gay" by Juno Dawson, and "Sister Outsider: Essays and Speeches" by Audre Lorde.

2. **Documentaries:** "Disclosure" (2020), "Paris is Burning" (1990), and "The Death and Life of Marsha P. Johnson" (2017) provide powerful insights into LGBTQ experiences and the hidden oppression faced by the community.

3. **LGBTQ Organizations:** Organizations such as Human Rights Campaign, GLAAD, and The Trevor Project provide valuable resources and information on hidden oppression faced by the LGBTQ community.

4. **Research Journals:** "Journal of Homosexuality," "Sexuality Research and Social Policy Journal of NSRC," and "Journal of LGBT Issues in Counseling" publish research papers focused on LGBTQ experiences and hidden oppression.

Exposing hidden oppression is a critical step towards achieving full equality and justice for the LGBTQ community. By shedding light on these forms of discrimination, activists can challenge societal norms, empower marginalized individuals, and create a more inclusive and affirming society for all.

Unmasking False Allies

In the fight for LGBTQ rights, it is crucial to have allies who genuinely support the cause and are committed to creating meaningful change. However, not all allies are what they seem. In this section, we will explore the concept of false allies and uncover their motivations and behaviors. By understanding the signs of false allies, we can build stronger, more authentic relationships, and ensure that our movement remains focused on true progress.

Identifying False Allies

Unmasking false allies begins with recognizing the signs that someone may not be as supportive as they claim. Here are a few characteristics to watch out for:

- **Performative support:** False allies often engage in performative acts of support, such as posting on social media or attending events, without actually taking meaningful action or challenging harmful systems.

- **Conditional support:** False allies may only show support when it is convenient for them or when it aligns with their personal or political interests. They may withdraw their support in situations where they perceive potential backlash or personal risk.

- **Tokenism:** False allies may tokenize members of the LGBTQ community, using their support as a way to appear inclusive without actively advocating for systemic change.

- **Lack of understanding:** False allies often demonstrate a lack of knowledge or understanding about the LGBTQ experience and the history of the movement. They may make insensitive or uninformed comments that reveal their true level of commitment.

- **Inconsistent actions:** False allies may exhibit inconsistencies between their public statements and their private behaviors. They may support LGBTQ rights in some contexts but engage in discriminatory actions or conversations in others.

Motivations of False Allies

Understanding the motivations behind false allies can shed light on why they engage in performative support and fail to take meaningful action. Some common motivations include:

- **Desire for social capital:** False allies may seek to enhance their own social status or reputation by aligning themselves with causes that are currently in the spotlight. They may prioritize their image over genuine support for the LGBTQ community.

- **Fear of exclusion:** Some individuals may claim to be allies to avoid criticism or social isolation. They may be motivated by a desire to fit in, rather than a true commitment to dismantling oppressive systems.

+ **Political expediency:** In some cases, false allies may leverage LGBTQ support for political gain, using it as a way to appeal to certain demographics or secure votes. Their allegiance may waver when it conflicts with their political agenda.

+ **Ignorance and indifference:** Lack of education or awareness about the LGBTQ community can also contribute to false allyship. Some individuals may simply be uninformed about the issues at hand and fail to fully grasp the importance of authentic support.

Addressing False Allyship

Unmasking false allies is crucial for maintaining the integrity and effectiveness of the LGBTQ rights movement. Here are some strategies for addressing false allyship:

+ **Education and awareness:** Increasing awareness about the LGBTQ community, its history, and the ongoing struggles it faces is essential. By providing accurate information, we can better equip individuals to understand the importance of authentic allyship.

+ **Challenging performative actions:** Calling out performative allyship and urging individuals to go beyond surface-level support can help hold them accountable. By encouraging them to take substantive action and challenging their misconceptions, we can foster more genuine allyship.

+ **Building genuine relationships:** Investing in authentic relationships with individuals who truly support the LGBTQ cause is essential. By prioritizing connections built on trust, shared values, and active support, we can create a strong network of allies who are committed to lasting change.

+ **Promoting inclusivity and intersectionality:** Emphasizing the importance of inclusivity and intersectionality can help combat tokenism and ensure that true allyship extends to all members of the LGBTQ community, regardless of race, gender identity, or socioeconomic background.

+ **Celebrating true allies:** Recognizing and celebrating individuals who demonstrate genuine allyship can serve as an example for others. By highlighting the positive impact of authentic support, we can inspire others to follow suit.

Conclusion

Unmasking false allies is an ongoing process in the fight for LGBTQ rights. By identifying the signs of false allyship, understanding the motivations behind it, and addressing it head-on, we can cultivate a more robust and dedicated network of genuine allies. Remember, true allyship is not performative or conditional—it is rooted in empathy, education, and an unwavering commitment to equality for all. Together, we can create a more inclusive and just world for the LGBTQ community and beyond.

Reclaiming LGBTQ Narratives

In the battle for LGBTQ rights, one of the key challenges faced by activists is the need to reclaim LGBTQ narratives. For far too long, these narratives have been overshadowed by societal prejudices and stereotypes. It is essential to challenge these harmful narratives and rewrite the story of the LGBTQ community in a way that reflects the true diversity and richness of queer experiences.

The Power of Representation

Representation plays a crucial role in reclaiming LGBTQ narratives. When individuals see themselves reflected in media, literature, and other forms of art, it validates their existence and helps break down stereotypes. Positive and authentic representation not only provides visibility but also empowers LGBTQ individuals to embrace their identities.

For instance, the inclusion of diverse LGBTQ characters in popular TV shows and movies has made a significant impact on viewers. Series like "Pose" and movies like "Love, Simon" have portrayed LGBTQ characters as complex individuals with their own unique stories, struggles, and triumphs. This kind of authentic representation not only educates the public but also fosters empathy and understanding.

Challenging Stereotypes

One of the significant obstacles to reclaiming LGBTQ narratives is the prevalence of stereotypes. Stereotypes, such as the flamboyant gay man or the butch lesbian, fail to capture the full spectrum of queer experiences. Activists must challenge these stereotypes and present a more nuanced and accurate portrayal of LGBTQ individuals.

By showcasing the diverse range of LGBTQ identities and experiences, activists can break down preconceived notions and reshape public perceptions. For example, highlighting the achievements and contributions of LGBTQ scientists, artists, athletes, and leaders showcases the talent and potential within the community, debunking stereotypes that suggest queerness is a barrier to success.

Sharing Personal Narratives

Personal narratives are a powerful tool in reclaiming LGBTQ narratives. Sharing stories of LGBTQ individuals allows for a more intimate and human connection, making it harder for others to dismiss their experiences. These personal narratives can inspire empathy, challenge prejudices, and create a sense of community.

Online platforms and social media have provided a space for LGBTQ individuals to share their stories and experiences. Through blogs, videos, and podcasts, people can engage with diverse narratives and learn about different aspects of the LGBTQ experience. The act of storytelling allows for the validation of individual experiences and paves the way for a broader societal understanding of queer lives.

Redefining Language and Terminology

Language plays a crucial role in shaping narratives, and it is important to critically examine and redefine the language used to describe LGBTQ experiences. Historically, derogatory terms and slurs have been used to marginalize and demean queer individuals. By reclaiming and redefining these terms, activists can challenge the harmful narratives perpetuated by discriminatory language.

For example, the use of the word "queer" has been reclaimed by the LGBTQ community as an umbrella term that embraces all non-heteronormative identities. This reclaiming of language allows for self-empowerment and dismantles the negative connotations associated with the term.

Additionally, it is essential to respect individuals' preferred pronouns and gender identities. Using correct pronouns and inclusive language helps create a safe and affirming environment for LGBTQ individuals, allowing them to share their stories authentically.

Amplifying Untold Stories

In reclaiming LGBTQ narratives, it is crucial to amplify the stories of marginalized individuals within the community. Intersectionality plays a significant role in shaping LGBTQ experiences, with individuals facing multiple layers of discrimination based on race, ethnicity, class, and other factors. By elevating the voices of those at the intersections of various identities, activists can ensure that these stories are heard and validated.

For example, transgender people of color often face heightened levels of violence and discrimination. By centering their narratives and experiences, activists can shed light on the issues unique to this community and work to eradicate the systemic injustices they face.

Empowering LGBTQ Youth

Empowering LGBTQ youth is a vital aspect of reclaiming LGBTQ narratives. By providing resources and support, activists can ensure that the next generation of LGBTQ individuals feels empowered to share their stories and challenge the status quo.

Creating safe spaces in schools, community centers, and online platforms allows LGBTQ youth to express themselves freely. It is through these spaces that young individuals can find solidarity, build confidence, and develop their own narratives.

In conclusion, reclaiming LGBTQ narratives is an essential facet of LGBTQ activism. By challenging stereotypes, sharing personal stories, redefining language, amplifying marginalized voices, and empowering youth, activists can reshape the narrative surrounding the LGBTQ community. Through these collective efforts, we can create a world that recognizes and celebrates the diversity and lived experiences of all queer individuals.

Intersectionality: Uniting Social Movements

Intersectionality: it's a term you've probably heard before, but do you really know what it means? In this chapter, we explore the concept of intersectionality as a powerful tool for uniting social movements and achieving true equality for all. But first, let's start by understanding what intersectionality is all about.

1.   Understanding Intersectionality Intersectionality is a framework that recognizes and analyzes the overlapping and interconnected systems of oppression and discrimination that individuals may face. It acknowledges that different forms of oppression (such as racism, sexism, homophobia, transphobia, ableism, etc.) are not separate, but rather intersect with one another, resulting in unique experiences of discrimination and privilege for individuals at various intersections of identity.

2.   The Importance of Intersectionality Intersectionality is crucial for understanding and addressing the complex and multifaceted nature of social justice issues. It recognizes that the experiences and needs of marginalized communities cannot be adequately addressed by focusing on one aspect of their identity alone. By considering the interconnectedness of different forms of oppression, intersectionality empowers us to create more inclusive and effective strategies for social change.

3. Applying Intersectionality to Social Movements Intersectionality has the power to transform social movements by fostering collaboration and solidarity among diverse groups. Here are some key ways in which intersectionality can be applied:

3.1 Recognizing and Amplifying Voices Intersectionality calls us to actively listen to and center the voices of individuals who experience multiple forms of marginalization. By acknowledging their unique perspectives and experiences, we can ensure that our movements are truly inclusive and representative.

3.2 Building Alliances Intersectionality encourages social movements to form alliances and work together in pursuit of common goals. Recognizing that different forms of oppression are interconnected, activists can find common ground and support one another's struggles, ultimately creating stronger and more impactful movements.

3.3 Challenging Power Structures Intersectionality challenges the dominant power structures that perpetuate inequality and discrimination. By examining how different forms of oppression intersect, activists can identify and confront the root causes of injustice, working towards systemic change rather than surface-level reforms.

3.4 Education and Awareness Intersectionality emphasizes the importance of education and awareness about the interconnected nature of discrimination. By promoting dialogue and understanding, we can challenge biases, break down stereotypes, and foster empathy across diverse communities.

4. Examples of Intersectional Activism Let's explore some real-world examples of intersectional activism to help illustrate the power and impact of this approach:

4.1 LGBTQ+ Rights and Racial Justice Activists fighting for LGBTQ+ rights have recognized the need to address the specific challenges faced by LGBTQ+ individuals of color. By bringing attention to the unique experiences of racialized LGBTQ+ communities, these activists have contributed to a more inclusive and intersectional understanding of queer liberation.

4.2 Feminism and Disability Rights Intersectional feminists have highlighted the experiences of disabled women and the ways in which ableism intersects with sexism. Their advocacy has helped bring attention to the barriers faced by disabled women in accessing education, healthcare, and employment, contributing to a more inclusive feminist movement.

4.3 Environmental Justice and Indigenous Rights Intersectional activists have fought for environmental justice by highlighting how environmental degradation disproportionately affects Indigenous communities. Their work emphasizes the intersection of colonialism, racism, and environmental issues, creating more comprehensive approaches to environmental activism.

5. Challenges and Critiques of Intersectionality While intersectionality has brought significant advancements in social justice movements, it is not without its challenges and critiques. Some common critiques include:

5.1 Simplification and Essentialization Critics argue that intersectionality sometimes oversimplifies complex issues and essentializes identity categories, potentially leading to the erasure of individual experiences and diverse perspectives.

5.2 Tensions and Divisions within Movements Intersectionality requires acknowledging and addressing tensions and divisions within social justice movements. This can pose challenges as activists navigate different priorities, strategies, and needs within diverse groups.

5.3 Co-optation and Tokenism There is a risk of intersectionality being co-opted by those in power, leading to tokenism and surface-level diversity without addressing underlying systems of oppression. It is crucial to ensure that intersectionality remains a tool for liberation and not a means of maintaining the status quo.

6. Embracing Intersectionality: Moving Forward To fully embrace intersectionality and create lasting change, we must:

6.1 Center Marginalized Voices Actively listen to and uplift the voices of individuals at the intersections of multiple forms of marginalization. Their experiences and perspectives must be central to our movements.

6.2 Continuously Educate Ourselves Commit to lifelong learning and understanding of intersectionality and its nuances. Continuously expand our knowledge to challenge our own biases and assumptions.

6.3 Embrace Collaboration and Solidarity Work together across movements and communities, recognizing that no form of oppression exists in isolation. By embracing collaboration and solidarity, we can build stronger and more resilient movements.

6.4 Take Action Intersectionality is not just a theoretical framework; it calls us to take concrete action. Advocate for policies and practices that address intersecting forms of oppression and work towards eradicating systemic inequalities.

By recognizing and embracing the power of intersectionality, we can create a more inclusive and equitable world for all. It's time to unite our efforts, amplify diverse voices, and dismantle the interconnected systems of oppression that hold us back. Together, we can build a future where every individual can live authentically, free from discrimination and prejudice.

The Importance of LGBTQ History and Education

In the ongoing fight for LGBTQ rights, it is crucial to recognize the significance of LGBTQ history and education. This section delves into the reasons why understanding and learning from LGBTQ history is vital for the progress of the community. By examining the struggles and triumphs of past activists, we can build upon their legacy and continue moving towards equality and acceptance.

Understanding the Past

To appreciate the progress that has been made and to acknowledge the challenges that lie ahead, it is important to understand LGBTQ history. This includes learning about the Stonewall Riots of 1969, a pivotal moment that sparked the modern LGBTQ rights movement. By studying this event, we gain insight into the power of collective action and the impact it can have on social change.

LGBTQ history also reveals the contributions of individuals who fought for their rights even in the face of adversity. From Harvey Milk, the first openly gay elected official in California, to Marsha P. Johnson, a transgender activist who played a significant role in the Stonewall Riots, their stories inspire us to persevere despite obstacles.

Countering Ignorance and Prejudice

Education is a powerful tool in combatting ignorance and prejudice. By integrating LGBTQ history and education into school curricula, we can promote inclusivity and empathy from an early age. This can help dismantle stereotypes and promote acceptance, fostering a society where everyone's identity is respected.

Furthermore, LGBTQ history can serve as a counter-narrative to prevailing prejudices. By highlighting the accomplishments and contributions of LGBTQ individuals throughout history, we challenge the notion that the LGBTQ community is somehow lesser or abnormal. This can empower LGBTQ individuals to embrace their identity and contribute to society without fear of judgment or discrimination.

Building Allies and Coalitions

Knowledge of LGBTQ history can also help in building alliances and coalitions with other social justice movements. Intersectionality is the understanding that oppressions, such as race, gender, sexuality, and class, intersect and compound one another. By studying LGBTQ history, we gain a deeper understanding of the ways in which these oppressions interact, enabling us to form more inclusive coalitions. This unity strengthens the collective power of marginalized communities, amplifying their voices and advocating for change on multiple fronts.

Empowering LGBTQ Youth

LGBTQ history and education are especially crucial for LGBTQ youth. By learning about the struggles and achievements of previous generations, young LGBTQ individuals can gain a sense of pride and belonging. It provides them with role models to look up to and can inspire them to continue fighting for equality. Additionally, LGBTQ history education in schools nurtures empathy among non-LGBTQ students, fostering a culture of acceptance and support.

Addressing Ongoing Issues

Understanding LGBTQ history allows us to confront ongoing issues faced by the community. For example, by examining the historical criminalization of homosexuality, we can better advocate for the decriminalization of same-sex relationships worldwide. By highlighting the struggles faced by transgender individuals throughout history, we can address the urgent need for trans rights and representation today.

Moreover, LGBTQ history sheds light on the persistence of discrimination and violence faced by the community. It underscores the significance of anti-discrimination laws, hate crime legislation, and comprehensive LGBTQ healthcare. Armed with this knowledge, activists and allies can work towards eradicating systemic injustices and creating a more equitable society.

Unconventional Yet Relevant: Interactive Time Travel

One unconventional yet relevant way to engage with LGBTQ history is through interactive time travel. In this virtual experience, participants are immersed in pivotal moments of LGBTQ history, allowing them to witness the events firsthand. By interacting with historical figures and taking on their perspectives, participants can gain a more profound understanding of the challenges faced by the LGBTQ community throughout history.

This interactive time travel experience not only brings history to life but also fosters empathy and encourages participants to reflect on their own role in creating a more inclusive future. It challenges them to actively participate in the ongoing fight for LGBTQ rights and provides a unique way to educate and engage a broader audience.

Conclusion

LGBTQ history and education play a crucial role in the fight for LGBTQ rights. By understanding the struggles and triumphs of the past, we can learn valuable lessons and build upon the legacy of previous activists. LGBTQ history challenges ignorance and prejudice, fosters empathy, and promotes inclusivity. It empowers LGBTQ youth, assists in building alliances, and addresses ongoing issues faced by the community. Through unconventional approaches, such as interactive time travel, we can further engage with LGBTQ history and continue working towards a future of equality and acceptance.

New Frontiers

Embracing Intersectionality

In the fight for LGBTQ rights, embracing intersectionality is crucial. Intersectionality recognizes that individuals can experience multiple forms of oppression based on their intersecting identities, such as race, gender, sexuality, and class. By acknowledging the interconnectedness of these systems of discrimination, we create a more inclusive and comprehensive approach to activism.

Understanding Intersectionality

Intersectionality acknowledges that each person's experiences are shaped by the unique combination of various social identities. For instance, a black transgender woman may face discrimination and violence based on her race, gender identity, and transgender status. Understanding intersectionality means recognizing and addressing the distinct challenges faced by individuals who belong to multiple marginalized groups.

By embracing intersectionality, LGBTQ activists can ensure that our movement is inclusive and representative of the diverse experiences within the queer community. This understanding helps us foster solidarity among different social justice movements, creating a stronger collective effort towards equality.

Inclusive Activism

Embracing intersectionality in activism means actively engaging with and supporting communities that face multiple forms of discrimination. It involves listening to and centering the voices of those at the intersections of marginalized identities. By doing so, we recognize the importance of a collective, inclusive fight for justice.

To practice inclusive activism, LGBTQ activists can:

1. Collaborate with Other Movements: Intersectionality calls on us to form alliances with other social justice movements, such as those focused on racial justice, gender equality, and economic justice. By building bridges and working together, we can amplify each other's voices and challenge the interconnected systems of oppression.

2. Educate Ourselves: Intersectionality requires continual learning and self-reflection. It is crucial to educate ourselves about the experiences and struggles faced by marginalized communities beyond our own. This knowledge helps us understand the complex ways in which various systems of oppression intersect and inform our activism.

3. Address Privilege: Intersectionality calls on us to confront our own privileges and biases. It requires us to acknowledge that certain social identities afford privilege, while others face systemic disadvantages. By actively working to dismantle our own prejudices and leveraging our privileges to uplift others, we can contribute to a more equitable society.

4. Challenging Stereotypes: Intersectional activists challenge stereotypes and biases within and outside the LGBTQ community. By interrogating and breaking down harmful generalizations, we create space for more inclusive narratives and experiences. This includes recognizing that queer individuals exist across races, genders, ethnicities, abilities, and socioeconomic backgrounds.

Case Study: Intersectionality in Action

Consider the case of a queer person of color experiencing discrimination in their workplace. Embracing intersectionality means recognizing that their experience is shaped by both their queerness and their racial identity. Advocating for their rights requires addressing both forms of discrimination while acknowledging the unique challenges they face due to the intersection of these identities.

To combat this, LGBTQ activists could collaborate with racial justice organizations to develop workplace policies that address discrimination based on race and sexuality. By creating inclusive policies, businesses can foster environments that celebrate diversity and provide equal opportunities for all employees.

Unconventional Perspective:

Intersectionality challenges us to question the idea of a single, universal queer experience. It reminds us that the battles for LGBTQ rights are not one-size-fits-all, and that our movement should be as diverse and multifaceted as the communities we seek to uplift. Embracing intersectionality means recognizing the unique struggles and contributions of each individual and standing in solidarity with all marginalized groups.

Exercises

1. Reflect on your own social identities and consider how they intersect. How might these intersections shape your experiences and perspectives?

2. Research a social justice movement that is different from the LGBTQ rights movement. How does this movement advocate for intersectionality and inclusion?

3. Engage in conversations with individuals from different marginalized communities to learn about their experiences. Listen actively and respectfully, and seek to understand the unique challenges they face at the intersections of their identities.

By embracing intersectionality, LGBTQ activists can advocate for a more inclusive and equitable society. By recognizing the interconnectedness of our struggles, we can work towards a future where no one is left behind in the fight for equality. Remember, our fight is not just for LGBTQ rights, but for justice for all.

Fighting for Trans and Non-Binary Rights

In this chapter, we delve into the important fight for trans and non-binary rights, exploring the challenges faced by these communities and the strategies employed by activists like Zion Ellis to advocate for change. We explore the concepts of gender identity and expression, the experiences of discrimination and prejudice faced by trans and non-binary individuals, and the ongoing efforts to secure their rights and recognition in society.

Understanding Gender Identity and Expression

Gender identity refers to a person's deeply held sense of their own gender, which may or may not align with the sex they were assigned at birth. For example, a person who was assigned female at birth but identifies as male has a male gender identity. Non-binary individuals, on the other hand, identify as neither exclusively male nor exclusively female.

Gender expression, on the other hand, refers to how individuals express their gender identity through their appearance, behavior, and mannerisms. This can include clothing choices, hairstyles, and other forms of self-expression. It is important to understand that gender identity and expression exist on a spectrum, and individuals may express their identities in a variety of ways.

Challenges Faced by Trans and Non-Binary Individuals

Trans and non-binary individuals face numerous challenges and forms of discrimination in their daily lives. These challenges can include:

+ Legal and institutional barriers: Many countries lack comprehensive legal protections for trans and non-binary individuals, making it difficult for them to access necessary healthcare, change their gender markers on identification documents, and navigate legal systems that may not recognize their identities.

+ Social stigma and discrimination: Trans and non-binary individuals often face high levels of social stigma, prejudice, and discrimination. This can manifest in various ways, including verbal abuse, physical violence, exclusion from social spaces, and difficulties finding employment or housing.

+ Limited access to healthcare: Trans and non-binary individuals may face significant barriers when seeking healthcare, including inappropriate or inadequate treatment, lack of access to gender-affirming care, and medical professionals who are unfamiliar with their specific needs.

+ Intersectional discrimination: Trans and non-binary individuals who also belong to marginalized communities, such as people of color or disabled individuals, may experience compounded discrimination due to the intersectionality of their identities.

It is crucial to recognize and address these challenges in order to create a more inclusive and equitable society for all.

Advocacy for Trans and Non-Binary Rights

LGBTQ activists like Zion Ellis have been at the forefront of advocating for trans and non-binary rights. Their tireless efforts have resulted in significant progress, but there is still much work to be done. Here are some of the key strategies employed in the fight for trans and non-binary rights:

1. **Raising awareness and education:** Activists work to raise awareness about the challenges faced by trans and non-binary individuals through educational campaigns, public speaking engagements, and media appearances. This helps to debunk misconceptions and promote understanding and empathy.

2. **Legal advocacy:** Activists push for comprehensive legal protections that recognize and respect the rights of trans and non-binary individuals. This includes advocating for gender identity and expression to be legally recognized, supporting gender-affirming healthcare access, and combating discriminatory laws.

3. **Creating safe spaces and support networks:** Activists strive to create safe spaces and support networks where trans and non-binary individuals can find community, support, and resources. This can include LGBTQ centers, support groups, online forums, and mentorship programs.

4. **Collaboration and coalition-building:** Activists understand the power of collaboration and often work alongside other social justice movements and organizations to amplify their advocacy efforts. By building strong alliances, they can advocate for trans and non-binary rights intersectionally and address the root causes of discrimination.

5. **Promoting accurate representation:** Activists aim to increase positive and accurate representation of trans and non-binary individuals in media, arts, and popular culture. This helps challenge stereotypes and promotes visibility, allowing for a better understanding and acceptance of diverse gender identities.

Real-World Examples and Solutions

To illustrate the challenges faced by trans and non-binary individuals and the efforts undertaken to address them, let's explore a real-world example:

Problem: Limited access to gender-affirming healthcare is a significant barrier for many trans and non-binary individuals.

Solution: Activists like Zion Ellis have advocated for improved healthcare access by:

1. Pushing for better training for healthcare professionals to ensure they are knowledgeable about the unique needs of trans and non-binary individuals.

2. Campaigning for changes in healthcare policies to remove barriers to gender-affirming treatments and surgeries.

3. Supporting initiatives that provide financial assistance for gender-affirming healthcare to make it more accessible and affordable for those who need it.

By addressing these issues, activists can help create a healthcare system that is inclusive and affirming of all gender identities.

Unconventional Approach: Art as Activism

Art has always been a powerful tool for social change, and many trans and non-binary activists have embraced creative forms of expression to advocate for their rights. Whether through visual arts, performance art, or written word, art can challenge norms, spark conversations, and humanize the experiences of trans and non-binary individuals. It creates a space for dialogue and can reach a broader audience, helping to foster empathy and understanding.

Conclusion

The fight for trans and non-binary rights is gaining momentum, thanks to the passionate activism of individuals like Zion Ellis. By understanding the challenges faced by trans and non-binary individuals, advocating for legal protections and social acceptance, and promoting education and representation, we can work towards a more inclusive society. Let us join hands in this ongoing fight for equality, justice, and respect for all gender identities.

Confronting the Challenges of Queerness

As Zion Ellis dives deeper into his activism journey, he confronts unique challenges that come with being queer in a society that often marginalizes and discriminates against LGBTQ individuals. In this chapter, we explore some of the key challenges faced by queerness and how Zion, along with the LGBTQ community, works towards overcoming them.

Understanding the Complexity of Queerness

Queerness is a complex and multifaceted concept that goes beyond simple definitions of sexual orientation or gender identity. It encompasses a wide range of identities, expressions, and experiences. To confront the challenges of queerness, it is crucial to understand this complexity and recognize that the LGBTQ community comprises individuals with diverse backgrounds and needs.

Navigating Discrimination and Prejudice

One of the primary challenges faced by queerness is the prevalence of discrimination and prejudice. LGBTQ individuals often encounter social stigma, bias, and systemic barriers in various aspects of their lives, including education, employment, healthcare, and housing. Zion's activism focuses on empowering the community to fight against discrimination and work towards creating inclusive and accepting spaces.

Example: To illustrate the challenges faced by queerness, Zion shares the story of Lila, a transgender woman who faced discrimination in the workplace. Despite her qualifications and skills, Lila encountered subtle acts of discrimination and microaggressions from colleagues and superiors. With Zion's support, Lila takes legal action against the company and becomes a symbol of resilience and strength in the face of adversity.

Mental Health and Well-being

Queer individuals often face higher rates of mental health challenges due to societal pressures, rejection, and the internal struggle to reconcile their identity with societal norms. Zion advocates for the importance of mental health support within the LGBTQ community and works towards creating accessible resources and safe spaces for individuals to seek help.

Explanation: Zion highlights the need for mental health services that cater specifically to the LGBTQ community, providing counseling and therapy that address the unique challenges faced by queer individuals. He shares resources and strategies for self-care, emphasizing the importance of self-compassion and community support in fostering mental well-being.

Intersectionality and Queerness

Intersectionality recognizes the interconnected nature of social identities and how they intersect to create unique experiences of discrimination and marginalization. Zion emphasizes the importance of considering intersectionality when addressing the challenges faced by queerness. He collaborates with other social movements to create inclusive spaces that recognize and uplift the voices and experiences of LGBTQ individuals who are also marginalized based on their race, class, disability, or other identities.

Example: Zion discusses his collaboration with a local organization that focuses on supporting queer individuals of color. Together, they organize events that celebrate and highlight the experiences of queer individuals who face multiple forms of discrimination. By centering these marginalized voices, they challenge the dominant narrative and work towards a more inclusive society.

Challenging Heteronormativity and Gender Binaries

Heteronormative standards and gender binaries perpetuate limiting and exclusionary ideas about identity and relationships. Zion challenges these societal norms and advocates for a more inclusive understanding of gender and sexuality. He promotes education and awareness to debunk myths and misconceptions surrounding queerness, encouraging individuals to embrace their authentic selves.

Explanation: Zion explores the impact of heteronormativity on the LGBTQ community, emphasizing the need to dismantle the assumptions that place heterosexuality and binary gender as the norm. He shares personal stories and experiences that demonstrate the power of embracing diverse forms of love and self-expression, challenging societal expectations and norms.

Promoting Self-acceptance and Empowerment

Self-acceptance is a crucial aspect of confronting the challenges of queerness. Zion shares his own journey towards self-acceptance and highlights the power of embracing one's true identity. Through his activism, he encourages individuals to celebrate their queerness and recognize their worth, inspiring them to become agents of change in their own lives and communities.

Explanation: Zion offers tips and strategies for self-acceptance, including practicing self-love, surrounding oneself with supportive communities, and seeking therapy or counseling if necessary. He emphasizes the significance of empowering oneself and others by creating safe spaces, promoting positive representation, and fostering a culture of acceptance and diversity.

Conclusion

Confronting the challenges of queerness requires a collective effort to challenge societal norms, dismantle discrimination, and create inclusive spaces. Zion's journey as an LGBTQ activist highlights the importance of recognizing and addressing these challenges while empowering queer individuals to embrace their identities and advocate for change. The fight for equality and acceptance continues, inspiring future generations to confront the challenges of queerness with resilience and determination.

Remember, your story matters, and your voice can make a difference. Let your queerness shine and embrace the challenges as opportunities for growth, change, and empowerment. Together, we can create a world that celebrates and uplifts all identities. Move forward with pride, strength, and resilience – the world needs your unique perspective.

Exploring Gender Fluidity and Identity

In this chapter, we delve into the complex and fascinating world of gender fluidity and identity. As society becomes more aware of the diversity of gender experiences, it is crucial to understand and accept the fluid nature of gender. We will explore the concept of gender fluidity, its impact on individuals, and the challenges faced by those who embrace non-binary identities. Through empowering stories, personal narratives, and thought-provoking insights, we will open the door to a deeper understanding of gender identity.

Breaking the Binary: Understanding Gender Fluidity

Traditionally, society has operated within a binary framework, viewing gender as strictly male or female. However, gender fluidity challenges this rigid perception by acknowledging the existence of a spectrum of gender identities. Individuals who identify as gender fluid may experience their gender identity fluctuating over time, shifting between masculine, feminine, and non-binary expressions. It is important to recognize that gender identity is deeply personal and can differ from assigned sex at birth.

To better understand gender fluidity, it is helpful to explore some key terms:

+ **Non-binary**: A term used to describe individuals whose gender identity does not exclusively align with male or female.

+ **Genderqueer**: An umbrella term encompassing non-binary individuals who reject or challenge traditional gender norms.

+ **Bigender**: Individuals who identify with two distinct gender identities.

+ **Androgynous**: Individuals whose gender expression and/or identity combines both masculine and feminine characteristics.

By exploring these terms and the experiences of those who identify with them, we can foster a more inclusive and understanding society.

Navigating the Challenges of Non-Binary Identity

Individuals who navigate non-binary identities often face unique challenges in a society grounded in a binary framework. One significant challenge is the constant pressure to conform to societal expectations of gender expression. Non-binary individuals may face scrutiny or disbelief, as their identities challenge deeply ingrained assumptions about gender.

Moreover, gender-fluid individuals may struggle with a lack of representation and understanding within institutions, such as healthcare, education, and the workplace. Limited recognition of non-binary identities can lead to feelings of isolation, exclusion, and inadequate support.

To support non-binary individuals, it is crucial to create spaces that validate their experiences, acknowledge their identities, and provide necessary resources and support. Education and awareness efforts play a vital role in dismantling gender stereotypes and fostering understanding and acceptance.

Embracing Gender Fluidity in Relationships

Exploring gender fluidity extends beyond personal identity and expression—it also encompasses the realm of relationships and partnerships. In a binary-focused society, relationships are often categorized as either heterosexual or homosexual. However, gender fluidity challenges these rigid categorizations, allowing for a broader spectrum of relationships.

Non-binary individuals may be attracted to individuals across the gender spectrum, breaking free from traditional notions of attraction based solely on binary gender. This fluidity enables greater openness, freedom, and acceptance in intimate relationships.

Embracing gender fluidity in relationships requires understanding, communication, and a willingness to challenge societal norms. Partners who support one another's gender journeys create a safe and empowering environment that fosters growth, self-discovery, and love free from the constraints of traditional expectations.

Promoting Inclusivity and Empathy

Accepting and understanding gender fluidity requires a multifaceted approach that involves education, advocacy, and empathy. It is essential for individuals, communities, and institutions to actively engage in promoting inclusivity and challenging binary frameworks.

Education plays a crucial role in debunking myths and addressing misconceptions about non-binary identities. By incorporating LGBTQ-inclusive curriculum in schools and universities, we can foster empathy and understanding among future generations.

Advocacy efforts should focus on encouraging systemic changes that recognize and protect the rights of gender-fluid individuals. This includes advocating for legal protections against gender-based discrimination and ensuring access to inclusive healthcare and other services.

However, the most impactful way to promote inclusivity is through empathy. By actively listening to the stories and experiences of gender-fluid individuals, we can deepen our understanding and cultivate compassion. Creating spaces for genuine dialogue, promoting visibility, and challenging our own biases are essential steps toward a more inclusive future.

Embracing the Exploration

As we delve into the world of gender fluidity and identity, it is crucial to approach the topic with an open mind and heart. Embracing the exploration of gender identities allows us to challenge societal norms, broaden our understanding of human experiences, and create a more inclusive and accepting world for all.

Remember, gender is a deeply personal and unique experience, and individuals should be respected and supported in their exploration of self. By embracing gender fluidity, we honor the diversity of human identity and take a significant step toward a more equitable and compassionate society.

Now, let's explore some practical exercises and reflections to deepen our understanding of gender fluidity and identity:

- Reflect on your own gender identity journey: How have your experiences shaped your understanding of gender? How can you challenge binary thinking in your own life?

- Engage in conversations with individuals who identify as non-binary or gender-fluid: Listen to their experiences, ask questions respectfully, and learn from their stories. This can be done through joining local LGBTQ+ organizations or attending virtual events and workshops.

- Challenge gender norms: Take a moment to reflect on the ways you may perpetuate binary thinking in your language, attitudes, or behaviors. How can you actively challenge and disrupt these norms in your daily life?

- Educate yourself: Read books, watch documentaries, and engage with resources that explore gender fluidity and non-binary experiences. Seek out diverse voices and perspectives to broaden your understanding.

- Advocate for inclusivity: Use your voice to push for systemic changes that recognize and protect the rights of gender-fluid individuals. Write to your local representatives, support LGBTQ+ organizations, and amplify marginalized voices.

By actively engaging in these activities and conversations, we can play a part in creating a more inclusive and accepting world for individuals of all gender identities. Let us continue this exploration with an open heart and mind, embracing the beauty and diversity of gender fluidity.

Dismantling Cisnormativity and Transphobia

Dismantling cisnormativity and transphobia is a crucial step in creating a more inclusive and accepting society for all gender identities. In this section, we will explore the underlying principles of cisnormativity and transphobia, the impact they have on transgender and gender non-conforming individuals, and strategies for challenging and dismantling these harmful beliefs.

Understanding Cisnormativity

Cisnormativity is the assumption that being cisgender (identifying with the gender assigned at birth) is the "normal" or default gender identity. This assumption is deeply ingrained in our society, perpetuating stereotypes, prejudices, and discrimination against transgender and non-binary individuals.

One of the key problems with cisnormativity is that it reinforces the idea that transgender and non-binary identities are invalid or abnormal. This invalidation can have detrimental effects on the mental health and well-being of transgender individuals, leading to higher rates of depression, anxiety, and suicide.

To challenge cisnormativity, we need to promote education and awareness about the diversity of gender identities. This includes debunking the myth that gender is solely determined by biological sex and recognizing that gender is a complex and deeply personal experience.

Addressing Transphobia

Transphobia refers to the fear, hatred, or discrimination against transgender individuals. It manifests in various forms, such as verbal abuse, physical violence, denial of healthcare access, and employment discrimination. Transphobia is often rooted in ignorance and a lack of understanding about transgender identities.

To dismantle transphobia, we must first educate ourselves and others about transgender experiences and issues. This includes learning about different gender identities, the challenges faced by transgender individuals, and the rights and legal protections they deserve.

Supporting and promoting transgender voices and representation is also crucial in challenging transphobia. By amplifying their stories and experiences, we can humanize transgender individuals and challenge stereotypes and misconceptions.

To address transphobia, we must also work towards creating safer spaces for transgender individuals and advocating for their rights. This can involve supporting policies that protect gender identity and expression, improving access to healthcare and mental health services, and actively working to reduce discrimination in all areas of life.

Challenging Gender Binaries

One way to dismantle cisnormativity and transphobia is to challenge the restrictive gender binaries that limit our understanding of gender. Traditional notions of gender often categorize individuals into rigid and binary categories of male and female, ignoring the existence of non-binary, genderqueer, and other gender-expansive identities.

We need to encourage a more nuanced understanding of gender and recognize that it exists on a spectrum. This includes acknowledging and respecting the self-identified gender of individuals, regardless of whether it aligns with societal expectations or traditional gender roles.

By challenging gender binaries, we can create space for transgender and non-binary individuals to exist authentically and without fear of judgment or discrimination. This can lead to a more inclusive society that celebrates and values the unique diversity of gender identities.

Allies and Advocacy

Dismantling cisnormativity and transphobia requires the active participation of cisgender individuals as allies and advocates. Allies are individuals who support and stand up for the rights of transgender and non-binary individuals, using their privilege to create change.

As an ally, it is important to listen to and learn from transgender individuals, respect their identities, and use correct names and pronouns. Education is key, so allies should actively seek out resources and information to better understand the experiences and challenges faced by transgender individuals.

Advocacy is another important aspect of dismantling cisnormativity and transphobia. This involves speaking out against discrimination, supporting transgender-inclusive policies, and engaging in activism to create change. By using our voices and platforms to raise awareness, we can help challenge harmful beliefs and promote acceptance and equality.

Conclusion

Dismantling cisnormativity and transphobia is a continual process that requires education, awareness, and collective action. By challenging gender binaries, addressing transphobia, and acting as allies and advocates, we can create a society that celebrates and embraces the full spectrum of gender identities. Let us join together to dismantle cisnormativity and transphobia, creating a world where everyone can live authentically and without fear of discrimination.

A Never-Ending Journey

The Future of LGBTQ Activism

The future of LGBTQ activism is a topic that sparks both hope and concern. As we move forward, the fight for equality and acceptance continues to evolve, presenting new challenges and opportunities. In this section, we will explore the key areas that will shape the future of LGBTQ activism and offer insights into how we can navigate these uncharted territories.

1. Intersectional Activism: Building Bridges and Solidarity

One crucial aspect that will shape the future of LGBTQ activism is the intersectionality of social justice movements. Intersectionality recognizes that different forms of oppression, such as racism, sexism, ableism, and homophobia, are interconnected. It emphasizes the importance of understanding and addressing the overlapping systems of oppression that affect individuals.

The future of LGBTQ activism lies in building strong alliances and collaborative efforts with other marginalized communities. By recognizing the common struggles and goals shared with other social justice movements, we can amplify our collective voices and create meaningful change on a broader scale. This requires us to actively listen, learn, and uplift the experiences and stories of those who face multiple forms of discrimination.

2. Rights for Trans and Non-Binary Individuals: A Focus on Gender Inclusivity

The fight for transgender and non-binary rights will continue to be at the forefront of LGBTQ activism. As society becomes more aware of gender diversity, it is crucial to advocate for legal protections, healthcare access, and cultural acceptance for these individuals.

In the future, we must work towards creating inclusive policies that respect and affirm the self-identified gender of transgender and non-binary individuals. This includes advocating for legal recognition of gender identity, eliminating discriminatory practices, and empowering trans and non-binary voices in decision-making processes. Education and awareness campaigns that challenge misconceptions and promote understanding will also be essential to achieving equality for all gender identities.

3. Addressing Global LGBTQ Rights: A Worldwide Movement

While progress has been made in many countries regarding LGBTQ rights, there is still much work to be done on a global scale. In the future, LGBTQ activism must extend beyond national borders to address the challenges faced by LGBTQ individuals worldwide.

Advocacy for global LGBTQ rights involves pressuring governments and international organizations to address human rights violations, decriminalize same-sex relationships, and protect LGBTQ individuals from discrimination and violence. Collaboration with local activists and organizations in different parts of the world is vital to gather accurate information, provide support, and amplify the voices of those advocating for change.

4. Embracing Technology and Digital Activism

Advancements in technology and the rise of social media have revolutionized activism. The future of LGBTQ activism will heavily rely on utilizing these digital platforms to spread awareness, mobilize communities, and advocate for change.

To harness the power of technology, LGBTQ activists must adapt to evolving social media trends, engage with online communities, and utilize data-driven strategies. This includes creating compelling multimedia content that educates and inspires, organizing virtual campaigns, and leveraging online platforms for fundraising and organizing events.

However, it is crucial to remember that digital activism should not substitute physical activism. To create lasting change, it is essential to combine online efforts with offline actions, such as protests, lobbying, and community organizing.

Conclusion: A Call to Action

The future of LGBTQ activism is bright but requires continuous dedication, innovation, and collaboration. By embracing intersectionality, advocating for trans and non-binary rights, addressing global LGBTQ issues, and harnessing the power of technology, we can pave the way for a more inclusive and accepting world.

As we move forward, it is essential to remember that progress is not linear, and setbacks may occur. However, through resilience, unity, and an unwavering commitment to equality, we can overcome obstacles and create a future where every member of the LGBTQ community feels safe, respected, and celebrated.

Remember, as LGBTQ activists, we have the power to shape our own destiny and create a world where love and acceptance transcend boundaries. So, let us stand together, continue to fight, and inspire future generations to carry the torch of LGBTQ activism forward. The journey continues, and our voices will be heard.

Paving the Way for Social Change

In the final chapter of Zion Ellis's biography, we delve into the crucial role he played in paving the way for social change in the LGBTQ community. His relentless activism and vision for a more inclusive and accepting society led him to spearhead initiatives that transformed the landscape of LGBTQ rights. This section explores the strategies, challenges, and accomplishments of Zion Ellis in his journey to create lasting social change.

Creating Intersectional Alliances

One of the key strategies employed by Zion Ellis in his pursuit of social change was his emphasis on intersectionality. Recognizing that social justice movements are interconnected, Zion actively sought to build alliances with other marginalized communities. By bringing together diverse voices and shared struggles, he advocated for a more inclusive and intersectional approach to activism.

Zion believed that collaborating with different movements, such as racial justice, gender equality, and disability rights, would amplify and strengthen the LGBTQ movement. He initiated dialogues and partnerships with organizations working towards these goals, facilitating mutual support and understanding. Through these alliances, he aimed to break down barriers and challenge systemic oppression on multiple fronts, fostering a more equitable society for all.

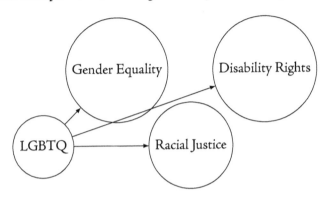

Figure 0.4: Intersectional Alliances for Social Change.

Addressing Health Disparities

Zion Ellis recognized that health disparities within the LGBTQ community posed significant obstacles to achieving social change. In his efforts to pave the way for a better future, he prioritized advocating for LGBTQ-inclusive healthcare policies and services. He tackled issues such as access to gender-affirming healthcare, mental health support, and HIV/AIDS prevention and treatment.

Zion understood the importance of comprehensive healthcare that catered to the unique needs of LGBTQ individuals. He collaborated with medical professionals, policymakers, and LGBTQ health organizations to push for inclusive policies and funding. Through education and awareness campaigns, he worked to destigmatize LGBTQ health concerns and empower individuals to seek the care they deserved.

Promoting LGBTQ-Inclusive Education

Education played a fundamental role in Zion Ellis's journey towards social change. He recognized that fostering understanding, empathy, and acceptance from an early age was crucial to a more inclusive society. Zion fought tirelessly for LGBTQ-inclusive education, advocating for curriculum reforms that acknowledged the contributions and struggles of LGBTQ individuals throughout history.

Zion championed policies that ensured LGBTQ students felt safe, respected, and represented in schools. He conducted workshops and training programs for educators and administrators, emphasizing the importance of inclusive teaching practices. By challenging heteronormative expectations and fostering a supportive environment, Zion aimed to empower LGBTQ students and pave the way for a generation that saw diversity as a strength.

Leveraging Technology for Activism

Zion Ellis understood the immense power of technology in amplifying LGBTQ voices and mobilizing for change. In the modern digital age, he recognized that social media platforms, online campaigns, and virtual spaces provided unprecedented opportunities for activism. Zion leveraged these tools to reach a wider audience, sparking conversations and mobilizing support for LGBTQ rights.

Through strategic social media campaigns, Zion effectively highlighted LGBTQ stories, experiences, and challenges. He harnessed the power of storytelling to cultivate empathy and understanding among those who may not have previously recognized or acknowledged LGBTQ struggles. By embracing technology and its potential for global connectivity, Zion Ellis inspired a new era of digital activism that transcended boundaries and resonated with diverse audiences.

The Legacy of Zion Ellis

As Zion Ellis reflects on his life's work in this final chapter, his profound impact on the LGBTQ movement becomes undeniable. Through his unwavering dedication, Zion paved the way for social change and laid the foundation for a more inclusive and accepting world. His emphasis on intersectionality, health equity, LGBTQ-inclusive education, and technology-driven activism set the stage for future generations of activists to carry forward the fight for social justice.

Zion Ellis's legacy serves as a reminder that progress is not achieved in isolation but through collective action. By fostering alliances, embracing diversity, and utilizing every available tool, we can continue to pave the way for social change in the ongoing pursuit of equality and justice for all. The story of Zion Ellis inspires us to champion inclusivity, challenge norms, and create a society where everyone's voice is heard and valued.

Exercises

1. Reflect on the challenges you see in your community or society that need addressing. How can you apply the principles of intersectionality to create alliances

and work towards social change?

2. Research the current healthcare disparities faced by the LGBTQ community in your region. What are some actionable steps you can take to advocate for LGBTQ-inclusive healthcare policies and services?

3. Explore the curriculum in your educational institution. Are there any gaps or missed opportunities to include LGBTQ contributions and experiences? Design a proposal for LGBTQ-inclusive education in collaboration with teachers and administrators.

4. Utilizing social media platforms, create a campaign to raise awareness about an LGBTQ issue that you care deeply about. Consider using storytelling techniques and interactive elements to engage your audience and inspire action.

Remember, social change starts at the grassroots level. It is up to each individual to take an active role in creating a more inclusive and accepting world.

The Legacy of Zion Ellis

Zion Ellis's legacy as an LGBTQ activist is an inspiring testament to the power of perseverance and dedication in the fight for equality. Throughout his life, Zion made significant contributions to the LGBTQ movement, leaving behind a lasting impact on society.

One of the key aspects of Zion's legacy is his unwavering commitment to intersectionality. He understood that LGBTQ rights are intertwined with other social justice issues, such as race, gender, and class. Zion recognized the importance of breaking down barriers by promoting inclusivity and understanding among different communities. His advocacy efforts focused on highlighting the experiences of marginalized groups within the LGBTQ community, such as trans and non-binary individuals, people of color, and those facing economic hardships.

Zion's legacy is also defined by his ability to mobilize and empower others. As a mentor and advocate, he inspired a new generation of LGBTQ activists, nurturing their potential and guiding them on the path to creating change. He understood that the fight for equality requires collective action, and he tirelessly worked to build strong networks and coalitions, both locally and globally. Zion believed in the power of community and encouraged collaboration among diverse organizations to amplify the voices of the LGBTQ community.

In addition to his advocacy work, Zion's legacy can be seen in his efforts to bring LGBTQ history and education into the mainstream. Recognizing the importance of understanding the past to shape the future, he championed LGBTQ-inclusive education as a means to combat discrimination and foster acceptance. Zion fought for comprehensive curriculum reforms that would broaden perspectives and challenge heteronormative narratives. His goal was to create an educational system that celebrates diversity and embraces individuals for who they are.

Zion's legacy also shines through his use of modern technology and digital platforms. He understood the power of social media and its ability to reach a wide audience, sparking conversations and raising awareness. Zion leveraged these platforms to initiate meaningful dialogues, share personal narratives, and counter misinformation. He recognized that the digital age presents both opportunities and challenges for LGBTQ activism, and he actively addressed the unique issues arising in this new landscape.

To honor Zion's legacy, it is vital for future LGBTQ activists to continue his work and build upon his achievements. They must remain committed to intersectionality, ensuring that diverse voices within the community are represented and heard. By embracing and understanding the complexities of different identities, LGBTQ activists can create a more inclusive movement that strives for justice and equality for all.

Furthermore, aspiring activists should focus on fostering unity and collaboration. Zion understood that change cannot be achieved in isolation. By forming alliances with other social justice movements, such as feminism, racial equality, and disability rights, LGBTQ activists can amplify their impact and build a stronger foundation for societal change.

In order to continue Zion's work, it is crucial to prioritize education. LGBTQ-inclusive curriculum reforms must be advocated for at all levels of education, from primary schools to universities. By incorporating LGBTQ history and narratives into educational institutions, future generations will gain a better understanding of the challenges faced by the community and be better equipped to promote equality and acceptance.

Finally, future activists should embrace technological advancements and find innovative ways to engage with the public. Social media, online platforms, and digital storytelling can all be powerful tools in shaping public opinion and fostering understanding. By adapting to the ever-changing technological landscape, activists can ensure that their messages reach a broader audience and inspire real change.

Zion Ellis's legacy serves as a reminder that the fight for LGBTQ equality is ongoing. His tireless dedication, intersectional approach, and commitment to education and inclusivity have laid the groundwork for future generations to continue the struggle. By building upon his legacy, LGBTQ activists can strive for a world where everyone is treated with dignity, respect, and equality, regardless of their sexual orientation or gender identity.

Let us carry the torch of Zion's legacy and work together towards a future where love, acceptance, and equality are the foundation of our society.

Queer Organizing in the Digital Age

In our fast-paced, interconnected world, the digital age has revolutionized the way we communicate, share information, and organize for social change. The LGBTQ community has embraced these technological advancements to create new avenues for activism, advocacy, and community building. In this section, we will explore the impact of digital tools and platforms on queer organizing and how they have reshaped the landscape of LGBTQ activism.

The Rise of Social Media

Social media platforms like Facebook, Twitter, Instagram, and TikTok have become powerful tools for queer organizing, enabling activists to share their messages, connect with others, and mobilize support on a global scale. These platforms facilitate the rapid dissemination of information, allowing LGBTQ activists to raise awareness about important issues, share personal stories, and promote inclusive narratives.

Hashtags, such as #LGBTQrights or #LoveIsLove, have become rallying cries for the community, bringing together individuals from different backgrounds and regions. They allow activists to participate in online conversations, contribute to ongoing discussions, and amplify marginalized voices. By utilizing these hashtags strategically, queer activists can drive social change and engage with a wider audience.

Digital activism also empowers individuals to shape public opinion and challenge mainstream narratives. It provides a platform for LGBTQ individuals to share their experiences, dispel stereotypes, and educate others about the diverse realities of queer lives. In turn, this increased visibility fosters empathy and understanding, ultimately leading to greater acceptance and support for LGBTQ rights.

Virtual Communities and Online Support

The internet has given rise to virtual communities and online support networks that provide crucial resources and connections for LGBTQ individuals. Online forums, chat rooms, and social networking groups offer safe spaces for individuals to express themselves, seek advice, and find support from others who share similar experiences.

These virtual communities have been especially impactful for LGBTQ youth who may lack supportive environments in their offline lives. Online support networks provide a lifeline to those facing bullying, discrimination, and social isolation. LGBTQ youth can connect with peers, receive guidance from mentors, and find the necessary support to navigate their unique journeys.

Additionally, digital platforms have played a pivotal role in connecting individuals in geographically remote areas or countries where LGBTQ rights are limited. By utilizing encrypted messaging apps and online video conferencing tools, activists can collaborate, exchange resources, and organize collective actions regardless of their physical location. This has facilitated the emergence of global solidarity among LGBTQ activists and has allowed for the sharing of best practices and strategies.

Mobile Apps and Accessibility

Mobile applications have also emerged as invaluable resources for the LGBTQ community. Dating apps like Grindr, Her, and Tinder have not only provided platforms for connection and relationships but have also carved out spaces for queer individuals to explore their identities and express their desires openly.

Beyond dating, mobile apps have also been developed to address specific needs of the queer community. Apps like Lyft and Uber have implemented features that ensure safe transportation options for LGBTQ individuals, particularly during Pride events or in neighborhoods that may be less accepting. Crisis helplines and mental health support apps tailored to the unique challenges faced by LGBTQ individuals have also emerged, providing valuable resources to those in need.

However, it is important to acknowledge that the digital age has its limitations and challenges. Online spaces can be fraught with harassment, hate speech, and the spread of misinformation. LGBTQ activists often face trolling, doxxing, and other forms of online bullying, which can have severe psychological and emotional impacts. It becomes crucial for platforms to implement effective moderation policies and ensure the safety of LGBTQ individuals in digital spaces.

Revolutionizing Online Activism

Queer organizing in the digital age goes beyond social media and support networks. Digital activism has seen the rise of online petitions, email campaigns, and virtual protests, allowing activists to mobilize their networks and put pressure on decision-makers.

Online petitions have proved to be a powerful tool for LGBTQ activists to collect signatures and demonstrate public support for various causes. They have been instrumental in influencing policy decisions, challenging discriminatory laws, and demanding change. Additionally, email campaigns have allowed activists to flood the inboxes of elected officials, urging them to take action in support of LGBTQ rights.

Virtual protests and livestreamed events have also gained traction, especially in the wake of the COVID-19 pandemic, which limited in-person gatherings. Activists have utilized video conferencing platforms and live streaming technologies to organize virtual rallies, panel discussions, and Pride events, reaching larger audiences and engaging participants from different parts of the world.

Ethical Considerations and Moving Forward

As we embrace the potential of queer organizing in the digital age, it is essential to address the ethical considerations attached to these advancements. Privacy concerns, data security, and algorithmic biases must be taken seriously to ensure that LGBTQ activists and communities are protected from harm.

Moving forward, it is crucial to prioritize digital literacy and media literacy among LGBTQ individuals and activists. Education and training on online safety, fact-checking, and constructive digital engagement can equip the community with the necessary skills to navigate the digital landscape effectively.

Furthermore, it is essential to develop and promote inclusive digital spaces for the diversity within the LGBTQ community. Intersectionality must be at the forefront of queer organizing online, ensuring that the voices and experiences of marginalized individuals are heard and amplified.

In conclusion, queer organizing in the digital age has opened up new possibilities for LGBTQ activism, advocacy, and community building. Social media, virtual communities, mobile apps, and online platforms have become powerful tools for sharing information, mobilizing support, and driving social change. However, it is imperative to navigate the digital landscape responsibly and ethically, ensuring the safety and inclusivity of LGBTQ individuals in online spaces. By harnessing the full potential of the digital age, queer organizing can continue to push boundaries, challenge norms, and fight for a more inclusive and equitable world.

The Importance of Self-Reflection in Activism

In the fast-paced world of activism, it is easy to get caught up in the constant action and the urgency of fighting for change. However, amidst the chaos, it is crucial for LGBTQ activists like Zion Ellis to take a step back and engage in self-reflection.

Self-reflection is not just about looking inward; it is about taking the time to assess one's beliefs, actions, and impact on the movement.

Understanding Our Motivations

Self-reflection allows activists to understand their motivations for being part of the LGBTQ movement. It is essential to ask ourselves why we are involved and what drives us to fight for equality. By understanding our motivations, we can align our actions with our values and ensure that we are making a genuine and lasting impact. This process helps us maintain authenticity and avoid performative activism.

Example Problem: Sarah, an LGBTQ activist, is participating in a pride march. However, upon self-reflection, she realizes that her motivation is driven more by seeking validation from others rather than a genuine desire for change. How can Sarah reevaluate her motivations and channel her efforts more authentically?

Solution: Sarah can engage in self-reflection by asking herself why she wants to be involved in activism. Through introspection, she can identify her authentic motivations, such as fighting for LGBTQ rights. Sarah can then shift her focus to actions that align with her true values, such as organizing educational events or volunteering at LGBTQ support organizations.

Examining Our Biases

Self-reflection also prompts activists to examine their own biases and prejudices. It is essential to recognize that no one is immune to bias, including within the LGBTQ community. By examining our biases, we can challenge them and work toward a more inclusive movement. This process requires humility, open-mindedness, and a willingness to learn from others' experiences.

Example Problem: James, an LGBTQ activist, notices that he unintentionally excludes the perspectives of bisexual individuals when advocating for LGBTQ rights. He realizes that this bias stems from a lack of understanding and empathy. How can James address this bias and become more inclusive in his activism?

Solution: James can start by educating himself about bisexuality and the unique challenges faced by bisexual individuals. He can engage in conversations with bisexual activists, read literature on the topic, or attend workshops that focus on bisexual issues. By actively seeking out diverse perspectives and questioning his biases, James can unlearn his exclusionary behavior and advocate for a more inclusive LGBTQ movement.

Avoiding Burnout

Engaging in self-reflection is crucial to avoid burnout, which is a prevalent issue among activists. The emotional toll of fighting for equality can be exhausting, and without self-reflection, activists may neglect their well-being. By regularly reflecting on their experiences, emotions, and boundaries, activists can identify signs of burnout and take necessary steps to prevent it. Self-care practices should be an integral part of an activist's routine.

Example Problem: Michael, an LGBTQ activist, has been dedicating all his time and energy to advocating for LGBTQ rights. He feels overwhelmed and drained, and his motivation is waning. How can Michael utilize self-reflection to prevent burnout and restore his passion for activism?

Solution: Michael can start by setting boundaries and establishing a work-life balance. He can reflect on the activities that give him joy and energy beyond activism. Michael should schedule regular breaks and engage in self-care practices, such as exercise, meditation, or spending time with loved ones. By understanding his limits and taking care of his well-being, Michael can recharge and continue fighting for LGBTQ rights with renewed vigor.

Learning from Mistakes

Self-reflection provides activists with an opportunity to learn from their mistakes and grow as individuals. It is crucial to acknowledge that activism is a learning journey, and no one has all the answers. By reflecting on past actions, activists can identify areas of improvement and make amends when necessary. This process fosters personal growth and helps build a stronger, more inclusive movement.

Example Problem: Emma, an LGBTQ activist, inadvertently made a hurtful comment that excluded transgender individuals during a panel discussion. She realizes the impact of her words and wants to address the mistake. How can Emma utilize self-reflection to learn from her mistake and take appropriate action?

Solution: Emma can start by acknowledging her mistake and reflecting on the underlying biases that led to the comment. She can seek guidance from transgender activists and immerse herself in literature on transgender experiences. Emma should issue a public apology and use the opportunity to educate others about transgender inclusivity. By learning from her mistake, Emma can become a more effective ally and advocate for transgender rights.

Finding Balance

Self-reflection is not only about evaluating one's impact on the movement but also about finding balance in activism. It is easy to become consumed by the cause and neglect other aspects of life. By reflecting on their priorities, activists can ensure that they are nurturing all aspects of their well-being, including personal relationships, hobbies, and mental health. This balance allows activists to sustain their passion for advocacy in the long run.

Example Problem: Ethan, an LGBTQ activist, finds it challenging to balance his activism with his personal life. He feels guilty whenever he takes time off and believes it is a sign of weakness. How can Ethan use self-reflection to find a healthy balance between activism and personal well-being?

Solution: Ethan can begin by reflecting on his values and priorities beyond activism. He should assess the areas of his life that require attention, such as relationships, self-care, and personal growth. Ethan needs to remind himself that taking breaks and setting boundaries is not a weakness but a necessary part of being an effective advocate. By finding a healthy balance, Ethan can sustain his passion for the LGBTQ movement and prevent burnout.

Conclusion

In the tumultuous world of activism, self-reflection plays a vital role in maintaining authenticity, challenging biases, preventing burnout, and fostering personal growth. By dedicating time to understand their motivations, biases, and impact on the movement, LGBTQ activists can be more effective leaders and allies. Self-reflection is not an isolated activity but a continuous journey that empowers activists to create lasting change and work towards a more inclusive and equitable world for the LGBTQ community.

Index